Public Sector Financial Management

Public Sector Financial Management

Second edition

H. M. Coombs
BSC (ECON), M. PHIL, IPFA
Principal lecturer,
Department of Law and Finance,
University of Glamorgan

D. E. Jenkins
BA (ECON), MSocSc (ACCOUNTING), IPFA
Principal lecturer,
Department of Law and Finance,
University of Glamorgan

INTERNATIONAL THOMSON BUSINESS PRESS
I ⓣ P® An International Thomson Publishing Company

London • Bonn • Boston • Johannesburg • Madrid • Melbourne • Mexico City • New York • Paris
Singapore • Tokyo • Toronto • Albany, NY • Belmont, CA • Cincinnati, OH • Detroit, MI

Public Sector Financial Management

 A division of International Thomson Publishing Inc.
The ITP logo is a trademark under licence

British Library Cataloguing-in-Publication Data
A catalogue record for this book is available from the British Library

First edition published by Chapman & Hall 1991
Second edition published by Chapman & Hall 1994
Reprinted 1995
Reprinted by International Thomson Business Press 1997 and 1999

Typeset by EXPO Holdings, Malaysia
Printed in Croatia by Zrinski d.d.

ISBN 1-86152-206-1

International Thomson Business Press
Berkshire House
168–173 High Holborn
London WC1V 7AA
UK

http://www.itbp.com

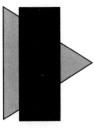

Contents

Preface

In the period since 1979 the public sector has faced significant challenges caused by the rapid pace of change enshrined in a welter of new legislation and government directives and exhortations. As significant, however, is a change in general attitudes both towards, and within, the public sector which has resulted in the emergence of a new managerial culture. This culture places greater emphasis on economy, efficiency and effectiveness in all spheres of the public sector where services are delivered. As greater pressure is placed on the public sector to provide services in this new environment increased demands are being put on the financial management skills of service managers. These service managers are also frequently asked to exercise these skills with financial management information systems which were often designed more to produce the financial accounts than to provide them with the information they need to run their services.

A demand thus exists for financial information which is directly relevant to the decision makers. There is also a need for the service manager to become more actively involved in financial management than he or she has been previously and to develop interpretive skills. This problem is further compounded by a lack of financial training for many service managers who have traditionally relied on a central finance department for financial advice but are now expected to make their own financial decisions. Finally, students training for both financial and general managerial positions in the public sector also must be aware of the increased need for financial management skills in order to manage adequately the resources that will be within their control.

It seemed to us that in writing this book we should attempt to address these problems by examining the financial management techniques that are considered appropriate to the public sector manager, and use these as a base to develop interpretive skills. In undertaking this task it might be thought that the natural starting point would be to begin with the existing literature. There was, however, no obvious place to begin as the area of financial management in the public sector has been substantially ignored by previous writers. This situation was not exactly unexpected as we have taught public sector financial management for a number of years and developed our own examples and illustrations based on our professional training and experience. This approach is, therefore, adopted in this book with substantial discussion of the practices undertaken in public sector financial management. This approach is complimented with exhibits and examples to show the techniques in practice, and discussion of the non-financial factors which affect any service operating in a political environment. Importantly it must be remembered that a technique only provides a financial result; particular emphasis must be given to the interpretation of that result, especially where non-financial factors are important. This clearly is the case with the public sector.

It is obviously not possible to cover every area of the public sector due to its size and variability but it is hoped that the exhibits, examples and general text will enable the reader to see direct applications in any area of the public sector with which he or she is directly familiar. It will be noted by readers that many of the financial management techniques discussed are directly related to those currently used in the private sector. It is thought that this is particularly important given the increased emphasis on private sector management techniques that the public sector needs to develop if it is to compete successfully in a competitive tender situation. We believe that these techniques will play an increasingly important role in public sector financial management, but stress also that they must be used in the correct context whilst bearing in mind the special factors which affect policy decisions in the public sector.

Each chapter concludes with a number of questions. The objects of those which are of a computational nature are, first, the calculation of the accounting solution to the problem and, secondly, as important, the consideration of the wider implications of the results of the calculations. This combination of the provision of financial results and the subsequent interpretation of those results together with relevant advice on a course of action to be followed are the true financial management challenges created by the changing times faced in the field of public sector financial management for trained accountants, service managers and students.

Finally, we are grateful to the Polytechnic of Wales and the Chartered Institute of Public Finance and Accountancy for permission to reproduce past examination questions.

Preface to second edition

Since the first edition of this book was published the speed of changes affecting the public sector show no sign of slowing down. Indeed, it might be argued that the only constant in the environment of the public sector manager is change. Certainly the need for all managers, potential managers, and students of public sector management to be equipped with the skills of financial management can no longer be seen as a virtue but as a necessity. We have therefore updated and expanded the original text in line with this objective while attempting to retain much of the style of the first edition, which attracted many favourable comments from readers and reviewers.

A major new feature in this second edition is the inclusion of a number of short case studies which pull together the themes of financial management developed in the individual chapters. These case studies are based on our experiences in acting as consultants to various public sector organizations and thus represent 'real world' financial problems faced by public sector managers. In these problems we have kept the main features of each scenario without overwhelming the reader with complex financial calculations. This is to allow the reader to understand the principles of financial management and to develop skills of interpretation. More complex financial calculations, as in the first edition, are contained within the questions at the end of each chapter. In this respect an accompanying teacher's guide has been prepared with solutions to all these problems and to provide guidance with respect to the case studies as there are in many of these cases no unique solutions, as would be expected, in the real world.

Finally, we would like to thank all those who spent time commenting on the first edition of this text and whose constructive ideas have been most helpful in undertaking this revision.

1 ▷ Introduction

Key learning objectives

After reading this chapter you should be able to:

1. Appreciate the increased importance of financial management to the public sector.
2. Distinguish between the different definitions of public expenditure and have gained an understanding of the mechanisms for deciding the overall levels of public expenditure.
3. Recognize the elements of the major initiatives in the public sector which contribute to the increased importance of financial management in the public sector.

The present government has as one of its major policies the restoration of market forces as far as possible throughout the economy. In his budget speech of 9 March 1982 Sir Geoffrey Howe stated 'It remains our purpose, wherever possible, to transfer to the private sector assets which can be better managed there.' Since 1982 significant assets which were in the public sector have been transferred into private ownership; for example British Telecom, British Steel, British Gas, the Electricity Boards and the water authorities. There still remains, however, a significant public sector, as can be seen in Table 1.3 and as is discussed later in this chapter. In those areas of the economy that remain within the public sector the object has been to introduce the concept of a bottom line comparable with the profit and loss concept of the private sector and the private sector management techniques that go with this concept. This may take the form of a set return to be earned on assets from a contract won under conditions of competitive tendering, the reorganization of management along private sector lines, the development of an internal market for services or the increased emphasis on management's responsibility to achieve a balanced cash limited budget often under severe financial constraints due to inadequate allowances for inflationary pressures. In addition, these pressures may not necessarily operate in isolation.

The government, in addition, is determined to introduce private sector capital into public sector projects both independent of the public sector and in partnership with the public sector. In such joint ventures the government expects the private sector to take the lead (Autumn Statement 1992, paras 2.111–2.117) (HM Treasury, 1992). These ideas will lead to an injection of private sector ideals into public sector attitudes which may in itself cause conflict. Value for money (VFM) is defined as the achievement of:

Economy   The practice of management of sound housekeeping and the virtue of thrift. An economical operation acquires resources of appropriate quality and quantity at the least cost.

Efficiency   Making sure that the maximum useful output is gained from the resources devoted to each activity or, alternatively, that only the minimum level of energy and work necessary is used for a given level of output.

Effectiveness   Ensuring that output from any given activity is achieving the desired result.

In any operation, VFM is no longer seen as a virtue but as a necessity for all public sector managers. In the government's words public expenditure 'should take a declining share of national income over time, while value for money is constantly improved' (HM Treasury, 1992, para 2.14).

Such individual or, indeed, combination of factors have all placed managers under increasing pressure to perform and deliver, often with financial information systems which are based on the need to produce published accounts rather than on the manager's need for financial information. Further, the manager's decision-making environment in many areas of the public sector is one where objectives are difficult to state or are ambiguous, market prices are inappropriate, ability to pay irrelevant to consumption, and the political consequences of decisions may seriously undermine the electoral chances of the party in power whether nationally or locally. Clearly all these factors represent challenges to be overcome but the role of the management accountant is to provide information to service managers in the form that they require, in sufficient detail and with sufficient accuracy to enable decisions to be made. In addition these tasks have to be performed in an appropriate timescale to enable the decision process to be activated, and the decision reached to be relevant to the circumstances facing the service manager as they arise. In the chapters which follow examples of management accounting techniques applied to the public sector are examined and discussed. Management accounting is not, however, seen as synonymous with financial management.

Financial management is seen in this text as being proactive in the use of financial and other information to actively manage the public sector enterprise to achieve goals and laid down objectives and not merely as the provision of financial information. The remainder of the introduction, however, takes an overview of the public sector spending decision-making process and then examines a number of the major initiatives that the government has taken to further its belief that the public sector will operate more economically, efficiently and effectively with an injection of private sector managerial skills. These private sector management skills demand sound financial information systems.

1.1   The public sector planning process

The proper planning of public expenditure is clearly an important mechanism in the government's overall control of the levels of public sector spending. The Plowden Committee, reporting in 1961, recommended that: 'Regular surveys should be made of public expenditure as a whole, over a period of years ahead, and in relation to prospective resources; decisions involving substantial future expenditure should be taken in the light of those surveys' (Plowden Report, 1961). An outline of the annual public sector spending planning process is given in Table 1.1.

Table 1.1   The public expenditure planning process

1992	
November	1992 Autumn Statement. Expenditure plans 1993–94 to 1995–96.
1993	
January–February	Examination of results of previous plans.
March	Budget 1993 (financial year 1993–94).
April–June	Government departments prepare bids based on Treasury guidelines. Treasury analysis of bids made.
July	Cabinet decides overall expenditure totals. Finance Bill 1993 Royal assent.
September–November	Bilateral negotiations between departments and the Treasury. In the event of a dispute the 'Star Chamber' will sit to adjudicate claims. The 'Star Chamber' is a Cabinet Committee made up of senior ministers normally without departmental spending responsibilities – appeals can be made to full Cabinet. Departmental totals agreed. Consideration of financing of expenditure and the public sector borrowing requirement.
30th November	Budget (financial year 1994/95) and expenditure plans 1994–95 to 1996–97 published.
1994	
January	Finance Bill published.
February	Departmental reports and statistical supplement to the budget published.
March	Detailed estimates presented to Parliament.

As a result of the government accepting the recommendations of the Treasury and Civil Service Select Committee the publication previously of the Public Expenditure White Paper in January of every year was discontinued. Summary information on public expenditure plans, at the time of writing, is contained in the Autumn Statement made to the House of Commons by the Chancellor of the Exchequer. The detail of the spending plans of individual government departments is contained in documents published separately. This process is, however, subject to change which is related to moving the annual Budget from March to November. This is so that it coincides with the publication of expenditure plans in order to provide a direct link with the financing of planned expenditure. These changes have been incorporated into Table 1.1 and are now discussed in detail.

Until the 1960s the budget was the time when the government presented both its tax and expenditure plans to Parliament although the detailed estimates and Financial Secretary's memorandum on public spending where normally presented to Parliament a little earlier. Following the Plowden report, mentioned earlier, the publication gap between expenditure plans and the financing of those plans began to grow. This division between expenditure and financing was given greater emphasis by the earlier presentation of more and more detailed information concerning expenditure in the Autumn Statement. This problem did not go unnoticed and was discussed in the Treasury and Civil Service Committee (1982). In 1992 the government concluded that while it was still right to publish spending plans well before the start of the financial year there were substantial advantages in bringing tax and spending plans together. These advantages included:

1. Ministers would be better placed to judge expenditure plans in the light of the overall fiscal and tax position.
2. Presentation would be improved in that policy would appear more consistent and coherent.
3. A more informed debate could take place.
4. The early announcement of tax proposals would enable taxpayers to better plan their affairs and reduce the administrative burden on employers of changes in tax and national insurance contributions.

(Budgetary Reform, 1992)

From 1993 therefore the budget statement will be accompanied by the following documents:

1. A summary of the main Budget tax and spending changes.
2. An analysis of departmental spending plans for the next three years.
3. A description of the main tax and national insurance contribution measures and their revenue implications.
4. A statement of the government's medium term financial strategy.
5. A short-term economic forecast.
6. Detailed material on the likely out-turn for the public Finances in the current year and a forecast for the year ahead.
7. Information on the cost of tax reliefs.

A number of terms are used to describe public expenditure. These are discussed in the following sections.

General government expenditure

This is the expenditure of central and local government excluding transfers between them such as the Revenue Support Grant to local authorities. This is the key public spending aggregate used in the government's medium-term financial strategy.

Table 1.2 General Government Expenditure – £Million (excluding privatization proceeds)

Categories of expenditure	1991–92 Out-turn	1992–93 Estimated out-turn	1993–94 Plans	1994–95 Plans	1995–96 Plans	Real terms				
						1991–92 Out-turn	1992–93 Estimated out-turn	1993–94 Plans	1994–95 Plans	1995–96 Plans
Central government expenditure	144 537	158 700	166 100	171 600	176 400	144.5	152.2	155.1	155.2	155.3
Central Support for local government	53 359	58 900	58 700	62 000	64 300	53.4	56.5	54.8	56.1	56.6
Local Authority self-financed expenditure	10 830	10 900	11 100	11 000	10 800	10.8	10.4	10.4	9.9	9.5
Financing requirements for public corporations	2 496	3 360	3 880	1 910	1 690	2.5	3.2	3.6	1.7	1.5
Reserve			4 000	7 000	10 000			3.7	6.3	8.8
Adjustment		100					.1			
New control total	211 222	232 000	243 800	253 600	263 300	211.2	222.5	227.6	229.3	231.7
Cyclical social security	11 023	13 000	15 500	16 500	17 000	11.0	12.5	14.5	15.0	15.0
Central government debt interest	16 320	17 700	20 000	24 500	27 500	16.3	17.0	19.0	22.0	24.0
Accounting adjustments	5 245	6 000	7 500	8 500	9 000	5.2	5.8	7.0	7.5	8.0
General government expenditure	243 810	268 800	286 600	302 500	316 400	243.8	257.8	267.6	273.5	278.4

Source: Tables 2A.3 and 2A.4 Autumn Statement 1992 Cmd 2096 (HM Treasury, 1992).

Table 1.3 New Control Total by Department – £Million

Departments	1987–88 Out-turn	1988–89 Out-turn	1989–90 Out-turn	1990–91 Out-turn	1991–92 Out-turn	1992–93 Estimated out-turn	1993–94 Plans	1994–95 Plans	1995–96 Plans
Ministry of Defence	18 922	19 221	20 777	21 797	23 015	23 800	23 520	23 750	23 220
Foreign and Commonwealth Office	718	772	898	968	1 133	1 360	1 220	1 210	1 220
Overseas Development	1 293	1 544	1 672	1 748	1 991	2 250	2 270	2 310	2 360
Agriculture Fisheries and Foods	1 833	1 607	1 487	2 137	2 219	2 280	2 820	2 930	3 110
Trade and Industry	894	934	1 626	2 342	1 880	1 650	2 590	1 130	1 060
ECGD	153	116	358	372	216	110	-30	-60	-30
Department of Employment	3 891	3 828	3 744	3 787	3 636	3 640	3 740	3 700	3 730
Transport	2 633	2 733	3 498	4 634	5 354	6 750	6 430	6 070	5 860
DOE – Housing	2 984	2 914	3 113	6 907	7 729	8 610	7 880	8 190	8 190
DOE – Environment	903	620	965	1 216	1 307	1 560	1 440	1 210	1 130
DOE – PSA				62	52	60	120	20	50
DOE – Local Government	18 238	18 823	19 531	20 392	28 177	30 880	29 380	30 900	32 560
Home Office	3 376	3 635	4 137	4 911	5 573	5 970	6 120	6 330	6 490
Legal Department	983	1 142	1 373	1 635	2 000	2 400	2 590	2 780	2 940
Education	3 228	3 519	4 865	5 655	6 342	6 980	9 520	10 120	10 500
National Heritage	631	687	713	782	889	1 020	990	1 010	1 040
Health	16 799	18 486	20 003	22 523	25 657	28 280	29 880	31 240	32 300
Social Security	41 221	42 806	46 000	48 821	54 722	61 200	65 000	67 100	70 800
Scotland	7 876	8 530	8 985	9 770	11 744	12 670	13 450	13 960	14 400
Wales	3 272	3 580	3 801	4 441	5 307	6 020	6 300	6 560	6 780
Northern Ireland	4 474	5 086	5 380	5 496	5 984	6 580	6 910	7 100	7 340
Chancellor's Department	2 480	2 692	3 154	3 346	3 394	3 560	3 390	3 560	3 650
Cabinet Office – OPSS	731	788	903	989	1 060	1 140	1 250	1 320	1 350
Cabinet Office – other, etc.	218	240	264	303	349	450	480	480	490
Local authority self-financed expenditure	9 226	10 809	15 550	15 062	10 830	10 900	11 100	11 000	10 800
European Communities	1 661	1 006	2 316	2 013	662	1 770	1 410	2 650	2 000
Reserve							4 000	7 000	10 000
Adjustment						100			
Panning Total	148 638	156 118	175 113	192 109	211 222	232 000	243 800	253 600	263 300

Source: Table 2A.5 Autumn Statement 1992 Cmd 2096 (HM Treasury, 1992).

New Control Total

For the 1992 autumn statement the government made a number of changes in the system of public expenditure control. These changes were designed to improve control to help ensure that the government achieved its medium-term financial objective of reducing over time the share of national income taken by public spending. To help achieve this the government set what is termed the 'New Control Total'. This replaced the former Planning Total.

The Planning Total included central government's own spending, central government support for local authority expenditure, the finance requirement's of the nationalized industries and other public corporations and a Reserve and was net of privatization proceeds. It excluded local authority self-financed expenditure, central government debt interest and various accounting adjustments. The New Control Total in comparison with the Planning Total makes the following main changes:

1. excludes cyclical social security payments in an attempt to isolate expenditure resulting from the economic cycle;
2. includes local authority self-financed expenditure as it is seen as not being cyclical and under significant government influence though grants, the ability of the government to cap local authority spending and, control over capital receipts;
3. excludes privatization proceeds.

The New Control Total is cash limited as was the previous Planning Total. It should be pointed out that the Planning Total had in fact been revised in 1990 following A New Public Expenditure Planning Total (HM Treasury, 1988). This was in an attempt to distinguish between that expenditure which was the responsibility of central government and that which was the

Table 1.4 Reconciliation between the former planning total and the new control total and general government expenditure

Former planning total	New control total
Social security – Non-cyclical – Cyclical	Social security – Non-cyclical
Other programmes	Other programmes
Privatization proceeds	Local authority self-financed
Reserve	expenditure
Planning Total	*New Control Total*
Local authority self-financed expenditure	Cyclical social security
Debt interest	Debt interest
Accounting adjustments	Accounting adjustments
General government expenditure (excluding privatization proceeds)	General government expenditure (excluding privatization proceeds)

Source: Autumn Statement 1992.

responsibility of local authorities. The 1990 White Paper, The Government's Expenditure Plans 1990–91 to 1992–92 (HM Treasury, 1990) represented the first time the definition had been used. A reconciliation between the former Planning Total and the New Control total with General Government Expenditure is set out in Table 1.4.

Supply Expenditure

Supply Expenditure is the annual expenditure by central government that is voted by Parliament in the Supply Estimates. Supply Expenditure does not cover all central government expenditure, the biggest exclusion being that which is financed by the National Insurance Fund which covers approximately half of the spending on Social Security. Other exclusions include payments to the European Community and the salaries of judges and the Comptroller and Auditor General. Supply estimates are the means by which the government seeks authority for its expenditure in the next financial year. Statutory authority is given in the annual Appropriation Act passed before the parliamentary summer recess. This authority is for cash expenditure in relation to those items for which the liability to pay has arisen and the method of payment issued. Money spent before the passing of the Appropriation Act is authorized by means of a system of 'Votes on Account'. (A summary of the supply procedure is set out in the Appendix at the end of this chapter.)

There was always considerable overlap between Supply Expenditure and the Planning Total. This was further enhanced by A New Public Expenditure Planning Total (HM Treasury, 1988) mentioned earlier. This overlap has been retained in the New Control Total. If a department's spending needs change unexpectedly during the year and extra provision is needed then a supplementary estimate must be sought. This requires Treasury and parliamentary approval. Since 1983 departments have been able to carry forward 5% of their capital expenditure and certain major maintenance programmes with a subsequent re-vote on any monies carried forward by Parliament. In 1988 this provision was extended to revenue subject to Treasury approval although as can be imagined the scope for slippage on revenue costs is not as great as with capital projects.

The total of public expenditure is illustrated in Tables 1.3 and 1.4. Table 1.3 shows the New Control Total and the total of General Government Expenditure. This table of General Government Expenditure shows planned expenditure in cash terms and contrasts it with plans in real terms. The figures have been adjusted to 1991–92 price levels by excluding the effects of inflation as measured by the gross domestic product deflator.

It can be seen from Table 1.1 that the planning process is one which takes a considerable time. At one time plans were made for up to five years ahead but this has now been reduced to three years. Obviously, however, the political expediencies of the day will take precedence over the political contingencies of tomorrow. In the early days of the planning process figures were given in constant prices or volume terms. Planning in volume terms had advantages in that, for example, constant prices directly related to the operational decisions of managers on recruitment and other physical resources and revealed the 'real' trend over time. By 1976, however, it had become increasingly apparent that the use of constant prices in times of high inflation and tight monetary control caused problems in terms of planning and monitoring public expenditure as cash spending resulted in programmes costing often considerably more than anticipated. Under the volume planning system of planning and control there was no automatic reduction in the volume of the programme; if prices for a programme rose extra cash was made available and government expenditure rose accordingly. Cash limits were, therefore, introduced and the cash limit figure became the determinant of expenditure during the year. The reasons given for the introduction of cash limits in the White Paper, Cash Limits on Public Expenditure (HM Treasury, 1976) included the need to:

1. give greater financial discipline;
2. ensure that resources consumed by the public sector were related to the ability of the economy as a whole to support this level of consumption;
3. control the sum spent in the financial year so that it relates directly to the plan set out in the annual budget;
4. contribute to the government's counter inflation policy by constraining the ability of managers to pay higher prices;
5. relate the budget to the cash that would be spent during the year even if inflation was significantly higher than predicted.

It should be remembered, however, that not all government expenditure can be cash limited as certain items are demand led. An example of demand led expenditure is the social security budget as a legal entitlement to benefit exists as long as the conditions of the benefit are met. Other examples of demand led expenditures include pensions and child benefits. As an illustration of another means of controlling this type of expenditure child benefit has not been fully uprated for inflation over time. Cash limits have also been imposed on certain areas of the social security budget effectively limiting entitlement to benefits; for example, the social fund. It was also stated in Regina v Secretary of State for the Environment, *ex parte* Greenwich Borough Council that the Secretary of State's obligation to fund the Housing Revenue Account under the Local Government and Housing Act 1989 was subject to the extent of the state's available resources (*The Times*, 27.8.90).

The reasons why a particular item makes an appearance in the spending plans of the government are complex. It would also be a mistake to ignore the behavioural implications of the whole process, as for example when expenditure bids are offered as sacrificial lambs in order to protect the core ambitions of the spending departments. This process has been described as 'haggling in a Turkish Bazaar' (Thain and Wright, 1990, p. 51). More conventional reasons for the inclusion of particular items of new expenditure include:

1. clear political commitments as set out in the party manifesto;
2. changing departmental objectives;
3. pressures from influential bodies including non-governmental pressure groups, other government departments, Members of Parliament and the EC;
4. ministerial judgement and initiative;
5. commitments created from past expenditure decisions;
6. rational investment appraisal indicating that the planned expenditure will result in savings.

Clearly, the game is one played in an atmosphere of political intrigue in which the ministers and the civil service mandarins are involved in wheeling and dealing to protect their own interests and advance their own causes (for a full and interesting discussion on this process see Likierman, 1988).

The 1993 public expenditure rounds was a particularly difficult one for the government. These difficulties were caused by the size of the public sector borrowing requirement and an economy still struggling to come out of recession with tax increases ruled out in the government's election manifesto although clearly the extension of value added tax in the March 1993 budget represented an increase in indirect taxes. A review of public sector expenditure was therefore launched and at various stages 'kites were flown' in terms of, for example, the extension of prescription charges to the elderly and children and the imposition of hospital hotel charges. At the time of writing these issues are still to be resolved although an option could also be to increase direct taxes possibly in a more hidden manner by restricting tax allowances to the basic rate of income tax as happened with mortgage interest tax relief in the March 1993 budget.

Finally, in order to conclude this section mention should be made of the Contingency Reserve. The object of the reserve is to allow expenditure to be undertaken which has not been planned for specifically without upsetting the Budget plans. If possible any additional spending on behalf of a programme is met by savings elsewhere in that programme. Where this is not possible increased expenditure resulting from ministerial decisions is charged to the Contingency Reserve. Examples of its use might include a decision to launch a new initiative or to meet the costs of such events as natural disasters like severe weather. The Contingency Reserve should not be confused with the Contingency Fund. The role of the Contingency Fund is to provide money for payments, which in the public interest, cannot be postponed until the money has been voted by Parliament. The Fund is repaid as soon as possible, for example, if expenditure has to be incurred before a Supplementary Estimate can be passed by Parliament then the Fund is repaid as soon as provision in Supplementary Estimates becomes available.

1.2 The Citizen's Charter

Before turning to examine a number of the major areas of spending within the public sector and the individual policy initiatives affecting them it is first necessary to examine the Citizen's Charter because, as will be seen, this government policy has implications throughout the public service. The Citizen's Charter was announced by John Major in 1991. The aims of the Charter are to achieve better quality in the provision of public services and make them more responsive to public demands. The key to this is seen as 'to listen to what people say' with the motto of the 'customer comes first' (Citizen's Charter, 1992, p. 1). The government again states that resources to fund public services are limited and that taxpayers have a right to expect that the money spent is used to maximum effect. The first report on the Citizen's Charter (1992) points out that new management structures are being developed, competition being introduced or extended and arrangements for pay changing rapidly. All these changes being in line with 'the pursuit of a single worthwhile cause: the safeguarding and improvement of our public services for the benefit of those who use them at a cost which the nation can afford' (p. 1).

Charters have been published in a wide variety of fields including railways, schools, tax offices and the Health Service. In the Health Service the Patient's Charter sets out key rights and entitlements. These include the right to:

1. receive health care on the basis of clinical need, regardless of the ability to pay;
2. enjoy respect for privacy, dignity and religious and cultural beliefs;
3. to be given a clear explanation of any treatment proposed, including any risks and alternatives, before agreeing to the treatment;
4. have access to personal health records, and to know that those working for the Health Service will, by law, keep those records confidential;
5. be given information on local Health Service quality standards and maximum waiting times;
6. be guaranteed admission to hospital for virtually all treatments by a specific date;
7. specific times for out-patient appointments and a maximum waiting time of 30 minutes;
8. a named qualified nurse, midwife or health visitor responsible for the patient's care.

As examples of standards being set by organizations the following are some of the targets set:

1. BT local offices aim to resolve problems and enquiries within two working days or, if this is not possible, to agree with the customer a plan of action.
2. Parcel force aims to respond to telephone enquiries the same day.
3. British Gas aims to reply to letters within five working days.
4. Westminster City Council Library Service aims to provide a good quality service to its membership by a prompt response to requests.

In local government the Audit Commission under Part 1 of the 1992 Local Government Finance Act was charged with the responsibility of drawing up a set of indicators for measuring the performance of local authority services. The Audit Commission list of indicators was published in December 1992 and covers such services as education, social services, libraries, planning and housing benefit. The indicators were selected on the basis of:

1. the ability of the public to comprehend them without over simplification and without creating incentives for authorities to distort them;
2. making comparability between authorities possible;
3. enabling the measurement of how effectively services meet the needs of different groups of local citizens;
4. the ability to compare the service for one authority over a period of time.

The Audit Commission aims to publish its first national report in 1995 (Citizen's Charter, 1992).

An important part of the Citizen's Charter is the market testing of services provided by civil servants in terms of comparison with the private sector of quality and cost. The government aims to market test services in, for example, the Ministry of Defence to the value of £323m involving 12 200 members of staff, the Home Office to the value of £120 involving 3850 members of staff, and the Department of the Environment to the value of £58m involving 700 staff. The total value of this market testing is £1449m and involves the jobs of 44 250 civil servants (Citizen's Charter, 1992, p. 61). The type of services covered includes computing services, internal audit, vehicle maintenance and professional property services.

For the policy to be successful it can be argued that there will be a need to:

1. give managers greater freedom of action by allowing them to set local pay and conditions for staff;
2. give operational managers budget holding responsibilities enabling them to negotiate such matters as cleaning services, training services and financial services;
3. encourage delegation to the lowest possible managerial level and provide these individuals with the necessary skills to do the job;
4. provide the rewards of enterprise to managers with clear promotional routes for those who have the capacity to do the job.
5. encourage a major cultural shift towards customer responsiveness, achieving value or money, quality in service delivery and accountability.
6. provide vision as to the direction of the initiative in order to provide a focus for expectation of each service.

Whether unrealistic expectations will be developed in clients will only be known in time. The Citizen's Charter initiative does, however, have important implications for public sector managers in that the implementation of the measures called for represent another demand on scarce resources.

1.3   The Financial Management Initiative

In line with its general objective of improving efficiency in the Civil Service the Government developed its Financial Management Initiative (FMI) in 1982. The aims of the FMI are to improve the management, allocation and control of resources. In detail the White Paper, Efficiency and Effectiveness in the Civil Service (Treasury and Civil Service Committee, 1982) the aims of the FMI were to give managers:

1. A clear view of their objectives; and means to assess, and wherever possible measure, outputs or performance in relation to these objectives.
2. Well-defined responsibility for making the best use of their resources, including a critical scrutiny of output and value for money.
3. The information (particularly about costs), the training and access to expert advice which they needed to exercise their responsibilities effectively.

Prior to the FMI the Rayner scrutinies (National Audit Office, 1986) had attempted to look at value for money in central government. The objectives of these scrutinies were:

1. To mount an eye-catching and public demonstration of how the citizen, business and industry were overburdened with forms and requests for information.
2. To examine the general practice and conventions in government which were barriers to the effective management of business resources by ministers and their officials.
3. To examine, in collaboration with ministers, selected specific activities and functions in particular departments which might be unnecessarily costly or wasteful. This examination was to question all aspects of the work normally taken for granted.

In its report 'The Rayner Scrutiny Programmes 1979–1983,' the National Audit Office (1986b) recorded annual savings of £421m identified by the scrutiny programmes. A more recent example of the results of a scrutiny exercise is contained in Learning from Experience (report to the Minister of State for Defence Procurement, Ministry of Defence, 1988) where it was reported after a scrutiny exercise that between £3bn and £4bn of the Ministry of Defence's annual expenditure related to costs which were unforeseen when projects started. The report also criticized the lack of clear responsibility, authority and accountability of the managers of major defence projects (quoted in *Public Finance and Accountancy*, 20/5/88).

At about the same time that the Rayner exercises were getting off the ground an attempt had been made to introduce a management information system (MINIS) into central government by Michael Heseltine for the use of Ministers. The idea was to enable Ministers to gain information on their departments to allow better control and more informed decision making. The key features of MINIS were the preparation of annual statements summarizing performance and plans for each of the department's activities; the examination of these by Ministers, top management and the managers directly responsible for the activity; and the requirement to follow up with agreed action. Effectively, the FMI combined the relatively simple Rayner studies and MINIS into a more sophisticated financial management framework.

The National Audit Office (NAO) reported that in respect of management accounting and budgetary control systems developed under the FMI an investigation in respect of 12 departments revealed that:

1. All departments had found it necessary to develop their systems for the budgeting and control of administrative costs and for informing managers of the cost of the resources allocated to them and of their performance in using these resources particularly as regards measures of output.
2. The range of costs covered by departmental budgetary control had varied but had become more comprehensive as the systems had developed.
3. The extent to which managers could exercise control over the components of their budgets varied as did the opportunities to transfer provisions between budget heads.
4. Departments had made encouraging progress in developing budgeting as an effective control over administrative costs, although more still needed to be done to achieve the full potential benefits. In particular, the area of developing links between input costs and the value of outputs.

(National Audit Office, 1986a)

The NAO study established that the FMI had resulted in departments identifying the need to enhance existing management systems or to introduce new ones. For this they had produced sound plans which, when fully implemented, should result in systems capable of supporting managers at all levels in operating according to FMI principles.

Thus it can be seen that some progress seems to have been made. It should be noted, however, that the above comments relate to the control of administration costs and say little about departmental programmes where the largest sums of government money are spent. Clearly, there will be greater difficulties here as government policy may be questioned and, also there are many complex connections between programmes. These links exist not only within each department but also with other departments and agencies within the public sector.

The latest initiative that the government has taken in respect of central government is the establishment of agencies as outlined in the proposals of the Efficiency Unit report on the Civil Service, 'Improving Management in Government: The Next Steps' (1988). Agencies have been established, for example, in respect of the Department of Trade and Industry for Companies House (October 1988), the National Weights and Measures Laboratory (April 1989), the Warren Spring Laboratory (April 1989) and the Laboratory of the Government Chemist (April 1989). At the time of writing one of the newest agencies was the Medicines Control Agency which operates the medicines licensing system in the UK on behalf of the Department of Health and became a trading fund on 1 April 1993. Turnover is approximately £20m per annum and it employs some 350 staff. Costs will be recovered from fees paid by the pharmaceutical industry for licence applications and other services. Expenditure will not be controlled by a cash limit so the agency will have to adjust its expenditure in line with its income. It will be allowed to finance capital expenditure from revenue and create a reserve. It has been stated that some 350 000 civil servants now work in agencies (*Public Finance and Accountancy*, p. 17, 11 June 1993).

In 1992 the National Audit Office reported that the Vehicle Inspectorate (the first executive agency) had achieved a 9% increase in its efficiency and saved £3.5m (*Public Finance and Accountancy*, p. 9, 21 February 1992). There had also been an improvement in its service to clients. Research carried out by Dopson (Dopson, 1993, pp. 17–23) in the HMSO may not, however, be so encouraging as a number of staff comments were negative, although, this was a small scale study. In contrast Kemp's comment was that 'in terms of fun, the place to be is the Agency. There the people have the opportunity to develop new services, be innovative and give a better service to the public' (Kemp, 1990). The 'jury' is thus still out until further research is done but the government needs to consider closely whether on the one hand it can advocate freedom and initiative yet at the same time establishing rigid guidelines setting out restrictions on trading performance as with HMSO.

The basis of the proposals to establish agencies is to give managers increased managerial and operational freedom to meet defined targets. Each agency is required to produce a corporate plan which sets targets for the quality of service and productivity. Chief executives are appointed for each agency and financial and managerial responsibilities are delegated to them. While there are wide implications for the staff envolved in these changes it is clear that the agencies will need sound systems for performance monitoring with, again a major role for the management accounting function and sophisticated financial management. It should also be borne in mind that the achievement of agency status might be an intermediate step before privatization. This appears to be the case with the Chessington Computer Agency responsible for the payment of payroll and pensions in that a couple of years as an agency will allow it 'to develop its business on sound commercial lines' (William Waldegrave quoted in *Public Finance and Accountancy*, p. 16, 11 June 1993).

1.4   The National Health Service

In the White Paper, Working for Patients (1989) it was stated that gross expenditure on the Health service will have risen from £8 billion in 1978–79 to

£26 billion in 1989–90. Given this rise in expenditure the government claimed that it desired to raise the performance of all hospitals and general practitioners to that of the best. The White Paper therefore proposed seven key measures. These were to:

1. make the Health Service more responsive to the needs of patients and to transfer power and responsibility to the local level;
2. allow hospitals to apply for the status of self-governing trusts;
3. allow hospitals to offer their services to other health authorities and charge appropriately;
4. reduce waiting times and improve the quality of services;
5. enable GPs with over 11 000 patients to apply for their own National Health Service (NHS) budget to buy a defined range of hospital services from either the private sector or the NHS;
6. improve the efficiency of NHS management by reducing it in size and reforming it along business lines;
7. make better use of resources, improve quality of service and value for money.

(Source: Working for Patients, Department of Health, 1989)

These concepts mean a significantly increased role for financial management as two of the underlying principles of the White Paper, as can be gleaned from the points above, are achieving better financial control and monitoring along commercial lines. This is of particularly importance in such areas as:

1. identifying the costs of patient care, as despite improvements in hospital financial information as a result of the Resource Management Initiative there is only a limited ability to link the diagnosis of patients to the cost of treatment;
2. appraising the opportunities that may exist in joint ventures with private developers;
3. managing capital assets and appraising capital investment decisions. This will be particularly important when charging is introduced for the use of capital assets as they have previously been regarded as a 'free good' for which no charge was made;
4. an education and training role in advising staff who may have had little or no experience of financial management.

These changes were incorporated in the National Health Service Community Care Act 1990. A number of the main features of the Act are detailed in the text which follows.

National Health Service trusts

Under the Act the Secretary of State may direct Regional Health Authorities to establish NHS trusts. These trusts assume responsibility for ownership and management of hospitals or other facilities. The trusts, while remaining within the NHS, have to arrange contracts for services but continue to provide treatment to NHS patients free at the point of delivery. The Secretary of State sets annual financing limits for each trust taking into account the trust's capital investment plans and needs for working capital. Trusts have the power to acquire, own and dispose of assets, borrow money subject to their external financing limit, build up reserves, establish pay and employment policies, enter into contracts to deliver health services, train their staff and accept gifts on trust or otherwise. Trusts are required to earn a 6% return on assets. If unsuccessful it can be wound up. The trust is accountable to the Secretary of State via the National Health Service Management Executive (NHSME). In 1992, six 'outposts' of the NHSME were set up to monitor trusts. Their duties include reviewing business plans, annual reports and capital investment plans. On 1 April 1991, 57 trusts became operational with a further 99 following in April 1992. The third wave of trusts in April 1993 was 128 with a fourth wave planned for April 1994. Table 1.5 summarizes the differences between a trust and a directly managed unit remaining under health authority management.

External financing limits

Capital expenditure by NHS trusts forms part of the public expenditure provision in the health programme. NHS trusts can only obtain finance from income they generate themselves or from borrowing. An annual external financing limit (EFL) controls access to external finance by the trust. The EFL is a net financing concept measured by new loans taken out by the trust less loans repaid adjusted for changes in deposits and other holdings of liquid assets. This will be set annually be the Department of Health. The EFL can be positive or negative. If the EFL is negative this means that the trust has to repay loans rather than develop new capital assets.

General practitioner (GP) fund-holding

GPs are allowed to apply for recognition as a fund-holding practice. The original size of practice was a minimum of 9000 registered patients but this has since been reduced to 5000. GPs must prove that they have the ability to manage a budget and have adequate administrative support (including a computerized information system). The budget for each GP is received from the Regional Health Authority although the whole year's budget is not provided upfront and is based on the relative need of patients registered with the practice. These funds can then be spent on such items as drugs, payments to trusts and private hospitals, and goods or services on an approved list. Overspending on the budget up to 5% in any one year is allowable although persistent overspending will be investigated. Money allocated to GP fund-holders is deducted by the Regional Health Authority from its allocation to District Health Authorities. In the financial year 1993/94 drug budgets were set on the basis of capitation bench marks rather than historic cost adjusted for price and volume changes. It is probably inevitable that as the system of GP fund-holding evolves that refinements will take place in budget allocation methods as the government pursues its quest for value for money. Practices will thus feel additional pressure for sound financial management procedures in particular in the area of budgetary control.

It should be noted that the district health authority will be in the position of being a purchaser authority in terms of the services it needs as well as a provider authority. This effectively extends the client and contractor arrangements which have existed in local government since 1980 to another area of the public sector, although it will be noted above that the number of trusts is increasing at a very rapid rate.

Table 1.5 A comparison between NHS trust hospital and directly managed units

Issue	NHS trust	Directly managed units
Management	Each trust is run by its own Board of Directors. The trust is free to determine its own management structure. Senior professional staff must be involved in management.	The district health authority (DHA) is responsible for the unit with the Unit General Manager (UGM) being responsible for day-to-day management. Internal management arrangements are subject to DHA approval.
Accountability	Each trust board is directly accountable to the Secretary of State via the NHSME.	Each unit is accountable to its managing DHA. The DHA is accountable to the RHA and the RHA is accountable to the Secretary of State via the NHSME.
Funding	Each trust's income is largely derived from contracts with health authorities, GP fund holders and the private sector.	Each unit's income is largely derived from contracts with health authorities, GP fund holders and the private sector.
Services	Each trust is free to determine the range and extent of servicesit wishes to provide, except that where a service must be provided locally, a trust can beobliged to provide it if it is the only unit able to do so.	The range and extent of services offered by a unit are determined by the managing DHA.
	Each trust provides the services which it is contracted to provide.	Each unit provides the services which it is contracted to provide.
	There is no requirement for a trust to consult the Community Health Council on closure or changes of use.	Closure and changes of use are subject to formal consultation with the Community Health Council.
Employment of staff	Each trust sets its own staffing structure and levels. It employs all its own staff including consultants.	Each unit determines its own staffing structure but its staff are employed by the DHA or RHA.
	Each trust is free to determine the pay and conditions of employment of all staff it employs. Staff to a transferring trust retain their existing terms and conditions of service until changes are negotiated.	Pay and other terms and conditions of employment of nearly all staff are subject to Review Body or national Whitley Council agreementsor departmental determination.

Table 1.5 (*cont'd.*)

Issue	NHS trust	Directly managed units
Financial duties	Each trust has a statutory duty to break even, taking one year with another. It is also required to achieve a 6% return on assets and keep within its agreed EFL.	The managing DHA has a statutory duty to balance its budget each year. The UGM has a managerial imperative to ensure that the units break even. The unit has to pay capital charges equivalent to depreciation and 6% interest on its fixed assets.
Prices	Each trust prices to cover running costs, depreciation and return on assets.	Each unit prices to cover running costs and capital charges (depreciation and interest).
Surpluses	Trusts may retain surpluses.	Units cannot retain surpluses.
Borrowing	Each trust is free to borrow within its agreed EFL.	Units have no power to borrow.
Insurance	Trusts do not insure for clinical negligence. They may insure for other insurable risks.	Units do not insure for clinical negligence or other insurable risks, with certain limited exceptions.
Ownership of assets	Each trust owns its own assets. It is generally free to acquire and dispose of assets and retains the proceeds from any sales.	Each unit's assets are owned by the Secretary of State or the health authority. Acquisition and disposal of assets are subject to control and regulation by the Department of Health, the RHA and the managing DHA. Retention of proceeds from sale is subject to decisions by the RHA.
Capital	Each trust makes its case for capital development to the NHSME. It funds the agreed programme from its own resources or by borrowing within its agreed EFL.	Each unit makes its case for capital developments to the DHA or RHA. Funding is dependent on allocations from the regional capital programme.

From 1977 money was allocated to Regional Health Authorities in England on the basis of a complex formula which was known as RAWP (Resource Allocation Working Party). The RAWP formula included such elements as morbidity (sickness), size of population, population structure, cost weightings and cross-boundary flows where patients moved from one health district to another for treatment. This formula has now been replaced by the funding of regional health authorities on a capitation basis, weighted to reflect the health and age distribution of the population and the relative costs of providing services on a regional basis. Where cross-boundary flows exist for patient care, regions will pay each other directly and in full. In 1992 a report produced by the Association of Community Health Councils in England and Wales indicated that the new formula will result in inner city districts making large cuts in services unless regions take greater account of social deprivation in calculating district allocations. Clearly, if the Association's conclusions are correct, this will put additional financial pressure on some districts' resources.

With regard to the funding of hospital services each district health authority is responsible for buying the services it needs from its own hospitals, from other authority hospitals, from self-governing trust hospitals or the private sector. In this manner it is hoped that hospitals will deliver the best and most efficient service and the district will achieve value for money. Those hospitals which are the most efficient, it is claimed, will attract funds, while those which are inefficient will have a major incentive to improve – the fear of closure.

It has been pointed out (Masters, 1993, pp. 4–5) that the changes incorporated in the 1990 Act had significant implications for the finance function. Prior to this Act the Treasurer of in the NHS primarily saw that function as management of the cash limit. There was thus a need for a major change of financial culture to one of being more pro-active and providing financial management information and advice. Masters claims in a little over two years the finance function has moved to one which:

1. operates in a radically different revenue allocation system;
2. meets the challenges of the NHS trusts;
3. implements a completely new system of asset management;
4. creates costing and settlement systems to underpin the new contracts;
5. overhauls the financial planning, monitoring and reporting systems.

Importantly, 'General managers and chief executives…started to see the crucial role that finance can and should play in the overall management team.' With the reforms continuing as more hospitals apply for trust status it is unlikely that this recognition of the importance of sound financial management will stop at just the management team but will percolate throughout the organization.

1.5   Local government

The local government sector has had to deal with a considerable volume of legislation since the Conservative Party first came to power in 1979. Those measures of a financial nature include:

1. the Local Government Planning and Land Act in 1980 which established competitive tendering for Direct Labour Organizations;
2. the Local Government Finance Act in 1982 set up the Audit Commission for Local Authorities in England and Wales;
3. the Local Government Act 1988 which extended the principles of competitive tendering to a range of other services;
4. the Local Government Finance Act 1988 introduced the Community Charge in England and Wales;
5. the replacement of the Community Charge by the Council Tax under the Local Government Finance Act 1992.

Local government has been at the forefront of the government's desire to open the public sector to the principle of competitive tendering. As stated above this was first applied in 1980 to direct labour organizations (DLOs). A DLO is the authority's own workforce which it employs in order to provide specific services to the authority rather than employ private contractors. Under the 1980 Act authorities were required to:

1. compete for work in specified areas against the private sector (over time the original categories have been extended);
2. earn a rate of return of 5% on the current cost of capital employed by the DLO;
3. to keep separate accounts for each category of work and to publish these accounts by the 30 September in each year.

Failure by the authority to achieve the rate of return could result in the Secretary of State closing down the DLO. As a result of this power the DLO at Haringey was closed down. Similar competition provisions have now been extended to other DLO activities, although the new term is a direct service organization (DSO). The 1988 Act covers the collection of refuse, cleaning services, catering services, maintenance of grounds and the repair and maintenance of vehicles. Appropriate targets have been set in each case, for example, the target for the cleaning contract is to break even. Given the large amount of work involved authorities were given a staggered timetable to introduce the legislation. Under Statutory Instrument No. 1468 an authority such as Monmouth District Council was given the following timetable for action for each activity covered by the Act to prepare for competitive tendering:

Vehicle maintenance and repair	by 1.8.89
Cleaning (non-building)	by 1.1.90
Refuse collection	by 1.8.90
Catering	by 1.1.91
Building cleaning	by 1.8.91

A considerable amount of preparation needs to be done in order to prepare the in-house service for the process of tendering in any area. These steps include the need for detailed business plans to be prepared and tender documents completed. Given that many local authorities often had little comprehensive information on the total workload that the above functions face it can be seen that the preparation of tender documents represents a major challenge. If the tender is then successfully won there is then a need to introduce an organizational culture which requires motives which are both profit and service motivated since the DSO must earn profits to survive and achieve high standards to retain its client's loyalty. The financial information system must then be geared to these objectives. The areas of competitive tendering quoted above involve essentially blue-collar jobs. It was suggested in

Table 1.6 Proposed white-collar services tendering dates

	Consultation with local authorities	Laying of statutory instrument	Tendering process
Legal services	Dec. 93–Feb. 94	Mar.–May 94	Jun. 94–Sep. 95
IT	Aug. 93–Feb. 94	Sep.–Nov. 94	Dec. 94–Sep. 96
Finance	Nov. 94–Jan. 95	Feb.–April 95	May 95–Mar. 97
Personnel	Apr.–Oct. 94	May–July 95	Aug. 95–Mar. 97

the first edition of this text that there was no intrinsic reason why white-collar services, such as financial and legal, could not be put out to competitive tender. Table 1.6 outlines a proposed timetable for the main central activities.

Many local authorities had prepared for this action by concluding service level agreements with user departments establishing the standard of service, and its related cost, required. These agreements, where in place, could effectively form the basis of competitive tenders as the majority of the preparatory work has been done in advance of the legal requirement to submit to competitive tender.

It should be noted that the government has taken a firm stand on any practices which are considered by central government to favour the in-house bid for the contract for the service subjected to competitive tender. Powers under Section 14 of the Local Government Act 1988 allow the central government to intervene to negate the effect of such activities. In July 1990 the Secretary of State ordered the Knowsley Metropolitan Borough and East Lindsey District Council to re-tender their refuse collection contracts by July 1991 as a result of judged anti-competitive practices. In *Accountancy Age* for 23.8.90 it was reported that, in the words of the Audit Commission, many councils in terms of compulsory competitive tendering had wasted 'their efforts trying to avoid its effects'. This stresses the needs to meet the challenge of compulsory competitive tendering by sound financial management of the competition units. The powers of the Secretary of State were further enhanced under the Local Government Act 1992: Commencement (No. 2), Order 1992. This allows, for example, intervention at any time after a contract has been awarded rather than as previously after work had commenced. Local government can, however, report an 83% success rate by value of contracts put out to competitive tender since 1989. This statistic is based on 4421 contracts to the value of £1753m. (Public Finance and Accountancy, p. 5, 18 June 1993).

The Local Government Finance Act 1982 is discussed in Chapter 10. Suffice it to say here that the external auditor was given powers to investigate whether a local authority had made proper arrangements to secure value for money in its activities. In part, as a result of its activities in this field, the role of the Audit Commission has now been extended to the full range of organizations within the NHS and to new activities such as NHS Hospital Trusts as they develop (Local Government and Housing Act 1989, Part IX and the National Health Service and Community Care Act 1990). The objective of this process, as set out in Working for Patients, is that there should be more commitment to value for money studies, which would cover a wider range of the NHS than was previously covered, by an audit body that is demonstrably independent of the health authorities, the Family Practitioner Committees and the Health Department.

On 1 April 1990 a new system of financing was introduced for local government (in England and Wales) in the form of the ill-fated Community Charge which increased central control over local government financing both via the ability to cap the charge (by setting an upper limit on the charge that can be levied locally) and the control by central government of the national business rate and the level of government grant. The national business rate and the government grant account for approximately 75% of local government revenue finance. Thus, local government had an ability to control only 25% of its income and, even here, if the government felt an individual council was 'over-spending' against a centrally determined notional Community Charge it could intervene. This intervention could forceably reduce the level of Community Charge and thus make the local authority reduce its budgeted expenditure. These same control principles have been retained with the Council Tax introduced to replace the Community Charge on 1 April 1993 (Local Government Finance Act 1992, S. 54).

The reason for the reduction in the Community Charge and now the council tax is that a local authority must legally set a local charge which will balance its budget. If its grant is fixed and the income from the national business rate has been set by central government the local authority must cut its budget to the expenditure that the local tax can support. The only alternatives are to raise additional income from fees and charges, or to generate efficiency savings. In 1990/91, 21 local authorities were designated for charge capping. Sixteen local authorities challenged the power of the Secretary of State to cap the charge but lost in the House of Lords in a unanimous judgement. The effect of charge capping is illustrated in the case of the Avon County Council and the London Borough of Haringey. The original budgets for Avon and Haringey for 1990/91 were £533.7m and £216.5m respectively. These were reduced to capped figures of £507.1m and £206.5m resulting in reductions to the community charge of £37 for Avon and £71 in Haringey per adult. These changes to the level of the community charge clearly illustrate the power of central government over local authorities and the budget difficulties that charge-capped authorities created. In terms of the council tax capping as stated was retained and the councils shown in Table 1.7 were effected in 1993/94.

Table 1.7   Council tax – proposed caps 1993–94

Authority	Authority's original budget	Original council tax for 2 adults Band D dwelling	Proposed cap	New tax rate
	£m	£	£m	£
Castle Point	8 470	625	7.97	607
Gloucester C.C.	316 889	474–636	306.61	419–581
Harlow	17 953	987	11.20	699

Finally, in this overview of major financial changes in the local government sector a further initiative has taken place in the shape of the Education Reform Act 1988. This Act introduced local financial management into schools with the result that responsibility for day-to-day financial management is delegated to the lowest possible level, that is the school. Schools are formula funded based mainly on the number of pupils on the roll. This type of delegated financial management will place pressure on management accountants to provide appropriate information to managers delegated with responsibility to manage within the constraints of the formula-based budget. It also challenges the traditional structure of many local authority finance departments by placing budgetary control and monitoring at a much lower level than is traditional – in this case, the headteacher. In many local authorities this function was performed by the finance department and senior financial staff within the education department. This trend in wider distribution of financial management is further emphasized by the growth of distributed computer terminal facilities in service departments with on-line budget status enquiries. The accountant will thus no longer be the keeper of the keys to the information chest and, as information is power, his/her role will inevitably be diminished unless he/she rises to the challenge to interpret the information and provide relevant financial advice. In response to such challenges many finance officers are now seconding staff to service departments to meet this new need for interpretative skills. Only time will tell how successfully they meet these demands.

A further development is the number of schools which are opting out of local authority control. These schools will be funded by a Funding Agency for Schools which will allocate funds on the basis of a common funding formula from April 1994. The main component of this formula will be pupil numbers. This has obvious implications for opted out schools as they will have to manage services provided within their financial resources as allocated. Even small primary schools will be able to opt out on the basis of seeking grant maintained status as a 'cluster'.

It is also relevant in dealing with education to refer to changes in further and higher education. Under the Further and Higher Education Act 1992 from the 1 April 1993 colleges of further education, six form and tertiary colleges were removed from local authority control following the former polytechnics (now the new universities) in this respect (under the Education Reform Act 1988). These institutions are now funded by their respective funding councils (the Further Education Funding Council and the Higher Education Funding Council respectively). In order to demonstrate the importance of sound financial management in the university sector, for example, the government has already significantly changed the rules on student funding by altering tuition fees at short notice placing new financial pressures on these institutions. The universities, therefore, clearly need the financial expertise to be able to respond to such changes in order to ensure financial stability.

1.6 The nationalized industries and public corporations

Nationalized industries are publicly owned bodies usually set up by their own statute and having a substantial degree of independence from government. They are usually run by boards and report to the Minister responsible. The government's primary aim for the nationalized industries is that they operate as effectively and efficiently as private firms and to strengthen them to the point where either they can be transferred to the private sector or only where judged necessary remain within the public sector. The financial controls under which these industries operate are set out in The Nationalised Industries (HM Treasury, 1978). This framework includes:

1. Setting strategic goals and targets to provide the framework within which the industry is to operate.
2. Investment and appraisal based on a required rate of return on investment of 8% in real terms before the payment of tax and interest. This return was originally set at 5% in 1975 but 8% is seen as being comparable with private sector returns. Prices are set to cover the return demanded.
3. Financial targets and performance aims are the primary control on the industries. These are set for up to three years ahead.

4. As with NHS trusts discussed earlier an external finance limit is set to control the level of borrowing that the trading activities need. Any expenditure on capital projects above this level has to come from the industries own resources. Coupled with financial targets this results in price increases if the investment goes ahead unless it can be financed from efficiency savings or the sale of surplus fixed assets.
5. Monitoring is carried out by the sponsoring Minister and department. The industries are also subject to periodic monitoring by the Monopolies and Mergers Commission under the 1980 Competition Act.

As examples of the strategic objectives set, British Coal is required to develop a deep mine business that achieves sustainable profits, the British Waterways Board is to encourage the fullest practicable use of the waterways while at the same time acting commercially and Nuclear Electric strategic goals include increasing profit and reducing total and unit costs (HM Treasury, 1993, para. 6.5). Table 1.8 summarizes the required returns and performance to date for a number of the nationalized industries.

The management accounting systems generally employed by these industries are the most directly comparable with the private sector of those areas of the public sector discussed in this introduction. There is no evidence that the privatization programme is ending, confirming Sir Geoffrey Howe's statement in the opening paragraph of this chapter. Future privatization candidates include British Coal, British Rail, Parcelforce and various subsidiaries in London Buses Limited. Where operations cannot be privatized as with, for example, the BBC then internal markets have been introduced, notably the scheme known as 'producer's choice' giving producers the option to use 'in-house' services or go outside the Corporation. It should also be pointed out that NHS trusts are treated as public corporations in the public expenditure planning process.

In 1979 the nationalized industries accounted for about 9% of gross domestic producer (GDP), 11% of total investment and employed 1.8 million people. By 1991 the share of GDP had dropped to under 2.5%, investment had fallen to approximately 3% of total investment and employment levels were 0.5 million

Table 1.8 Nationalized industries financial targets and performance

Industry	Current target	Latest results
British Rail	by 1992–93 Public Subsidy for Regional Railways down to £345m and Network South East out of grant	1991–92 subsidy Regional Railways £550m and Network South East £350m
British Waterways	1992–93 Breakeven after grant	1991–92 Breakeven after grant
Civil Aviation Authority	8% Return on Capital 1992–93 to 1994–95	7.1% return for period 1989–92
London Transport	1992–93 £70m surplus	1991–92 deficit £123m
Scottish Nuclear	1992–93 4.3% return on capital	1991–92 2.8% rate of return

workers. The continued intention to privatize, and the on-going drive for greater efficiency, requires that management accounting systems are efficiently adaptable to meet the increased demands placed upon them.

1.7 Summary of text

Chapter 2 examines approaches to the measurement of the costs of specific services and discusses the problem of using costs in value for money studies and the apportionment and control of overhead costs. The importance of costs in the construction of service level agreements (SLAs) is considered as is the technique of full absorption costing. An examination of some of the costing problems which are specific to the NHS is also made.

Chapter 3 considers the use by the public sector of marginal costing and the practical limitations of the technique. It also examines the concept of relevant costing for decision-making purposes and considers it usefulness to the decision maker in the contracting process for services now found in the public sector.

Chapter 4 looks at budgeting processes in the public sector. It examines the traditional incremental approach to budget setting, considers developments, and contrasts the incremental approach with more modern approaches such as planned programme budgeting and zero-based budgeting. The chapter also discusses business planning and the formula based budget systems now becoming increasingly common in the public sector.

Chapter 5 studies the control process in budgeting by examination of expenditure profiling, variance analysis and standard costing in a competitive environment.

Chapter 6 studies the concept of sound working capital management and stresses the importance of the techniques available in generating the potential for savings to the public sector organization.

Chapter 7 examines the methods of financing capital expenditure available to public sector bodies and contains a study of three specialist areas: leasing, debt management and derivatives.

Chapter 8 examines capital budgeting in terms of the development of capital programmes in the public sector, the assessment of revenue implications and the consideration of non-financial factor in the capital budgeting decision.

Chapter 9 considers methods of investment appraisal available including discounted cash flow and cost benefit analysis. The problems of risk and inflation are also discussed. The concept of non-financial factors in the decision process is further developed.

Chapter 10 discusses the development of the audit function in the public sector and charts its movement from a role which was primarily one of stewardship to one of examination of the arrangements made by the organization to achieve economy efficiency and effectiveness in the conduct of its financial affairs.

The book concludes with a section containing a number of case studies. This section has been included in order to allow the reader to develop an understanding of the issues raised in the text in the context of potential problems facing public sector managers. The cases themselves present a number of scenarios but the important point is not the individual scenario and the circumstances described in each case. It is that the lessons to be learnt and problems to be solved have general applicability across the public sector for public sector financial managers and students of financial management.

Key points of chapter

This chapter examined:

1. The process of establishing the overall level of public sector spending.
2. The major initiatives that have taken place in the major parts of the public sector stressing their effect on financial management.
3. The importance of financial management to the public sector.

1.8 Conclusion

The introduction to this book has attempted to illustrate the many challenges that are facing the public sector financial manager be he/she a trained accountant or a service manager faced with dealing with demands for the achievement of economy, efficiency and effectiveness in performing the service. The new skills demanded in public sector financial management lie in the interpretation of financial information and the provision of financial advice to help achieve the goals of the organization for individual service goals. This, however, adds another dimension to the problem as, frequently, the goals of the public sector organizations cannot be accurately defined. The more complex the public sector organization the more difficult it is to define the goal of that organization and in addition its constituent elements may have conflicting goals. Clearly, the pace of change has also been rapid and at this point in time shows no sign of slowing down. It might be claimed that the very speed of these changes makes any attempt to plan irrelevant, but here lies the paradox. The greater the speed of change the greater the need for a planned approach to tackle it. An organization must know where it has come from in order to know where it is going an how far from any of its planned goals it is at any point in time. It is hoped that the techniques discussed in this book will enable public sector financial managers to deal with and master change by having the necessary financial skills to cope with change as it takes place.

1.9 Appendix: summary of the supply process

Parliament approves an individual supply estimate as a 'vote'. This can be defined as a coherent area of government expenditure which is the responsibility of one government department. A single vote will therefore cover expenditure which can be gathered under a particular main heading and which relates to a single department. Where responsibility for a particular area of expenditure spreads to another department it is reflected in the vote for that department. Each department is then accountable to Parliament for the expenditure detailed. A single vote is prepared in a standard format. This format follows and includes a brief description of the component parts:

1. *The introductory note*. This is used to put the vote in context giving details on the items of expenditure, whether the expenditure is cash

limited (see 4 below), details on any important changes in the expenditure from the previous year and an indication of the level of service to be provided.

2. *The ambit*. This describes the purpose for which the provision is made and effectively limits the ability to spend to the ambit. The wording of the ambit may not be changed without Treasury approval.

3. *Summary and subhead details*. This section breaks the estimated expenditure for the next financial year down into its component parts. In addition, comparison is possible with the last completed year for which figures are available and with the total provision and estimated results for the current year.

4. *Receipts*. Certain receipts can be used to finance some of the gross expenditure on a vote and thus reduce the sums drawn on the Consolidated Fund (the government's bank account). These receipts are known as 'Appropriations in Aid'. Other receipts and receipts above the level of the approved Appropriations in Aid are paid into the Consolidated Fund. These other receipts and extra Appropriations in Aid are detailed separately. Those Appropriations approved to be used to finance expenditure are related to expenditure and are given in the summary and subhead section of the supply estimates.

5. *Additional information* usually given in the form of supplementary tables.

Operational and service-based costing

Key learning objectives

After reading this chapter you should be able to:

1. Prepare and interpret a unit cost statement.
2. List the strengths and weaknesses of conventional approaches to efficiency comparisons.
3. Define and apportion overheads.
4. Understand the benefits and weaknesses of different ways of charging for overheads in a public sector environment.

This chapter takes a selective and critical view of the collection and use of costs within public sector organizations. It is concerned specifically with the everyday collection and measurement of the costs of individual services. These costs include both direct costs and indirect costs (overheads), and costs which are variable and those which are fixed. They are used for purposes such as cost recovery and cost control, and are used extensively in the analysis and evaluation of managerial performance.

Three distinct areas are singled out for discussion.

1. The use of costs in efficiency and value for money studies throughout the public sector.
2. The measurement, apportionment and control of overheads including charging for overheads via service level agreements.
3. A study of some of the specific problems of costing activity within the National Health Service.

Managers in any sector of the economy need to be able to assess performance in order to manage effectively the resources within their control. At the strategic level managers will be looking to formulate new policies or reformulate existing policies if a perceived need is not being met. At the operational level managers will be searching for improved administrative efficiency including the better use of resources within the existing policy framework. The problem for public sector managers is to define the output of a particular service in order to assess whether or not their service is performing within the value for money objectives of economy, efficiency and effectiveness. This chapter examines the contribution that the collection and measurement of costs makes to this process.

2.1 The use of costs in efficiency and value-for-money studies

Within public sector organizations there is rarely a bottom line figure such as profit which can provide a single evaluative measure of performance. This is because many services are provided out of taxation, either central or local, and do not generate sales revenue which can be the basis for calculating profit or loss. Examples include primary and secondary state education, defence, and the National Health Service. Other services are provided at a 'loss' with income frequently being related to clients ability to pay; examples include prescriptions issued by doctors, and the fees payable for the opthalmic and dental services. In the absence of profit, financial measures of performance tend to be cost-based. Different dimensions of 'output' are selected and cost is then related to such 'outputs' to produce a cost-based input/output ratio. Examples include the cost per patient day within a hospital, cost per vehicle operating mile for police vehicles and cost per school meal produced.

As you learnt in Chapter 1, during the past decade many services have been privatized or contracted out, or at least reorganized into self-contained trading profit centres. These include the local authority direct labour organizations (DLOs) which comprise construction and maintenance activities and the direct service organizations (DSOs) such as street cleansing, refuse collection and parks. In these services there is a bottom line profit figure, but organizations must still concern themselves with the detail of costs if they are to control costs as part of securing their profit objective.

At this point, it is necessary to stress the difference between throughputs (or intermediate outputs) and outcomes. Throughputs may be defined as an indicator of the level of activity in a particular service, for example, the number of hip replacement operations carried out in a hospital, the number of children receiving education in a school. Outcomes refer to the impact which the level of activity has on the recipients of the service, and which may be considered to be the whole objective of providing the service. For this reason, the ultimate measure of performance relates to outcomes rather than to units of service delivered. For example, the primary objective of providing a home for the aged would not be to provide, say, 15 000 resident bed days per year but is to improve the quality of life of those elderly people who are so accommodated.

However, the measurement of outcomes presents great difficulties within the public sector. For example, how does one measure the improvement in the quality of life of residents of an old persons home? Might their quality of life have been greater located within the community? The indicators of services delivered by a comprehensive school are many and varied. They include the broad education of pupils, the number of GCSE grades obtained by the pupils, the attendance rate of pupils, the number staying on beyond the age of 16 or finding employment, the preparation for a world of change, the development of self-discipline, and so on. Some of these are immeasurable, and it is impossible to combine the others into one measure of a school's performance.

The problem is aggravated because in education and health the initial intake of pupils or patients is not standardized. Pupils arrived with different abilities and come from different socio-economic backgrounds; patients may be admitted with smaller complaints but the severity of those complaints is different. These difficulties mean that in most cases, managers will be looking at the costs of throughputs and not final outcomes.

In a situation where market prices are available, as in the private sector and, where goods and services are freely traded, then outcomes may be equated with sales revenues. Economics tells us that consumers will purchase units of output until marginal utility equates with price. In a market situation, consumers will pay no more than the perceived benefit from the service received. However, in much of the public sector in the United Kingdom, in education, health and defence, for example, such market prices are simply unavailable.

In the health sector, it is thought by many that outcomes are related to the increase in the quality of life of the patient; indeed, the concept of quality adjusted life years (QUALY) has been developed as a measure of outcomes: a QUALY considers both the increase in life expectancy and the increased quality of life derived by the patient. This may possibly represent the measurement future for the outcomes of health care. However, QUALYs are not yet in operational use within the Health Service; in place of such a measure of genuine outcome, recourse is sought in throughput measures, such as the number of beds provided or the number of patient days. The difficulty of measurement relevant to outcomes or quality of service pervades much of the public sector with the result that there is a concentration on performance measurement and control based on throughputs.

Not all activities are so bedevilled; there are some where the problem of measuring output is absent. In appraising ambulance efficiency, for example, we can readily work with cost per ambulance mile for an individual vehicle which could be compared with its past performance or with other vehicles. Such information may indicate declining efficiency or have possible audit implications if, say, fuel cost per mile showed a significant increase.

The starting point for cost-based efficiency analysis is the definition of the unit of performance to be studied; these units may be single measures such as the number of schoolchildren taught and the number of meals provided, or multiple measures such as passenger miles. Thus, one may calculate the cost per child, per passenger mile, per meal, per motorway mile and so on. These are usually referred to as unit costs.

The analysis of differences in unit costs may be assisted by the preparation of a cost statement which disaggregates total cost into the detailed cost elements and expresses throughput in terms of each of the cost elements. Table 2.1 provides an example of such a statement; it examines the costs of cleaning three offices.

An immediate problem which has to be confronted in constructing a unit cost statement is that relating to the classification of the cost elements (that is, employees, cleaning materials, equipment, and so on). One approach is to use a format which is uniform across all organizations. In the National Health Service such a format is laid down for health authorities while most local authorities follow the CIPFA recommended standard form of accounts. The CIPFA standard form specifies in detail the classification of costs and the detailed content of each section. Both approaches adopt a subjective approach to classification in that costs are grouped according to the nature or subject of the expenditure. Thus, in the CIPFA system, the broad classification runs as follows:

Table 2.1 Example of a unit cost statement

Blaenwent BC Unit cost statement:	Cleaning services 9 months to 31 December 1988							

Costs	Office A		Office B		Office C			
	Total £	Per m² P	Total £	Per m² P	Total £	Per m² P	Total £	Average Per m² P
Employees' pay	9 000	150.00	50 500	325.81	13 500	450.00	73 000	297.96
Nl etc.	1 650	27.50	9 090	58.65	2 439	81.30	13 179	53.79
Travel	20	.33	5	.03	30	1.00	55	.22
Bonus	1 800	30.00	10 605	68.42	1 750	58.33	14 155	57.78
Employees sub-total	12 470	207.83	70 200	452.90	17 719	590.63	100 389	409.75
Cleaning materials	2 570	42.83	13 240	85.42	2 425	80.83	18 235	74.43
Equipment	430	7.17	1 270	8.19	230	7.67	1 930	7.88
Misc.	20	.33	40	.26	10	.33	70	.29
Subtotal	15 490	258.17	84 750	546.77	20.384	679.47	120 624	492.34
Contract window/ cleaning	900	15.00	3 050	19.68	750	25.00	4 700	19.18
Supervisor	3 120	52.00	3 120	20.13	3 120	104.00	9 360	38.20
Total	19 510	325.17	90 920	586.58	24 254	808.47	134 684	549.73
Statistical data								
Floor area (m²)	6 000		15 500		3 000		24 500	
Cleaners	3		17		4		24	
Floor area/cleaner	2 000		912		750		1 021	

employees, running expenses (premises, transport, supplies and services, agency and contracted services, transfer payments, and central, departmental and technical support services), and capital financial costs. In principle, uniform approaches, such as these, allow comparison between authorities. An alternative approach is to classify costs according to their behaviour and not their subject; this requires a knowledge of cost variability and is discussed in detail in Chapter 3. The advantage of this latter approach is that it aids decision making and control and can give a more informed insight when carrying out performance appraisal activities and value for money (VFM) studies.

2.2 Unit cost statements

Unit cost statements have three main uses as follows:

An indicator of relative efficiency

Unit costs serve as an indicator of efficiency relative to other establishments or organizations. The Audit Commission in England and Wales makes considerable use of unit costs for this purpose, generating batteries of comparative statistics which may act as a starting point for analysis. In Table 2.1 it is evident that the cleaning of office A is considerably more efficient in cost terms than is the cleaning of offices B or C. Its overall cost per square metre, 258p, is less than half that of B or C. Examination of the unit cost components reveals that office A's lower unit costs are largely the result of lower unit employee costs.

Efficiency over time

Unit costs serve as an indicator of efficiency over time. They allow us to compare the performance of the same organization from year to year, which can be a pointer as to whether efficiency is increasing or decreasing. The problem is that inflation will tend to increase the costs of providing a service over time. Therefore, in order to make a true comparison, the effects of inflation will need to be removed so that the 'real' trend may be observed. This may be done by using a price index, usually one which is specific to the cost element, such as the fuel cost index, or the appropriate wage index. However, the Treasury guideline for all central government services in the United Kingdom, including the National Health Service, is that the GDP deflator should be used. This is a general price index and its use is said to reflect the wider economy from which central government's resources are drawn via taxation.

Cost control

Unit costs provide a basis for cost control. They can be used to set unit cost standards against which actual performance can be monitored. As is illustrated in Table 2.1, their disaggregated nature highlights the cause of high total costs in A and B: the first cost which needs to be examined is the pay of employees.

The limitations of unit cost comparisons

However, unit cost measures such as those above need to be used with care. Their limitations, which are discussed below, are summarized as follows:

1. They use throughputs rather than outcomes.
2. They ignore the quality of performance.
3. They may ignore differences in case mix.
4. They should make comparisons against best practice.
5. There are significant inter-authority differences.
6. Overheads may be charged in different ways.
7. Differences in delegated budgets will impair comparison.
8. Capital financing methods may affect costs.

As has been indicated, throughputs are usually taken as a proxy for outcomes; this assumes that there is a direct and linear relationship between throughputs and outcomes. It also assumes that all outcomes are proxied by the throughput indicator but this is unlikely to be the case.

They tell us nothing about the quality of performance; cleaning may be carried out to different standards of performance in the three offices, and this may explain the variation. If differences in standard are laid down in the cleaning contract, the differences may be acceptable. If they are not, and differences in cleaning standards are observed, then either offices B and C are being cleaned too thoroughly or office A is not being cleaned to the required standard.

This is related to the problem of throughput mix. One cannot usefully compare the costs of two homes, one for the elderly and one for the elderly infirm. The latter will require more specialized staffing, certainly a higher staffing ratio, and quite probably different dietary requirements. Thus, we would compare homes for the elderly with one another, and homes for the elderly infirm with other for the same. However, the latter category includes a range of infirmities and disabilities, and the differences in case mix will clearly affect costs. In this specific case, allowing for the effects of case mix is almost impossible, because the costs associated with different types of infirmity are not known. In the case of a hospital, one solution is to compare the costs of different specialities, rather than the total unit costs of activities, and then make inter-hospital and inter-temporal comparisons on a speciality-by-speciality basis.

In making inter-organizational comparisons, one is not necessarily comparing performance against defined best practice. At the very least, it is necessary to compare actual unit costs against budgeted unit costs which do represent an assumption about the level of efficiency which is being sought. Ideally, comparison would be against a predetermined standard cost which would be based upon the standard amounts of time, materials and so on required to undertake a specific task efficiently. Within the NHS there have been pilot studies of the use of diagnosis related groups (DRGs), which are concerned with classifying acute patients (but not psychiatric, geriatric or community care services) according to their diagnostic status. These DRGs specify standardized units of workload for each diagnostic grouping and may, therefore, form a basis for establishing the standard costs of specific hospital activities; such standard costs can then provide a benchmark for the appraisal of actual unit costs. DRGs have been imported from the United States where they were originally intended as a basis on which insurers would reimburse hospitals. The aim of this was to cap the growth in health care expenditure by providing incentives for hospitals to carry out treatment as efficiently and economically as possible. However, there is some dissatisfaction with their use in the United Kingdom as it is argued that DRGs do not adequately reflect British medical practice, that classification systems for recording diagnoses and procedures are different in the UK and that DRGs must respond to local conditions. Therefore, there are moves within the NHS to measure hospital activity by grouping together sets of cases which meet specified criteria and the resources they consume. From this data it is possible to compare the work undertaken between hospitals and from year to year.

There are major differences between some local authorities. For example, labour costs in London and the South East of England may be very high compared with the North East; some local authorities are primarily rural (e.g. Dyfed in West Wales) while others are primarily industrial (e.g. Sandwell in the West Midlands); some local authorities on the south coast of England have a high proportion of retired people. The different factors impose different demands on local authorities and are likely to influence the cost of providing services. In rural areas, primary education is likely to be more expensive due to the prevalence of small schools and/or high costs of bussing pupils. In rural areas, refuse collection costs per tonne of refuse are likely to be high because of the distances which need to be covered. In industrial areas, street cleansing and road maintenance costs are likely to be high. Similar problems bedevil the Health Service where, for example, economic and social deprivation and sparsity of population will each have a significant impact on health costs. The solution to this problem is to compare like authorities with like authorities. The Audit Commission for England and Wales has identified family groups of like authorities using the Shaw Classification; this provides a focus of comparison by outside agencies but, more importantly, also provides service managers with specified comparator authorities with whom it may be worth establishing contact. Contact with like authorities which appear to be more efficient may yield useful lessons. Contact may expose better systems of service delivery, differences in methods of organization, different approaches to the management of staff, different approaches to the customer, that is, the general public.

Sometimes, unit costs are compared with a national average. This practice is not particularly useful as the average figure simply conceals the wide range of performance which underpins it, and makes no allowance for the factors identified in the preceeding paragraphs.

Finally, three specific accountancy related issues may weaken the usefulness of unit costs as efficiency indicators. The first of these is concerned with the charging of overhead costs to service activities. In the case of local authority homes for the elderly, there will be two sources of costs which are not directly related to individual homes: the managerial overheads of the Social Services Department, and the general overheads of the local authority (the main components of which are finance, legal, computerization, and local democracy; the last of these includes members expenses, the costs of committee meetings, the costs of elections, and so on and it is not practice to apportion these costs). There is no standard method by which central and departmental overheads are apportioned, although The Chartered Institute of Public Finance and Accounting does specify recommended practice. The absence of standardization means that different apportionment methods and bases can influence the costs charged to homes, or to any other managerial unit. Therefore, as far as possible, the results of such apportionments, normally included under the heading 'Central, Departmental and Technical Services', should be excluded when making inter-organizational comparisons of efficiency. However, charges based on service level agreements (SLAs) are gradually replacing arbitrary apportionment. The service providers (overhead departments) will negotiate levels of charges, volume of service, quality and timeliness with the service users. This involvement in the SLA by the management of the homes does mean that the overhead charges in these circumstances should be treated like any other cost as the expense should reflect the economic, efficient and effective management of the home.

The second point relates to the delegation of budgets to schools. Delegation is dealt with more fully in Chapter 4 but at the heart of delegated budgets is each local education authority's approved scheme of delegation. This will specify which of a number of discretionary items are to be delegated to schools and which are to be retained centrally by the authority. In one scheme a specific item may be delegated to schools; in another scheme this cost element may be treated as discretionary exception and managed centrally. As a result of such an absence of standardization inter-authority comparisons require great care.

The third point is that, currently, the method of financing local authority fixed assets dictates the treatment of the asset in the revenue accounts. Loan financing results in an annual charge for capital repayments and interest over the life of the loan; financing from capital reserves may result in a nil charge to a specific service's revenue accounts; financing from revenue results in a once and for all charge to the revenue accounts when the asset is acquired. Furthermore, any loan charges will be related to the amount raised when the asset was acquired; the system does not attempt to charge accounts with an estimate of the notional benefits resulting from the use of the asset. Therefore, the impact of high or low quality assets, some of which may have a pay off in terms of lower operating costs, is completely excluded from consideration.

However, change is on the way. CIPFA has proposed that capital accounting be based upon replacement costs rather than the current system based upon the method of finance; central government legislation has already specified replacement cost depreciation for DLOs and DSOs. With effect from the 1994/95 final accounts (Spring 1995) a fundamental change will have occurred in the capital accounting of local authorities. Local authorities will have set up asset registers allowing assets to be shown at their current value in the balance sheet. They will also have introduced service capital charges based on the current economic value of using assets in each service. This means that in the future the capital charge within the accounts will be useful in making comparisons as it will indicate the value of capital-related services which have been received by, say, the home in the year and one would expect that the higher the figure, the greater the benefit received in terms of more commodious or newer accommodation, for example.

In the past within health authorities and central government generally, capital expenditure has been completely separated from revenue expenditure. However, in hospital trusts a system of replacement cost depreciation is now in place and this provides a much improved basis for comparison.

To summarize, unit based costs are useful indictors of efficiency and may serve as a starting point in value for money studies, as long as the caveats noted above are taken into consideration.

2.3   The measurement and control of overheads

Direct costs are those which can be traced directly to units of output. Furthermore, they change directly and proportionately as output changes. For example, in the production of meals, provisions costs are directly related and traceable to the number of meals produced.

Overheads are those costs that cannot be traced directly to units of activity; in the production of meals, rents and equipment costs are examples of overheads. As overheads cannot be traced directly, then they are traced to units of output by a two stage process:

1. They are first apportioned or charged to cost centres where the final output or service is produced.
2. Then they are absorbed into the costs of final outputs or services by using a predetermined recovery rate.

In a hospital, the costs of nurses and clinicians, drugs, x-ray units and food, for example, are all directly traceable to patient care. However, there are other costs such as portering, maintenance, cleaning, administration and stock-holding which are not directly traceable, and are the overheads of the service.

In local authorities CIPFA has defined overheads as comprising of support services, corporate management, service management and regulation. These are discussed more fully below:

1. *Support services* are services which support the provision of services to the public. They are either obtained from colleagues or bought in, to help the users of support services to carry out their own main functions. They include a range of functions including accountants, architects, information technology, payroll, personnel staff and typists.
2. *Corporate management* includes all activities which local authorities engage in because they are multi-purpose authorities. It includes the following:
   (a) meetings of the council and of corporate policy-making committees and the staff and accommodation required to support such meetings;
   (b) chief executives, except for the time spent by them on specific services;
   (c) estimating and accounting for precepts, block grants and rates;
   (d) local elections.
3. *Service management* comprises the management of specific services to the public, DSOs and support services.
4. *Regulation* includes the duties which local authorities are required to carry out in order to maintain the standard of service. It also includes those chief officers with a statutory responsibility for the management of a particular service, for example directors of social services appointed in accordance with Section 6 of the Local Authority Social Services Act 1970.

The extent of apportionment

CIPFA's view on the extent of apportionment is contained in *The Management of Overheads in Local Authorities* which was published in 1991 (CIPFA, 1991a). The extent of apportionment depends on which of the above four categories a particular overhead item falls into.

Support services: all service users must pay for the support services which they use. Thus support services must be apportioned or charged to the users of services.

Corporate management: this cost should be allocated to a separate 'corporate management' expenditure head and should not be apportioned to other expenditure heads or to service users.

Service management: the costs of service management should be allocated to the services managed in the same way as support service costs.

Regulation: the cost of regulating any service to the public should be apportioned to a separate expenditure head within the accounts of the service and should not be apportioned to divisions or units of service.

2.4   The advantages of full apportionment

In the case of support services and service management it is recommended that costs be apportioned fully.

The arguments advanced in favour of making a full apportionment are as follows:

It shows the full costs of services

In this way members, officers and taxpayers may be informed of the full cost of providing services; without such apportionment, the costs of service provision would be understated, and this could give incorrect signals in resource administration. However, as the following chapter indicates, the emphasis on full costs can give incorrect signals in situations which require emphasis on marginal or incremental costs.

It ensures that maximum revenue is received

It ensures the receipt of the full amount of revenue in the case of services aided by a specific percentage grant from the government (such as the Police service which is funded via a 51 per cent specific grant), or where the service is provided under an agency agreement (such as the reinstatement of road surfaces by county councils when the road has been opened by one of the utility companies such as gas or water).

Compliance with legislation

Under the DLO and DSO legislation, referred to in Chapter 1, both DLOs and DSOs must compete fairly for work by submitting tenders to the client local authority in competition with the private sector. It is argued that their costs should include a share of the overheads of the 'host' local authority. Their accounts are duly charged with a share of overheads, and all costs have to be covered and a 5 per cent return on the current cost of assets earned. The requirement to earn a 5 per cent return ensures that, in tendering for work, DLOs and DSOs must make provision for the cost of central services.

It allows true cost comparisons

It permits the true comparison of the costs of local authority provisions of a service with the costs of a contracted-out service.

Inter-authority comparisons

If all authorities follow the full apportionment policy under identical rules or guidelines it permits the confident comparison of inter-authority accounts and statistics.

Aggregation at national level

Central Government makes use of the annual aggregated expenditure figures related to local authorities in its own planning. If the accounts all follow the principle of full apportionment, first there is a similarity in a major aspect of accounts preparation (which is strengthened by the use of the CIPFA Standard Form of Accounts), and secondly, the service accounts all show the full cost of service delivery.

Within the Health Service, the Griffiths Report recommended that overheads should be redistributed to units (to provide a full resource budget for units), and to departments and wards. Speciality costing, another development, requires the apportioning of all costs to each separate speciality within the hospital. However, such full reapportionment, which ignores the ways in which costs behave as activity changes, maybe of little use for planning and budgeting. It is possible that other developments, patient costing, charging costs to specific patients and the use of DRGs may make use of reapportioned costs but this depends on the purpose and use of the costings.

The bases for the apportionment of costs used in practice have been varied in nature but a typical pattern would be as follows:

Expenditure head	Basis of Apportionment
Employees	Time spent
Administration buildings	Floor area
Printing	Number of pages
Stores	Number or cost of issues
Computer:	
Punching	Time spent, 000s key taps
System Analysis	Time spent
Programming	Time spent
Special Stationery	Direct to user
Operating costs	All costs, including accommodation, collected and recovered on the basis of time used.

2.5   Criticisms of full apportionment

Apportionment as described above can be criticized as follows:

Cost control at the point of expenditure

If one is concerned with control of overhead items of expenditure, one cannot necessarily expect control to be exercised at the end point of the apportionment process. Hospital portering expenditure, for example, can best be controlled centrally by senior staff and by the specification of a budget which is adhered to. Indeed, there appears to be little incentive in the originating departments to control costs, if such costs are going to be apportioned elsewhere.

On the other hand, if one considers services such as photocopying, where it is possible to recover costs via a unit charge, then the charge does provide the best form of control as it appears within departmental budget and accounts.

It blunts the competitive edge

If a public sector service is competing with a private sector firm, as in the DLO case, there is evidence that DLOs are penalized by the weight of central charges which they carry in comparison with low overhead competitors. This is compounded by the 5 per cent real rate of return which must be earned.

Opposition from service managers

The apparent imposition of high central overhead appointments can create resentment among service managers; they appear to be unjust and arbitrary, especially in those services where a rate of return has to be earned.

Antidotes to the criticisms

The criticisms noted above can be partially countered in two, closely related, ways:

1. by workload charging;
2. by service-level agreements.

Workload charging

Costs may be charged on a workload basis. To take the photocopier example; if a charge of 5 pence per copy is specified in advance, and departments use electronic keys which provide a cumulative record of copies made, then the resulting charge appears fair and end-point departments have a role to play in controlling costs. A similar principle applies to X-ray and pathology services and a hospital laundry, where the costs can be allocated via measures of workload. Another advantage of workload charging is that it encourages the overhead units to plan in workload terms, and requires them to keep within the predetermined unit costs.

Chapter 3 investigates the ways in which costs behave as activity changes, and a basic distinction is made between fixed costs which do not change as activity changes, and variable costs which do so. If this idea is applied to charging on a workload basis, it gives rise to a two-part tariff very similar to the system used for charging for public utility services such as gas, electricity and telecommunication. In these cases a fixed charge is payable each quarter and represents the fixed rental for connection to the service, and this fixed rental may be seen as contributing to the fixed costs of the utility. Every user must pay the same fixed element in recognition of the fact that, whatever the use made, the infrastructure, cabling, and so on must be provided. On top of the quarterly fixed charge, a variable amount is payable and this is based upon consumption of gas, electricity and so on. This principle of a two-part tariff may be applied to workload charging so that, in the hospital laundry example, user departments would pay a fixed annual amount related to the annual fixed costs of the laundry and a variable amount per unit laundered. The two-part tariff system contributes more information to users of the service. Indeed, in the National Health Service Resource Management Budgeting model system it is recommended that all intermediate costs (not direct costs) should be recharged in two parts, fixed and variable, so that final budget holders can see readily see the net increases or decreases in expenditure that result from given changes in workload.

Service level agreements

The traditional basis of apportionment of costs of services normally provides for no written agreement between support service providers and users. The cost of all support services is simply apportioned between their users.

However, there has developed in local authorities the use of a very different approach to support services. The approach involves service level agreements. These provide for a written agreement between providers and users which covers:

1. the provision of a certain amount of service;
2. at a specified standard of quality and performance;
3. at a predetermined and agreed cost; and
4. for a specified period of time.

For example, the Treasurer may negotiate with the DLO manager a fee for the provision of payroll and invoicing services; the agreement specification will include the number of employees covered, the extent of the service, the duties required of the user in the provision of information, and a statement as to the timeliness of the service. Another agreement with the Education Department may specify the number of audit hours to be deployed and also the total audit cost.

Service level agreements have significant implications:

1. The basis of cost is clear to the service department and the amount which will be charged is known in advance, facilitating their budgeting.
2. Users and providers have to have some degree of freedom in negotiating charges.
3. They may encourage users to shop around for services which they may be able to obtain more economically from outside the organization.
4. They force careful planning and budgeting by central departments, including the necessity of operating efficiently and pricing competitively if they are to retain their customer base among the service departments, DLOs and DSOs.
5. There may be year end balances representing under-apportionment of costs. This may be the result of poor budgeting or poor cost control by support service managers. In an apportionment system, such costs are fully apportioned to user services. However, in a service level agreement system, they remain the responsibility of the support service providers, and they must make arrangements to manage such balances. Currently the law does not permit losses to be carried forward and they would be transferred to the general accounts of the authority.
6. Within the accounts of users, support service charges replace apportioned costs. These represent a much closer approximation of the economic costs of operating the service as they arise from negotiation on costs and services in which the service user has a full part to play.
7. After the period of the SLA expires, users are under no obligation to pay for the service, and this may result in losses to the providers.

Public sector organizations are now entering the post-SLA era. The next stage in the process of requiring value for money from support service providers is to be the contracting out of support services. In the NHS individual managers have applied market testing to a number of services including payroll, laundry and estates. In local authorities the contracting principles which have already been applied to DLOs and DSOs will next be applied to white collar and professional support services.

2.6 An example of overhead recovery

Table 2.2 presents relevant data and a traditional statement in which costs are first apportioned and allocated to a print unit and then secondly recovery rates (or absorption rates) are established for the purpose of achieving full cost recovery from user departments.

There are two machines and in the case of each machine, the budgeted recovery rate is obtained by dividing budgeted total costs by budgeted print hours. The budgeted recovery rates are calculated prior to the start of the financial year and user departments should be informed of the appropriate rates so that they may take decisions in full knowledge of the costs which they will be required to bear.

Table 2.2 Print unit: Budget for year ended 31 March 1995

Cost elements	Total costs £	Machine A £	Machine B £
	25 000.00	13 000.00	12 000.00
Labour	7 400.00	3 900.00	3 500.00
Electricity	2 100.00	1 300.00	800.00
Premises costs	8 400.00	4 300.00	4 100.00
Maintenance	1 800.00	890.00	910.00
Financing costs	4 775.00	3 610.00	1 165.00
	49 475.00	27 000.00	22 475.00
Budgeted print hours	2 950.00	1 500.00	1 450.00
Budgeted recovery rate per hour		18.00	15.50

It may be observed from the table that full cost recovery will only be achieved if the amounts recovered from user departments actually equal or exceed the costs of the print unit; thus, the unit must keep within its budget of £49 475, and ensure that it achieves its target usage. Alternatively, any reduction in activity should be met by reducing costs, although the absence of a two-part tariff approach means that there is no automatic link between cost reduction and a fall in income. Similarly, the absence of fixed/variable cost distinction renders difficult cost control when activity increases because the manager is unaware as to which costs may be allowed to increase, and by how much. However, the usual approach is one in which fixed and variable costs are subsumed within one recovery rate.

Three conditions are possible:

Full recovery

The unit exactly recovers all its costs. The total of costs recovered using the budgeted recovery rates exactly equals the actual costs incurred by the print unit during the period.

Under-recovery

The unit makes an under-recovery of costs. The total of costs recovered is less than the total of actual costs incurred by the print unit during the period.

			£
Let us assume that:			
Total costs incurred			50 000
Total activity	Recovered		
Machine A 1400 hours	1400 * £18	= 25 200	
Machine B 1500 hours	1500 * £15.5	= 23 250	
			48 450
	Under-recovered		£1 550

In this case two things may be done at year-end: either write off the balance to revenue, or carry forward and attempt to recover the amount in next year's charge, which will be increased as a result of the carry forward. There may be a degree of inequity about the latter approach as next year's users are unlikely to utilise the services of the unit in exactly the same proportions as they did in the current year.

Over-recovery

The unit makes an over-recovery of costs. The total of costs recovered is more than the total of actual costs incurred by the print unit during the period.

			£
Let us assume that:			
Total costs incurred			49 000
Total activity	Recovered		
Machine A 1400 hours	1500 * £18	= 27 000	
Machine B 1500 hours	1500 * £15.5	= 23 250	
			50 250
	Over-recovered		£1 250

The same treatment may be accorded to over-recoveries as in the previous case with the exception that, now, carrying forward the balance to next year would serve to reduce the charge for users in that period.

If overhead costs and recoveries are monitored during the year then any apparently large balances can be investigated. If it can be shown that the original budgeted overhead recovery rate was incorrect, it may be decided to revise the rate part way through the year in order to ensure that balances are minimized at year end. Any changes must, of course, be communicated to users.

There is a further worked example illustrating the processes of overhead recovery in Exhibit 2.2 at the end of this chapter.

Central Sterile Supply Department (CCSD) costs

One of the major practical problems, apart from forecasting usage and costs, and then controlling the latter, is that of actually collecting and charging an appropriate share of overheads. An illustration of this is provided by a hospital Central Sterile Supply Department (CSSD) Department. CSSDs are concerned with the production and issue of sterile packs. Packs usually comprise both sterile soft packs of dressings, non-disposable bowls, and so on and surgical instruments. Generally, the costs of raw materials and also of staff are readily traced to specific packs and the CSSD respectively. However, non-CSSD expenditure, which may be charged to non-CSSD budget-holders may also be involved in pack production: for example, energy to provide steam to drive the autoclave sterilizing process and linen which is used to cover the theatre trays. A typical situation might be as follows:

Cost element	Budget-holder
Energy	Works department
Linen and laundry	Linen services
Equipment	Works department

Unless appropriate proportions of these costs can be systematically reapportioned to CSSD, then the production costs of sterile packs will be understated and will reflect only raw material and CSSD employee costs.

Specialty costing

Specialty costing is a system whereby the costs of a hospital are reapportioned to each specialty according to the level of workload imposed by each specialty on wards, theatres, pathology laboratories and other support services. It was recommended by Korner that Districts should start collecting specialty cost data from April 1987, providing annual reports with effect from the following year. Examples of specialties are: inpatients: general medicine, general surgery, geriatric and paediatric; outpatients. The approach requires an information system capable of collecting costs at source, holding workload data, and then apportioning and reapportioning costs on the basis of workload or use. Such specialty costs and specialty unit costs would then be used in efficiency comparisons.

However, Jones and Prowle (1988) regard the system as flawed on two counts. First, the system is inflexible, producing costs only on a specialty basis; for example, it is not capable of producing costs relating to DRGs or to individual patients. Secondly, the activities of specialties are diverse as regards case mix (that is, the particular medical problems and severity of illness treated) and a single unit cost can conceal wide variations in the costs and quality of health care provided within a specialty.

Key points of chapter

1. The absence of a bottom-line profit measure in the public sector means that cost-based performance measures are emphasized.
2. Cost-based performance measures, such as unit costs, need to be used with great care.
3. Costs are usually related to throughputs rather than outcomes.
4. Overheads are usually fully apportioned in the public sector; this is of value but needs to be used with care.
5. Overhead apportionment is increasingly being replaced by service level agreements which define charges, volumes and quality.

2.8 Summary

It can be seen from the above discussion that a cost in itself may tell the decision maker little about performance. It is the manager who places an interpretation on the information in order to arrive at a decision as to the use of the information provided. It has also been pointed out that the provision of unit cost data can merely be seen as a measure of the resources devoted to an activity but says little of the quality of such output and is therefore a measure of throughput costs. Furthermore, inter-organizational comparisons are weakened by differences in location and environment and differences in accounting policies.

The apportionment of overheads is important if decision makers are concerned about the full costs of providing services. Rules and guidelines are required if such costs are to be aggregated or used as the basis of inter-organizational comparison. Increasingly, apportionment is being replaced by charging within the context of service level agreements. These have benefits for users and present a challenge to providers. They have required an examination of costs, service volumes and quality and timeliness of service.

Full cost recovery can only be obtained if costs are strictly controlled and if the use of an activity can be predicted with some degree of accuracy. Ideally, recovery should be related to the use of workload measures, and the use of a two-part tariff to reflect the distinction between fixed and variable costs would also be of benefit. The organization will need to decide how it is going to deal with over- and under-recovery of overheads at the conclusion of an accounting period (see CIPFA 1991a).

Exhibit 2.1

This is a short case study which illustrates the preparation and interpretation of unit cost statements.

You are employed as a financial advisor to the Director of Social Services of the Glamwent County Council. The Council operates three homes for the elderly each of which has a kitchen serving a dining-room. The Director has requested that you investigate the costs of operating the three kitchens in the last financial year.

On investigation, you discover the following operating costs for the last financial year:

	Kitchen A £	Kitchen B £	Kitchen C £
Cost of provisions	32 000	35 250	12 700
Heating and lighting	3 600	4 100	2 200
Number of employees:			
Cooks	1	1	1
Assistant cooks	1	2	1
Kitchen assistants	8	9	5
Capital costs of kitchens:			
Building costs	60 000	30 000	18 000
Equipment/Furniture	27 000	29 000	14 000
Number of meals produced	72 000	78 000	32 000

Notes:

1. Average annual earnings are Cooks £6500, Assistant cooks £5500 and Kitchen assistants £4000.
2. In addition to the above staff one supervisor has overall charge of the three kitchens and is paid an annual salary of £7500. This is to be apportioned over each of the kitchens.
3. Overheads on wages and salaries amount to 10% of total salaries and wages costs.
4. Administration costs are to be apportioned to each kitchen on a basis of 1 p per meal produced.
5. Building costs are written off over a 60-year period and equipment and furniture over 15 years. In order to calculate the annual charge to revenue, a 9% annuity basis should be adopted. The appropriate factor for 60 years is 0.09 and the factor for 15 years is 0.12.

Required:

Investigate the costs of operating the three kitchens for the Director of Social Services and draw appropriate conclusions from the costs.

Discussion

The first step is to prepare a unit cost statement as the basis for analysis. This is contained in Table 2.3 which has been prepared using the number of meals served as the denominator and the costs recorded against each item of expenditure as the numerator. Unit costs are provided for each kitchen, for each item of expenditure and a total column aggregates costs to give an average cost for each expenditure head.

Comments

1. The provisions costs vary by 5p, or 11% of the average cost of provisions. This may be caused by waste and inefficiency including over-ordering and an absence of efficient portion control. Dietary needs may also play a part in that one home may have a number of residents with special requirements. It could also be possible that kitchen C is underfeeding its residents. Finally, if there is no central purchasing, the cost differences might be attributable to different prices being paid for provisions.
2. There is some variation in lighting and heating costs and it may be appropriate as an energy conservation exercise to look at a wider sample of homes.
3. The numbers of staff vary considerably between the homes while the workload table shows that there is a particularly heavy burden on kitchen A. At the very best, kitchen C appears overstaffed and it may be possible to remove the kitchen assistant. Questions should also be raised about staffing policy in other homes.

Table 2.3 Unit cost statement: Homes for the aged (Glamwent CC)

	Kitchen A		Kitchen B		Kitchen C		Total	
	Cost £	Unit P	Cost £	Unit P	Cost £	Unit P	Cost £	Unit P
Provisions	32 000	44	35 250	45	12 700	40	79 950	44
Heat/light	3 600	5	4 100	5	2 200	7	9 900	5
Cooks	6 500	9	6 500	8	6 500	20	19 500	11
Ass. cooks	5 500	8	11 000	14	5 500	17	22 000	12
Kitchen asst.	32 000	44	36 000	46	20 000	63	88 000	48
Supervisor	2 500	3	2 500	3	2 500	8	7 500	4
Overheads	4 650	6	5 600	7	3 450	11	13 700	8
Admin. costs	720	1	780	1	320	1	1 820	1
Capital costs:								
Buildings	5 400	8	2 700	3	1 620	5	9 720	5
Furn/Fit.	3 240	5	3 480	4	1 680	5	8 400	5
Totals	96 110	133	107 910	138	56 470	176	260 490	143
No. of meals	72 000		78 000		32 000		182 000	
Workload (average meals served):								
Cooks			72 000		78 000		32 000	
Assistant cooks			72 000		39 000		32 000	
Kitchen maids			9 000		8 667		6 400	

4. The supervisor has been apportioned to each home on the basis of one third of the salary to each home. It would also be possible to apportion the supervisor's salary on the basis of the number of meals produced or on the basis of the number of staff employed in each kitchen. This also raises the question of the relevance of the apportionment as the supervisor is, at the kitchen level, a non-controllable overhead. Similar comments to the latter can also be made about the apportionment of overheads on salaries and wages, the administration charges and the capital costs.
5. It should be noted that no definite conclusions can be reached at this stage and no comments have been made as to the quality of meals provided. However, the Director is now in a position where a problem has been identified and further work can be undertaken to seek a solution. The investigation has also enabled areas of responsibility to be identified in that, for example, the cook is responsible for the preparation of meals and the possible lack of portion control.

Exhibit 2.2

Goldstar Windows is a subsidiary company of the X County Council which employed disabled workers to manufacture double glazed UPVC windows. The process consists of cutting the delivered lengths of raw material, manufacturing the window frame and finally fitting the glass to the double glazed units. For the year to 31 March 1994 the cost centre expenses and other relevant information is as follows:

	Total £	Cutting £	Manufacture £	Glass fitting £	Stores £	Maintenance £	Tool room £
Indirect materials	12 260	5 640	4 880	1 150	410	60	120
Consumable materials	5 500	1 500	2 000	1 100	–	600	300
Depreciation	70 000	35 000	13 000	12 000	1 000	8 000	1 000
Heat/light	14 250						
Insurance	12 000						
Rent/rates	19 000						
Power	48 000						
Floor area (m²)	9 500	3 000	2 500	2 500	500	500	500
Power use (%)	100	40	30	15	5	5	5
Value of building (£)	120 000	40 000	40 000	10 000	15 000	5 000	10 000
Direct labour (hrs)	20 000	5 000	8 000	7 000			
Machine hours	22 000	15 000	4 000	3 000			
Stores requisitions	8 000	1 000	3 000	3 500			500

Using the above information provided for Goldstar Windows, a three-stage process will now be undertaken which will culminate in the calculation of overhead recovery (or absorption) rates for the three production cost centres: cutting; manufacture; glass fitting.

Stage 1: This involves apportioning the total costs over the six cost centres within Goldstar Windows. In the case of indirect materials, consumable materials and depreciation, costs have already been allocated to cost centres. The remaining costs are apportioned as indicated in the following apportionment statement. The statement is termed an overhead analysis. The bases for apportioning the costs are indicated in the statement and a brief commentary on the reason for choosing the bases follows:

1. *Heat/light* expenditure is assumed to vary in relation to floor area. Other things being equal, the larger the area, the greater the heat and light required. Hence, the expenditure is apportioned to the cost centres on the basis of floor area.
2. *Insurance* is assumed to be related to the value of buildings and it is apportioned to the cost centres on this basis.
3. *Rent and rates* fall into the same category as insurance.
4. *Power costs* are apportioned to cost centres on the basis of the share of power use provided in the above data.

Stage 2: Following the initial apportionments, the total costs for all six cost centres are obtained. However, three of these cost centres are in the nature of support services and these provide services to the production cost centres. The support service cost centres are: stores; maintenance; tool room. None of these produce a saleable product but without them the production cost centres, cutting, maintenance and glass fitting are unable to function.

Stage 2 involves re-apportioning the support service costs to the production cost centres. The service centre costs are reapportioned as follows:

1. Stores are reapportioned to cutting, manufacturing, glass fitting and the tool room on the basis of the number of stores requisitions.
2. Maintenance costs are reapportioned on the basis of machine hours.
3. Tool room costs are also reapportioned on the basis of machine hours.

Stage 3: overhead recovery rates are established for each production cost centre. The process involves dividing budgeted costs by budgeted activity to provide a budgeted recovery rate or budgeted absorption rate. In the case of cutting, a rate based on machine hours has been used because the cost centre appears **to be very machine-orientated when the labour and machine hours are compared. With manufacture and glass fitting, the reverse applies and so the basis for the recovery rate which has been selected is labour hours.**

The rates are shown on the apportionment statement below. They will be applied to all work undertaken by Goldstar Windows. The cost of work which the unit undertakes will consists of direct costs (primarily labour and materials) plus a share of overheads derived by applying the rates to the amount of time each job spends in each of the productive cost centres.

Apportionment

The first stage is to apportion the costs to the three units.
This is effected by means of an overhead analysis statement.

	Basis of apportionment	Total £	Cutting £	Manuf. £	Glass fitting £	Stores £	Maintenance £	Tool room £
Indirect materials		12 160	5 640	4 880	1 150	410	60	20
Consumables		5 500	1 500	2 000	1 100		600	300
Depreciation		70 000	35 000	13 000	12 000	1 000	8 000	1 000
Heat and light	Area (M2)	14 250	4 500	3 750	3 750	750	750	750
Insurance	Value of Bldg	12 000	4 000	4 000	1 000	1 500	500	1 000
Rent and rates	Area (M2)	19 000	6 000	5 000	5 000	1 000	1 000	1 000
Power	Use %	48 000	19 200	14 400	7 200	2 400	2 400	2 400
Sub-totals		180 910	75 840	47 030	31 200	7 060	13 310	6 470
Reapportionment								
Stores			883	2 647	3 089	-7 060		441
Maintenance			9 075	2 420	1 815		-13 310	
Tool room			4 712	1 257	942			-6 911
Totals		180 910	90 510	53 354	37 046	0	0	0

The next step is to calculate recovery rates.

Machine hours			15 000					
Labour hours				8 000	7 000			
Rate per machine hour			6.03					
Rate per labour hour				6.67	5.29			

2.1 You are employed as financial advisor to the Glamwent County Council. The authority operates a large comprehensive school serving three separate dining rooms. The Director of Education has requested that you carry out a financial investigation using unit cost data into the three kitchens.

On investigation you discover the following information for the last financial year (19X1/X2):

| | Kitchen | | |
	A	B	C
Cost of provisions	£ 80 000	£ 98 500	£ 49 000
Heating and lighting	£ 2 600	£2 700	£ 1 900
Number of employees:			
Cooks	1	1	1
Assistant cooks	1	1	–
Kitchen maids	8	6	5
Capital costs:			
Buildings	£300 000	£300 000	£180 000
Equipment	£ 90 000	£ 90 000	£ 60 000
Total meals produced	60 000	66 000	30 000
Income	£ 30 000	£ 31 000	£ 15 000

Other factors

(a) Average annual earnings are £10 000 for a cook, £9 000 for an assistant and £5 000 for other staff.

(b) In addition to the above staff one supervisor has overall charge of all three kitchens. She is paid an annual salary of £18 000.

(c) Wage overheads are estimated to amount to 10% of total wages and salaries.

(d) Administration costs are to be allocated to each kitchen on the basis of 2p per meal produced.

(e) Buildings and equipment are depreciated on a straight-line basis. The appropriate periods are 60 years and 15 years respectively.

Required

Prepare a cost report to the Director of Education on the costs of operating the three kitchens in 19X1/X2. The report should contain appropriate recommendations based on your conclusions about the operating costs of the three kitchens.

Note:
You may make any reasonable assumptions in preparing the report but these should be stated in the report or your working papers.

(25 marks)

2.2 The Bedpan Health Authority administers 3 hospitals and, at each, maintains a catering service for both patients and staff.

The following information has been made available for the 9 months ended 31 December 19X2.

| | Hospitals | | |
	North £	South £	West £
Food Stocks: 1.4.–2	3 345	16 445	1 140
31.12.–2	3 680	22 610	935
Wages: Kitchen Staff			
– Patients Meals	96 600	201 250	21 000
– Staff Meals	47 750	263 500	10 000
Dining Room Staff	53 000	183 250	–
Hardware, Crockery etc.	6 000	17 500	1 450
Salaries Catering			
Management	15 000	25 000	
Income: Staff Meals	70 000 CR	394 090 CR	10 000
Sale of Waste	5 500 CR	1 650 CR	6 500 CR
Purchase of food in the			250 CR
year	168 905	556 600	22 780
Cost of food used for			18 000
patient meals	117 530	327 175	12 600
Patient Days	96 600	241 500	15 960
Staff Meals Served		141 680	354 200

Notes:
1. The DHA laid down the following cost limits for the financial year to 31.3.–3:
   (a) Food cost allowance for patients was £6.70 per patient week.
   (b) Staff meals price should be set so as to recover the cost of the food used plus 60%.
2. Inflation during 19X2/X3 affected food prices at an average rate of 10%.
3. All allocations of costs between patient and staff meals have been obtained from records kept by each catering manager.
4. Menus are at the discretion of each hospital catering manager, who is also responsible for his own purchasing.
5. Increases in pay are awarded with effect from 1 April. During 19X2/X3, however, a long dispute was not settled until the middle of December, the pay aware to all employees being 6.5% backdated to 1 April 19X2. The pay award did not find its way into salaries and wages paid out until the end of January 19X3.
6. Electricity and gas costs are not separately metered for the catering departments. However, based on floor area, in estimated apportionment of such costs for 19X2/X3 gives the following charges for the year:

	£
North	2 500
South	8 700
West	2 100

7. The total hospital catering budget for Bedpan HA for 19X2/X3 amounts to £1 718 000 and was apportioned as follows:

North	£435 000
South	£1 205 000
West	£78 000

Required

Prepare a report to the Senior Assistant Treasure comparing the efficiency of the establishment and examining the probable out-turn for 19X2/X3 with reference to the budget for the year.

2.3

	Oldhouse Hospital	Newtown Hospital	Manor-cottage Hospital
	£	£	£
Cleaning materials	3 980	19 440	910
Equipment	300	810	160
Cleaning staff – pay	6 000	139 860	15 000
– national insurance	600	12 150	1 320
– superannuation	480	7 830	600
– travelling expenses	–	810	–
Contract – general cleaning	31 460	2 430	240
Services – window cleaning	360	810	160
– other contract services	120	1 480	80
Miscellaneous	720	540	160
Statistics			
– Floor area 12 000 sq.m.	27 000 sq.m.	4 000 sq.m.	
– Average number of available staffed beds	100 beds	300 beds	25 beds

Notes:

(i) The costs of the Domestic Superintendent responsible for the three hospitals are to be apportioned on the basis of floor areas. The costs for 19X6/X7 were:

	£
Pay (including national insurance and superannuation)	4 300
Travelling expenses	430

(ii) Sundry creditors were:

	31 March 19X6	31 March 19X7
	£	£
Oldhouse Hospital		
– equipment	–	600
– general cleaning	500	600
Manorcottage Hospital		
– contract services, window cleaning	50	50
Newtown hospital		
– cleaning materials	250	–

(iii) During 19X6/X7 Newtown Hospital entered into an equipment maintenance contract for £600 per annum payable annually in advance on
1 December. The payment made on 1 December 19X6 is included in the
above figures under 'other contract services'.

(iv) Issues from the Central Store for cleaning materials issued during the last
week of 19X6/X7 have not been included in the above figures. These are:
Newtown Hospital £400, Oldhouse Hospital £80, Manorcottage Hospital
£10.

(v) Stocks of cleaning materials in hand were:

	31 March 19X6	31 March 19X7
	£	£
Oldhouse Hospital	250	350
Newtown Hospital	1 000	2 500
Manorcottage Hospital	50	50

The above details have been extracted from the accounting records of the
Somewhere Area Health Authority for the year ended 31 March 19X7. You are
required to:

(a) Prepare a statement comparing the cleaning costs for each hospital for
19X6/X7.

(b) Discuss the relative cleaning costs for each hospital and the possible
reasons for variances.

(c) Comment on a recent request from the Domestic Superintendent for an
additional cleaner at Manorcottage Hospital.

2.4 You are employed as a Principal Accountant at the London Borough of Mutton.
An opposition councillor is proposing to raise the question of efficiency in the
library service at the next meeting of the Arts and Libraries Committee. He has
information which shows that the gross costs of running Mutton's libraries is 49%
higher than in Lambden (usually regarded as a high spending authority) whereas
Mutton's population is only 27% higher. Your assistant has collected the
following further information.

		Mutton	Lambden
Population (000)		247	194
Gross Expenditure of Library Services	(£000)	3 889	2 560
including (1) Recharge of management			
and administration costs	(£000)	793	615
(2) Debt charges	(£000)	642	213
Income	(£000)	340	134
Number of libraries (mobile library vans)		11(1)	17(2)
Stock – books (000 items)		2 477	1 846
– other (000 items)		623	832
Issues – books (000)		8 451	6 314
– other (000)		1 937	2 865

Required

(a) Prepare a briefing note for the Assistant Director of Finance who will be
attending the Committee on behalf of the Director. The note should cover:

(i) The extent to which the available information supports the councillor's case; (8 marks)

(ii) the alternative explanations which exist for any apparent differences in performance between the two Boroughs. (6 marks)

(b) Why is it desirable to recharge the costs of management and administration to services? (6 marks)

(Total 20 marks)

2.5 Barkworth Health Authority is responsible for Armsworth Hospital, a purpose-built hospital for the mentally handicapped providing service for inpatients and outpatients. Callendar Health Authority provide a similar service in the Abell Wing of Delta Hospital.

The following figures are available for analysis:

	Armsworth Hospital		Delta Hospital– Abell Wing	
	Total cost £000	Out-patients share of total cost %	Total cost £000	Out-patients share of total cost %
Medical and dental	100	5	90	1
Nursing	1 800	1	1 200	3
Pharmacy and medical	130	5	80	8
Physiotherapy	50	6	–	–
Occupational therapy	90	5	150	20
Catering	300	–	310	8
Laundry and linen	80	–	80	–
Administration	200	3	50	10
Domestic and cleaning	150	3	200	12
Portering	30	–	20	–
Estate management	610	2	210	12
Energy and utilities	410	2	220	12
	3 950		2 610	

Statistics:

Average no. of beds	290	210
Average no. of occupied beds	190	208
No. of inpatient days	100 000	70 000
No. of outpatients attendance	3 000	7 000

Required

(a) From the figures given calculate for each expenditure head and for total expenditure:
   (i) the costs per inpatient day in each hospital, and
   (ii) the cost per outpatient attendance at each hospital.

(6 marks)

(b) State:
   (i) what conclusions you draw from your analysis of the figures, and

(8 marks)

   (ii) the reservations, if any, you have about these conclusions.

(2 marks)

(Total 16 marks)

3 ▷ Cost variability and relevant costs

Key learning objectives

After reading this chapter you should be able to

1. Classify costs by behaviour.
2. Explain why cost behaviour is so important to managers.
3. Make use of cost behaviour in decision-making problems.
4. List the difficulties of classifying costs by behaviour in a public sector organization.
5. Understand the benefits and limitations of classifying costs by relevance to the decision under consideration.
6. Make use of incremental analysis in decision-making problems.

Chapter 2 examined traditional approaches to the collection and use of costs within public sector organizations. It was partly concerned with the traceability of costs and the apportionment of overheads to units of output. It also outlined how unit cost statements could be organized on a subjective basis leading to classification by employee costs, materials costs, premises costs and so on.

However, neither classification by traceability nor by subject makes any reference to the ways in which costs behave, for example the extent to which costs increase as one additional pupil is admitted to a school, or as one additional patient is admitted to a hospital. Yet such information is clearly of value to managers concerned with decisions about increases or reductions in the services offered.

3.1 Cost classification by behaviour

To illustrate this, we will use two examples. Our first is of an infants school with 160 children in six classes; output or activity is measured by the number of children in the school. Our second example is of a large hospital of 750 beds where we shall take an extremely crude measure of activity, the number of inpatient days.

Costs may be classified into four main categories, as follows:

1. variable costs
2. fixed costs
3. semi-variable costs
4. step costs.

Variable costs

Variable costs (VC) are those which vary wholly and proportionally with an increase in output. Graphically, a variable cost is described in Figure 3.1. As may be seen, it commences at the origin and increases in a linear fashion.

In an infants school, the only cost which can be placed in this category is that relating to consumable materials – paper, paints, and so on. These are likely to increase proportionally as the number of children in the school increases by one.

In the hospital there are a number of variable costs: drugs, X-rays and sterile packs are obvious examples of costs which increase as the number of inpatient days increase.

It should be noted that there are some costs, such as heating costs, which do vary from month to month. However, the observed changes are not in response to the specified measures of activity in this case and must, therefore, be excluded from the VC category.

Fixed costs

Fixed costs (FC) remain unchanged as output or activity increases or decreases. Graphically, a fixed cost is described in Figure 3.2. As may be observed, the level of cost remains constant irrespective of the level of output.

Figure 3.1 *Variable costs.*

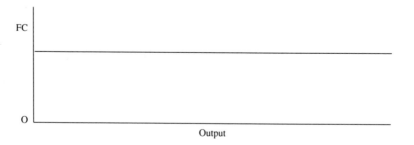

Figure 3.2 *Fixed costs.*

Using the infants school illustration, examples of fixed costs include the costs of caretaker and security, the external maintenance of buildings and grounds, heating costs, and the capital financing charges relating to the school. You will note that neither teachers' nor headteacher's salaries are included within this category. This is explained when step costs are considered below.

Within our hospital, the general manger's salary may be regarded as fixed, as will be the salaries of those senior managers immediately below that level. Building services, portering services, and equipment expenditure also come into this category.

Semi-variable costs

Semi-variable costs (SVC) contain a fixed component and a variable component which is related to output. Graphically, a semi-variable cost is described in Figure 3.3. As may be seen, it intersects the vertical axis at point A; the distance OA represents the fixed element of the cost. The linear slope to the right of point A, along the section to B, reflects the variable element of the cost.

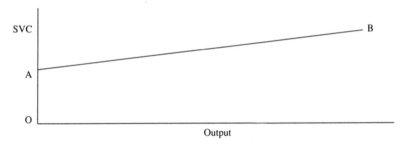

Figure 3.3 *Semi-variable costs.*

Within an infants school, examples include a photocopier where a fixed rental is payable and then a charge related to use, which one may assume is itself related to the number of children within the school.

Within a hospital, laundry costs present such an example. There is a fixed component and a variable element related to power, water, chemicals and so on which relate to activity which is itself tied to the number of inpatient days.

In both school and hospital, the overall catering cost is a semi-variable cost made up of food costs (variable), catering assistants (step), chef (fixed), heat (variable), and so on.

Step costs

Step costs (SC) are those which are fixed for a given level of activity, but at some critical level of output, they increase to a new level. Step costs are described diagrammatically in Figure 3.4. As may be seen, the cost behaves as a fixed cost up to activity level X, but thereafter shifts to a higher level of expenditure.

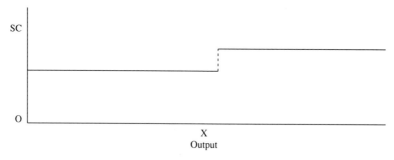

Figure 3.4 *Step costs.*

Whether a cost is a step cost or a fixed cost depends, crucially, on the range of output that is being considered. Over very large ranges of output almost all costs become step costs; for example, a very large increase in the potential pupil intake may require a temporary classroom to be installed, or a wing to be added to the school, and will probably require hiring new teachers on fixed salaries.

In our infant school illustration, the school currently admits 160 pupils. If the number falls to 139, say, the headteacher may suffer a salary reduction as the school slips down to a lower group. If the number of children falls to below 150, the headteacher may have to adopt the role of a teaching head, and, in consequence, there may be some loss in staff time and a reduction in staff costs. If, on the other hand, the number of pupils increases to 175, say, the school may be entitled to an additional part-time teacher. In both of these cases, it can be seen that relatively modest changes in pupil numbers can give rise to changes in staff costs.

Consider our hospital: an increase in patients (subject to the availability of funds) may require that a ward be opened; this may well increase nursing and clinician time so that staff costs, normally regarded as fixed, step up to a new level.

3.2 Revenue and contribution

So far in this chapter our two examples have made no reference to revenue. However, in the public sector of the 1990s, revenue and its relationship to costs is going to become increasingly important.

Table 3.1 shows the relationship between revenue, variable costs and contribution. It is usual to consider each of these per unit of output; this is possible

Table 3.1 The contribution approach

	Total £	Per unit £
Sales revenue	x	x^1
Less variable costs	y	y^1
Contribution	z	z^1
Less fixed costs	a	
Net profit	b	

because it is assumed that each of these three variables increases in a linear fashion so that the relationship between all three is maintained with consistency.

Any fixed costs which are applicable can then be deducted in total; these are not shown on a per unit basis because to do so would represent arbitrary averaging and may suggest to a manager that such costs are also variable on a per unit basis. It should be noted that this applies specifically to the unit cost statements outlined in Chapter 2. There, all costs were divided by the appropriate measure of throughput. As suggested in Chapter 2, more useful for management might be the disaggregation of costs into their variable and fixed components, with detailed examination of unit costs being concentrated on the variable cost elements. To some extent, low fixed unit costs may reflect that the unit is operating near to capacity – but this information can be communicated statistically rather than via unit cost measures.

In the short term, or where there is excess capacity, an organization may tolerate its failure to cover fixed costs. As long as revenue exceeds variable costs, some contribution will be made towards fixed costs, and some contribution may be better than none. Indeed, the desire to maintain the labour force, or hold on to a customer (department), may result in continuing operations if revenues only cover variable cost, if this is the best that can be obtained. In the short term, the aim might be to maximize contribution. However, at the end of the day, all fixed costs must be covered. Thus, long-term considerations would require that the total contribution from operations at least equals total overheads.

If the organization's operations can, in some way, be segmented Table 3.2 demonstrates how the layout in Table 3.1 can be expanded marginally. It is assumed that we have a refuse disposal DSO, and that its disposal activities are segregated into domestic refuse and trade refuse. In this situation, each activity may have overheads which are specific to that activity. For example, trade refuse may have a separate chargehand, and it may employ a different type of refuse vehicle – possibly a lorry as well as a refuse freighter. Such overheads are termed 'segmental fixed costs' or 'segmental overheads' and are designated by letters d and s in Table 3.2. After deducting segmental fixed costs from contribution, this gives rise to a segmental contribution (letters e and t) to the

Table 3.2 Segmented operations and contribution

	Domestic		Trade		
	Total	Per bin	Total	Per tonne	Total
	£	£	£	£	£
Sales revenue	a	a^1	p	p^1	
Less: Variable costs	b	b^1	q	q^1	
Contribution	c	c^1	r	r^1	
Less: Segmental fixed costs	d		s		
Segmental contribution	e		t		
					x
Less: Organizational fixed costs					y
Net profit					z

remaining overheads of the organization (letter y), resulting in the organization's net profit designated by letter z.

3.3   The importance of cost behaviour

Cost behaviour becomes important whenever the level of activity is expected to increase or decrease. As activity increases, variable costs, and the variable element of semi-variable costs, increase too. On the other hand, fixed costs will remain constant – unless, of course they are step costs within the activity range under consideration, in which case the point at which the step occurs becomes critical.

To illustrate the importance of cost behaviour, we take two examples from an environment which is very different from that of a school or hospital, namely an employees' canteen, and a grounds maintenance DSO.

An employees' canteen

A local authority runs a canteen for its workers, which must at least break even (no profit/no loss) on a year-by-year basis. During the last financial year, the costs of providing a meal in its canteen were as follows:

Variable costs per meal:	
food	45p
fuel, etc.	15p
Annual fixed costs:	
wages	£36 000
other overheads	£24 000
Average meal price	72p
No. of meals sold	700 000
Capacity (meals)	825 000

For the next financial year, it is anticipated that the cost of food per meal will rise to 50p, fuel, etc. to 16p, wages will increase to £38 000 and other overheads to £25 000. The catering manager wishes to know the answer to one question: how many meals must be sold to break even?

It is this kind of situation for which knowledge of cost behaviour is particularly useful, and understanding of the relationships outlined in Table 3.1 can be especially valuable. The catering manager's question can be dealt with in two stages:

Stage 1: Calculate the contribution from each meal:

Unit contribution = average meal price – variable costs
= 72p – (50p + 16p)
= 6p

Stage 2: Divide fixed costs by unit contribution to give breakeven output:

Total fixed costs/Unit contribution = (£38 000 + £25 000)/£0.06
= 1 050 000 meals to break even

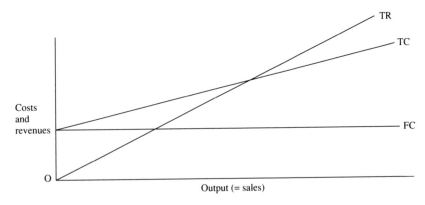

Figure 3.5 *Breakeven charts.*

The catering manager is now provided with information which gives some insight into the problems which need to be faced.

1. The breakeven output exceeds the capacity of the canteen by (1 050 000 – 825 000) 225 000 meals; quite apart from this, any increase in output would need to be sold.
2. The breakeven output level must be reduced. This can be attacked on two fronts. The first is by increasing prices. But what is the likely impact of a given price increase on demand? This can be answered only when we have some idea of the elasticity of demand for meals at the canteen. Secondly, the catering manager can try to find ways to reducing costs. Reducing variable costs will result in an increase in unit contribution; reducing the fixed costs will reduce the breakeven point for any given level of unit contribution.

These relationships can be illustrated diagrammatically in a breakeven chart as shown in Figure 3.5.

In the breakeven chart, the total fixed costs (FC) are drawn parallel to the horizontal axis. FC includes the fixed elements of semi-variable costs (SVC). Total costs (TC) are found by adding variable costs (VC) at each output level to FC. Therefore, when output is zero, TC are equal to FC because VC are also zero. The increase in TC in the range of output illustrated is wholly attributable to variable costs as there are no step costs present. The chart assumes that output is equal to sales. Total revenue (TR) from the sale of output is a straight line from the origin. As sales increase, revenues also increase.

The point of intersection of TC and TR indicates the breakeven level of sales. To the left of this point, a loss is made. To the right, a profit is made. The canteen discussed above is currently operating below breakeven. We saw that the breakeven level of output must be reduced by increasing selling price (increasing the slope of the line TR) or by reducing TC, either by cutting VC (the line would slope less steeply), or by cutting FC (shifting down vertically both FC and TC).

A grounds maintenance DSO

Blaenwent Borough Council has set up a separate shrub-growing section within its grounds maintenance DSO. The section is to be run as a separate trading

Table 3.3 Budgeted costs for shrub-growing operation

	Logard Blue	Faze Yellow	Hardy Berbarian	Berry Red
No. of shrub/acre	100	80	90	100
Selling price each	£4	£5	£6	£7
VC per acre:				
Seedlings	£150	£200	£225	£300
Wages	£30	£20	£25	£50
Fixed costs per annum		£3000		

activity and its objective is to maximize profit as this will help the department subsidize grounds maintenance in the event of poor performance. It is planned that the activity will supply shrubs to the parent authority and also to other public sector organizations within the confines of the Local Authority Goods and Service Act (which limits the ability of local authorities to compete outside the public sector). A total of 20 acres of land have been set aside for this activity and the department has prepared the budget shown in Table 3.3.

Wages may be treated as a variable cost as the shrub-growing section will buy in labour from the parent DSO on an acre-by-acre basis, as and when needed.

Discussion with the DSO manager reveals that the council, as client, has agreed to purchase 120 Logard Blues, 80 Faze Yellows, 72 Hardy Berberians and 100 Berry Reds. The manager feels, however, that such is the expertise within the department, and such the demand for the product, that it would be possible to sell up to 2000 shrubs of any type to the local and health authorities in the area. Given this, he wishes to investigate which variety represents greatest profit, and by bundling the host authority's needs along with sales of the most profitable shrub, he wishes to investigate the overall maximum profit that can be obtained.

This situation, like the last, can also be tackled in two stages. Stage 1 involves identifying the contributions per acre from the four types of shrub. The relevant calculations are shown in Table 3.4.

As may be seen, the greatest contribution per acre is provided by the variety Berry Red. Because the number of acres devoted to this activity restricts the number of seedlings that can be planted, the variety Berry Red is the most attractive financially because it makes the highest contribution per acre of this limiting factor. This suggests that any excess acreage, after meeting the authority's needs, should be devoted to this variety if the objective is to maximize contribution.

Table 3.4 Contribution per acre from the shrubs

	Logard Blue £	Faze Yellow £	Hardy Berberian £	Berry Red £
Revenue per acre	400	400	540	700
VC per acre	180	220	250	350
Contribution per acre	£220	£180	£290	£350

Table 3.5 Maximum contribution and profit available

	Logard Blue	Faze Yellow	Hardy Berberian	Berry Red	Total
Sales to host	120	80	72		
Acres required	1.2	1	0.8		
Acres available for Berry Red (20–3)				17	
	£	£	£	£	£
Contribution per acre	220	180	290	350	
Total contribution	264	180	232	5950	6626
Fixed costs					3000
Net profit					£3626

Stage 2 involves calculating the maximum contribution and profit that can be obtained from the operation. Relevant calculations are displayed in Table 3.5. As can be seen, after making allowance for the total of three acres which must be devoted to the first three types of shrub in order to supply the host local authority with the agreed mix of shrubs, the remaining 17 acres are used for growing the Berry Red variety.

By doing this maximum contribution and profit can be obtained because the Berry Red makes the greatest contribution per acre, which is the factor of production which limits output. This produces a total contribution of £6626 and a net profit of £3626 after meeting the fixed costs of the operation.

Conclusions

The two previous examples have demonstrated that knowledge of cost behaviour is valuable to management in both planning and decision-making.

In the first example, the breakeven position was established; extension of the approach would allow the prediction of required sales for any specified target profit – given by: (Fixed costs + Target profit)/Contribution per unit of output. As the assumed relationship between contribution and output is a linear one, once contribution per unit has been established, it is possible to estimate with some ease the total contribution from different levels of output. If price or variable costs are to be changed, the revised unit contribution can be assessed relatively quickly, and then applied to projected levels of output.

In the second example, the concept of the limiting factor was introduced, and it was demonstrated how contribution per unit of the limiting factor could be used to establish the optimum product mix.

One other valuable use of cost behaviour is found when budgeted costs are monitored against actual performance. If actual performance relates to different levels of activity than the budget, then there appears little point in comparing actual variable costs with budgeted variable costs. Instead, they should be compared with what budgeted variable costs would be expected to be at that actual level of output. This point is examined within the context of flexible budgeting in Chapter 5.

3.4 Problems relating to the cost behaviour approach

As has been demonstrated, the classification of costs by behaviour is very attractive, but its practical application has to face a variety of problems, as is indicated below:

Fluctuating nature of variable unit costs

The assumption underpinning the accountant's approach to variable costs is that they are constant per unit of output. However, increasing efficiency may result in decreasing variable costs per unit, and vice versa. The likelihood of this will differ for different components of cost; variable labour costs are likely to be the most liable to change, although all unit variable costs may change as a result of modifications in equipment or methods of organization.

The prevalence of step costs

As has been indicated, many costs fall into the step category over output ranges with which we may be concerned. Within the education service, the stepped elements of salaries are fairly easy to derive. The pupil numbers bands for determining headteachers' salaries are publicized; the ground rules for relating pupil numbers to staff numbers are also well known. However, within a secondary school, changing option preferences may require relatively complex projections of the resulting costs. Within a hospital, complexity is likely to be even greater. The size of many acute hospitals (many large ones have an annual expenditure in excess of £40m) and the integrated nature of operations may mean that the step cost implications of decisions may be widespread and complex to follow through. Take, for example, a decision to treat more patients within a specialty as day patients rather than as inpatients. This may result in freeing beds and, may also free nursing and clinician time (both indicating steps in a downward direction). However, the policy change is probably aimed at increasing the number of patients treated, so that drugs expenditure (a variable cost) will almost certainly increase, there may be an increase in admission costs, an increased demand on the non-emergency ambulance service, and a possible rearranging of clinician and nursing hours.

Disaggregation of semi-variable costs

Rarely are costs purely variable; many costs are semi-variable. Where there exists a two-part tariff, as with telephone and photocopier charges, the standing charge is clearly the fixed element, the metered charge the variable element. However, taking a school as an example, a large part of the telephone metered charge may remain substantially fixed over significant changes in pupil numbers. The management of the school will require telephone contact – with officers of the LEA, with examining bodies, with governors and so on. On top of this, increases in pupil numbers will necessitate use of the telephone to contact parents, the LEA and so on. Thus, the apparent simplicity of the metered element of the telephone charge conceals a cost which is semi-variable, and may be stepped as well.

There are two distinct approaches to dealing with the problem of semi-variable costs, both are concerned with segregating the fixed and variable elements:

An engineering approach

An engineering approach attempts to build up a cost after specifying the target inputs required. For example, from what is known about cooking, times, energy costs, ingredient costs and labour costs, it may be possible to build up a standard cost for a meal, segregating the costs into fixed and variable components. However, this approach may be expensive and time-consuming, and requires the expertise of a variety of specialists such as organization and methods experts and energy experts.

A statistical approach

A statistical regression approach takes a large number of observations of costs and activity levels and uses regression analysis to derive the equations giving the fixed and variable elements of cost. Diagrammatically, Figure 3.6 indicates the approach which is taken. The line AB, the least squares regression line, is so constructed as to minimize the vertical deviations between the observed values and the line. Thus it is said to be the 'line of best fit'. The distance OA then represents the fixed cost element, and the slope of the line AB represents the variable cost.

This approach can be carried out quickly, with a calculator or software package handling the calculations, but there are also a number of reservations, some of which are as follows. First, a number of observations are needed to give one confidence in the output of the model. Secondly, the line is essentially an average – it may never actually pass through any observed points. Finally, the model cannot be used as a basis for extrapolating beyond the limits of the data – in either a downward or an upward direction – thus the model cannot be used to predict variable costs if it is planned to expand output beyond past levels. (Further information about regression and its limitations can be found in most statistics textbooks.)

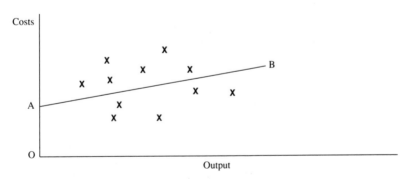

Figure 3.6 *Regression analysis and semi-variable costs.*

Costs of classification

Costs are not normally classified or collected on the basis of cost behaviour. Therefore, additional time and money has to be expended to collect the necessary information. Often, little better than rough estimates of variable elements of costs and of steps may be available. However, using such estimates is better than just ignoring cost behaviour.

3.5 Incremental analysis using relevant costs

The earlier sections of this chapter have been concerned with the distinction between variable costs and fixed costs and their relationship to changes in activity. We now move on to an approach entitled incremental analysis, and the concept of relevant costs – those costs which are relevant to a specific decision under consideration. This concept is much wider than that of classifying costs on the basis of behaviour; the idea of relevance/irrelevance cuts across the variable/fixed classification.

Relevant costs and relevant revenues are those that will change as the result of a specific decision. Non-relevant costs and revenues are those which are unaffected by a specific decision. Thus the concept of relevance is distinguished by two features:

1. Relevance is decision-specific: change the decision and the relevant factors change too.
2. Relevance is related to the future: a cost which has already been incurred is not relevant because it cannot be affected by the decision; we are not in a position to turn the clock back and alter a previous decision. Such past or historic costs are termed 'sunk' costs.

To expand on this idea, consider a healthy authority which is seeking to dispose of an obsolete ambulance in need of some repair. The ambulance originally cost £15 000 some years ago. There are two alternative ways of disposing of the vehicle, and it has to decide between these alternatives:

1. to transport it, at a cost of £50, to a motor auction where its sale can be expected to net £300;
2. to obtain spare parts costing £200 and incur labour costs of £400 to render the ambulance driveable. It would then be driven to the auction, where its sale can be expected to net £1000.

In either case, return travel from the auction may be expected to cost £15.

All the above information is given in Table 3.6. The relevance/non-relevance of each of the items is now examined. The list below refers to the 'notes' column in the table:

1. Revenues are relevant because they relate to the future and differ between the alternatives.
2. Original cost is irrelevant; it is a sunk cost and it cannot be influenced by the decision. As it is a sunk cost, it is also common between the two alternatives.
3. Transport to the auction is relevant as it represents a cost of one of the alternatives only.

Table 3.6 Alternative methods of disposing of ambulance

	Note	Auction now £	Repair and auction £
Revenues:			
Proceeds	1	300	1 000
Costs:			
Acquisition	2	15 000	15 000
Transport to auction	3	50	
Transport from auction	4	15	15
Spare parts/labour	5		600

Table 3.7 Relevant costs and revenues

	Auction now £	Repair and auction £
Relevant revenues:		
Proceeds	300	1000
Relevant costs:		
Transport to auction	50	
Spare parts/labour		600
Net relevant income	250	400

4. Transport from the auction is a future cost but, as it is common to both alternatives, it may be ignored as the decision is simply between those alternatives.
5. Spare parts and labour are relevant as they relate to one alternative only.

It follows from this that each of the following represents a sufficient condition for regarding a cost or revenue as being non-relevant:

1. All sunk costs/revenues are irrelevant.
2. All common costs/revenues are irrelevant.

The cost and revenue information has been recast in a relevant cost format in Table 3.7. As can be seen, the approach clearly identifies the relevant monetary factors with respect to a specific decision. In doing so, it strips away much confusing or irrelevant information and helps to clarify the issues for the decision maker.

Limitations of the incremental approach

There are two important limitations that need to be noted. First, a routine approach to cost collection is unlikely to provide relevant information because relevance depends on the current decision, and relates to estimates of future costs and revenues rather than to past costs and revenues, which are at the core of routine costing systems. Therefore, special *ad hoc* studies will be required to establish relevant costs for each decision, necessitating the expenditure of time and money.

Secondly, the approach is essentially short term. Overheads may or may not be relevant to a decision. If they are judged to be non-relevant, they will not be included within the costs with which relevant revenues are compared. Yet, in the long term, all such costs must be covered if an organization is to remain viable, or if it is to avoid the cross-subsidization of losses in one area, possibly from the core area of the business. This is not to say that the relevant costing approach is wrong but simply emphasizes the need to consider, when pricing, that viability eventually requires all costs to be covered.

3.6 Relevant costs and the 1990s

Management of the public sector in the 1990s is likely to exhibit the same trend towards increasing concern with commercialism, competition and internal markets as has occurred in the 1980s. Against this background, we can envisage the following situations within which the idea of relevance can be of great value.

The preparation of competitive tenders

Direct service organizations will need to obtain business by the submission of competitive tenders. Such tenders should initially be constructed by identifying the relevant costs which must, of necessity, be covered. This would then give a minimum tender price below which no bid should be made. To this should be added an amount which makes a contribution to overheads – the amount which can be added and still provide a competitive tender depends on the judgement of the estimator. An estimate of the full-cost price may provide some rough indication of the costs which may be under consideration by rivals in the field.

When tendering for the bulk of the DSO's business, then, overheads will become relevant; if the core contract is not obtained, the DSO may have to close and overheads will not then be incurred. Similarly, a tender for the core will require attention to the target return (breakeven point or 5%, depending on the service) as, again, failure to achieve this may result in closure.

Finally, the costing of tenders should always be carefully related to the specified standards of performance. For example, in the collection of domestic refuse, service standards will specify the number of collections weekly, the number of households, the type of refuse container (sack, dustbin, wheely bin), whether bin collected from pavement or from rear of house, and so on. If any element of standard performance is inadvertently excluded from the tender cost build-up, then if successful, actual completion of the contract will reduce net income, and may occasion losses.

The NHS internal market

The major responsibility of district health authorities now is with identifying the health needs of the local population and with purchasing health care services which are required to meet those needs. The supply of health care services is primarily provided by the trust hospitals.

Currently most services are purchased from local hospitals but health authorities are able to purchase services from outside their area and in the case of elective surgery one can envisage many patients travelling to where care can be provided. This is expected to increase as purchasers seek to obtain the best value for money out of their restricted funds. The purchasing health authorities will consider quality and timing of services as well as cost.

Currently, providers must engage in no cross-subsidization of services in the prices which they quote for undertaking work which in practice means that cost-based prices must contain a fair share of overheads. In addition, contracts are generally of a 'block' nature, covering a range of services which the purchaser buys; prices of individual procedures are not provided.

This would seem to be an environment which is alien to relevant costing. However, looking to the future one can see advantages from pursuing a relevant cost approach:

1. Prices quoted to purchasers would contain much more information on the cost of providing services. Purchasers, responding to the market would seek out the lowest price for the same level of quality. Relevant cost-based prices are likely to provide more informed prices in this process.
2. If relevant cost-based prices are lower because of more efficient medical procedures, then this would act as a catalyst for the more widespread use of those procedures as other providers seek to obtain the same benefits. Currently the implementation of more efficient procedures is not revenue driven and there is a time lag before all clinicians adopt such procedures.
3. Hospitals offering services should establish relevant costs with great care ensuring, as a minimum, that the price quoted covers relevant costs. It can then look for a competitive price in excess of that figure knowing that a contribution to overheads will be made.

However, a major difficulty within the NHS relates to the costing of activity. Relevant costing makes great demands on information systems and currently the information base is not generally available. It is also more difficult to audit relevant costs than apportioned costs which can be obtained from a routine cost system. Relevance is partly determined by the time period, is not routine and is difficult to audit yet cost audit is significant in the context of no cross-subsidization.

Service level agreements

As outlined in Chapter 2, many internal local authority services are now governed by service level agreements. These can apply to internal audit, computer services, payroll services, invoice-related services, architectural services, legal services and others. They represent a movement away from the traditional apportionment of costs and offer customer departments a level of service at a set price. Consumer departments can influence the costs borne by changing their demand of the support services or, possibly, by acquiring the service from a cheaper source such as an external body. One thing is certain, it focuses the user's attention on the cost of the support services, and on their perceived benefit. This is especially so when the customer department itself is subject to competitive pressure (such as a DSO).

The next step is for each support service to run a practice account, a form of trading account. In this situation, it is in the support service's long-term interests to ensure that its charges cover its costs. This suggests that for each aspect of the service provided, it needs to consider the relevant costs of service provision, so that the charge made is related to relevant costs and not to costs that are arbitrarily apportioned. Failure to do this may well mean that users will consume services which are (incorrectly and arbitrarily) under-priced and avoid services where the reverse occurs; this would be bad business for any support service which would see costs outstripping revenues.

3.7 Costing and survival

The contribution and relevant costing approaches are both relatively under-utilized in the public sector. Variable, fixed, semi-variable and stepped costs are not normally measured or reported in routine management accounting systems. However, as the public sector becomes more competitive, markets, whether external or internal, will force organizations to look carefully at costs and prices in order to survive. Within this environment, arbitrary apportionment of over-heads as the method of cost recovery and broad averaging of all costs to obtain a unit cost may prove of very limited use. Broad averaging may provide costs which are relatively meaningless if we are considering changes in the level of activity or examining specific decisions.

Of course, the decision-orientated techniques are not perfect and face significant difficulties on the cost collection side. However, even if estimated, they are related to decisions, to the future, to really examining which costs change and by how much, and are concerned with using cost information in order to earn a profit. They are also vitally important in an *ex post* capacity for VFM and performance studies whether this is carried out by management or an external monitoring body. For many of these organizations, examining the dynamics of cost behaviour may represent an important first step in ensuring survival.

Key points of chapter

1. Cost behaviour is important to managers.
2. Variable costs, contribution and fixed costs can be used to help solve problems relating to breakeven, price, output and mix.
3. There are practical difficulties in classifying costs by behaviour.
4. Relevant costs can make an important contributions to managerial decision-making.
5. Relevant costing has both uses and limitations when the organization must meet overheads to survive.

3.8 Summary

This chapter has examined the classification of costs by behaviour and by relevance to specific decision-making situations. It has emphasized the distinction between fixed and variable costs and introduced the concept of the contribution. Examples have indicated the power of the contribution approach, especially when changes in levels of activity, breakeven or target contribution, and optimal product mix are under consideration. Additionally, the powerful technique of incremental analysis has been demonstrated, including the way in which it can be used to eliminate non-relevant data from decisions.

The difficulties involved in implementing these costing approaches have also been noted, especially the ways in which they do not match conventional approaches to cost collection. We have also highlighted the dangers of ignoring fixed costs which must be covered in the long term. However, it is argued that these techniques can yield benefits in a variety of situations, including competitive tendering, internal market pricing and purchasing, and service level agreements. Indeed, in any competitive situation it is essential that an organization is aware of cost behaviour, and specifically which costs are relevant in different situations.

Questions

3.1 Didcot County Council has a community workshop which produces picnic baskets for sale to the general public. For the financial year ending 31 March 19X9 the production details were as follows:

Units produced and sold	4 950
Selling price (per unit)	£19.00
Fixed overheads	£20 000
Variable costs per unit:	
Wages	£8.00
Materials	£4.00
Variable overheads	£2.00

Estimates for the next financial year (i.e. 19–9/–0) show the following budgeted changes:

Units to be produced and sold	5 500
Fixed overheads to rise by	£7 000
Variable costs per unit:	
Wage costs to rise to	£8.80
Estimated materials costs	£4.26
Variable overheads to fall by	3%
Selling price per unit	£21.00

Notes:
1. The following analysis of results is given for the three years prior to 19X8/X9:

	[19X5/X6]	[16X6/X7]	[19X7/X8]
Selling price (unit)	£14.00	£16.00	£18.00
Actual sales (units)	6 000	5 000	4 800
Fixed costs	£15 000	£18 000	£18 000
Variable costs	£72 000	£65 000	£64 800

2. The fixed overheads are allocated to the area used by picnic baskets on the basis of production floor space utilized by the department. Total fixed overheads in 19X9/X0 are estimated at £36 000.

3. Normal sales are direct to the public but a major wholesaler has approached the community workshop with an offer to purchase 800 units. There is sufficient space capacity to absorb the order but the price is only £17 per unit.

Required

Prepare a report to the workshop manager advising him:

(a) on the breakeven level of sales for 19X9/X0 (indicate the results using an appropriate graph);

(b) in the light of past sales performance, a forecast of the profit or loss if the level of sales for 19X8/X9 is achieved in 19X9/X0;

(c) whether the special order should be accepted.

Your report should draw on both financial and non-financial factors in presenting your results, including pointing out the weaknesses of breakeven analysis and the implication of the results since 19X5/X6 on the forecasted sales for 19X9/X0.

3.2 A DSO, operating on commercial principles, receives an order for work at a price suggested by the prospective customer of £1600. The customer is a public sector organization. Acceptance of the contract will not affect the progress of existing contracts.

The following details emerge from an estimate of the requirements of the job.

1. Some of the materials required are in stock already as a result of a previous over-order; at present it looks as if there will be little alternative use for the materials. They originally cost £910 but can be sold for only £650.

2. Other materials will have to be purchased at a cost of £560, plus delivery costs of £10.

3. The job is estimated to need 32 labour hours and will be carried out on two successive Saturdays. The appropriate average wage rate is £2.45 per hour, and wage-related overheads amount to 55% of all wage payments. Saturday working is paid at time and a half.

4. The job will require the use of a lorry; the vehicle will be hired from the Plant DLO at a total cost of £100, driver included.

Required

(a) What is the estimated profit or loss?

(b) Should the job be accepted at the price offered?

3.3 Blaenwent Parks Department has been approached as a direct service organization to take an additional work to its existing contract. A price therefore has to be negotiated between the DSO and the client. In arriving at the contract price the following information was used:

Estimated direct labour hours p.a.	50 000
Estimated fixed overheads	£66 000
Estimated direct wages rate (hr)	£2.40

On the basis of the above the direct labour rate was calculated at £3.72 per hour (i.e. a 55% on-cost rate). There is still some spare capacity in the workforce and the unit aggressively seeks profitable work to fill this time. The current contract is on schedule and no problems are predicted in achieving the anticipated return.

The department has been approached by the Went Area Health Authority to undertake ground maintenance at one of its hospitals because it has cut back on its own workforce. This will envolve a gang of three men plus transport working Saturday and Sunday with time and a half paid on the Saturday and double time on Sunday. Estimated hours are as follows: Saturday, 8 hrs; Sunday,4 hrs.

Transport will be required to be hired for the weekend at a cost of £70 for the two days. In addition mileage will cost 45p per mile. Total estimated mileage is 75 miles. Direct materials will cost £140.

It is anticipated that a successful bid plus good quality work will result in the authority being invited to tender for the bulk of the health authority's work as its own DSO is closing down due to inefficiency.

Required

Calculate the minimum price the unit should tender. Why have you chosen this price?

3.4 The Getwellsoon Health Authority is responsible for eight separate establishments; a central laundry unit serves six of these and the other two have their own independent laundry facilities. The summarized final accounts for the unit for 19X3/19X4 are as follows:

	£	£
19X3–19X4		
Income:		
Recoveries		1 672 000
Expenditure:		
Staff costs – operatives	1 100 000	
– drivers	20 000	
– management	110 000	
Laundry materials used	200 000	
Repairs to premises	38 000	
Rent and rates	50 000	
Power and heat	100 000	
Vehicles – running costs	10 000	
– fixed charges	3 000	
Equipment (minor items)	20 000	
Water	25 000	1 676 000
Deficit 19X3–19X4		£4 000

You ascertain:

1. An error in the stocktaking of laundry materials at 31 March 19X4. The correct stock is £4000 less than that used in the accounts.
2. The number of articles laundered in 19X3/19X4 was:

April 19X3–September 19X3	3 000 000
October 19X3–March 19X4	4 000 000
Total	7 000 000

3. There was an increase of 15% in the charge per 100 articles laundered as from 1 October 1983.

4. No charge is made in the accounts for depreciation of laundry equipment and vehicles but the laundry is expected to return a surplus of 10% (at least) of the cost of equipment and vehicles used.

5. There are three vans in use whose cost and purchase dates are as follows:

Van	Cost	Year of purchase
	£	
A	2 500	19X4–19X5
B	4 000	19X0–19X1
C	6 000	19X2–19X3

6. Last year (19X2/19X3) the laundry made a surplus of £10 000 which was regarded by management as 'satisfactory'.

The Authority is considering inviting tenders for its laundry requirements for 19X5/19X6 onwards which prompts the Laundry Manager to produce the following memorandum:

> 'The accounts for 19X3/19X4 show the laundry producing a unit cost of less than £24 per 100 articles laundered. The major laundry plant and equipment will definitely need replacing in April 19X5 which will cost £515 000. However, the new equipment will enable us to cut the number of operatives by one-tenth.
>
> The unit supplies only four-fifths of the Authority's total laundry requirements. The new plant and machinery could cope with the other fifth without any increase in standing charges and it should be allocated to us.
>
> 'If this were done we should not need any additional vans or drivers; at present ours are under-employed at certain times of the week.'
>
> 'Should the Authority agree to the above I am sure we would be below the commercial rate which I understand is around £22.00 per 100 articles laundered.'

You are asked to produce a briefing note for the Treasurer, setting out the salient points of the situation (ignore inflation).　　　　(17 marks)

3.5 Crick CC is a widespread, rural authority which currently operates five establishments providing residential accommodation for children of school age. The total number of places provided at the establishments is 400, but recently the demand for places has fallen off, largely due to a change in population pattens within the county. The present occupancy is, consequently, 60% and this is expected to continue in 19X4/X5. The authority wishes to reduce the total number of places to 300 and it would also wish to cut its budget by at least 25%.

The following data are available:

Establishment	No. of places	Estimated average occupancy 19X4/X5	Estimated net cost 19X4/X5 £000
A	110	80	228
B	70	40	170
C	60	30	100
D	80	40	130
E	80	50	110
	400	240	738

Estimates 19X4/X5

	A £000	B £000	C £000	D £000	E £000
Staffing	110	106	64	81	67
Premises	20	22	12	11	17
Food	107	44	31	40	32
Other (variable costs)	7	4	1	4	4
	244	176	108	136	120
Income*	16	6	8	6	10
	228	170	100	130	110

*based upon parental ability to pay.

Staffing and premises costs are wholly fixed costs.

All establishments are fully financed and there are no outstanding debt charges.

Continued use of home E beyond 19X4/X5 is dependent on major repair work being carried out which will take 15 months to complete and cost an estimated £120 000.

Home C is only used five days per week but all other establishments are used seven days per week.

Required

With reference to financial and other considerations, analyse the above information. Consider available options and make appropriate recommendations.

3.6 A division of a public sector organisation operates an commercial principles and manufactures a small range of products, mainly to customers' orders. An enquiry is received for an order at a price suggested by the enquirer of £5000.

The following details emerge from an estimate of production requirements:

1. *Materials.* These are in stock entirely because of an estimating error on an earlier order. The materials cost £750 but have a realizable of £870.
2. *Production labour.* The division has normally sufficient orders to keep production labour occupied. Wages for production labour on the order are estimated to be £1300.
3. *Supervision.* The order would require a high degree of supervision, and one supervisor would be in full time attendance on the order for 12 weeks. Supervisors are paid £60 per week but for the high degree of attendance demanded by the order, temporary plus rates will have to be paid to other employees on other work to act as supervisors at a total cost of £360.
4. *Fixed overheads* apportioned on normal rates to the order would amount to £1500.
5. *Components* can be brought in for the order at a cost of £200 or made on otherwise idle equipment at a cost of £300 arrived at as follows:

Labour	£100
Materials	80
Fixed overhead	120
	£300

6. *Machine No. 1.* This is owned by the division, and £1000 depreciation, following normal depreciation policy would be apportioned to the order. The machine is however shortly due for replacement. If sold immediately, the machine is likely to realize £1200, but if used on the order would probably realize £700.
7. *Machine No. 2.* This machine is leased by the division at £100 per week on long period agreement. Acceptance of the order would mean withholding this machine from other work, and temporarily hiring a substitute machine. The only substitute machine immediately available from hires is an older model at a price of £80 per week for 12 weeks, and additional production labour to maintain output would be needed for that period at a cost of £30 per week. The estimator's report on the order is as follows:

	£
Materials	910
Production labour	1 300
Supervision	720
Overheads	1 500
Components	200
Machine No. 1 – Depreciation	1 000
No. 2	1 200
Total cost	6 830
Price offered	5 000
Loss	£1 830

You are required to advise, with reasons, whether or not in your view the order should be accepted.

3.7 The budget of a profit-making contracting unit in a public sector undertaking for the year ended 31 March 1990 is as follows:

	£000	£000
Direct costs: Materials	80	
Labour	70	
		150
Contracting unit overheads		60
Total CU costs		210
General overheads		70
Total costs		280
Income		315
Budgeted profit		35

The target profit achieves a return of 8% on the current cost of assets which is in excess of the 5% target specified by the Secretary of State.

After the budget has been drawn up, the unit, which has spare capacity, is invited to tender for a construction contract by a local health authority.

The unit's internal rules lay down that the price tendered is to be found by referring to the annual budget and:

1. adding to the direct costs of the job a percentage to cover unit overheads;
2. adding a further percentage to cover general overheads;
3. adding a profit margin amounting to 12.5% of total costs.

Required

(a) What is the price to be tendered by the unit?
(b) The direct materials cost includes £2750, the cost of 100 units of K already in stock; these are not likely to be required for any future jobs. However, if £75 is spent on conversion, they could be used as substitutes for 100 parts of M which would otherwise have to be bought in at a cost of £22 each, or they could be sold, without conversion, for £19 each.

The direct materials costs of the contract also include £1500, the cost of the required quantity of material R which is also in stock. The material is used frequently by the company and its current cost has increased to £1800.

All other direct costs are solely attributable to the contract.

The general overhead expenditure would be the same whether the contract is accepted or not, but acceptance would increase contracting unit overheads by £3250 for additional supervision, labour, fuel and power.

What is the minimum price to be tendered for the contract?

3.8 Your public sector organization has a contracting unit which operates on a trading basis; taking one year with another it is expected to break even.

In March 19X7 the unit is asked to undertake two jobs but the unit's resources do not permit the acceptance of both. Both jobs would commence on 1 April

19X7 and take one year to complete. The following financial statement has been prepared by the cost accountant attached to the unit:

	Job A £	Job B £
Materials: in stock 20/3/X7 (at cost):		
Type A	15 000	
Type B		6 600
to be purchased	16 000	20 400
Direct labour	33 000	49 000
Depreciation of plant on site	2 400	3 200
Total of direct charges	66 400	79 200
Office and admin. on-cost (6%)	3 984	4 752
	70 384	83 952
Agreed contract price	80 000	96 000
Surplus	£9 616	£12 048

Note:
1. If job A is accepted, the stock of type B materials can be sold for £12 500 (it is assumed that all stocks not required can be sold).
2. If job B is accepted, the stock of type A materials can be sold for £14 950 or, subject to the purchase of additional components for £500, can be used in place of 80% of the materials to be purchased for job B in 19X7/X8.
3. Depreciation of plant, charged in the financial accounts, is estimated to be £3200 per year (£2400 for A). The resale value at 1/4/X7 is £10 000 and this is expected to fall by £1000 for each quarter that passes.
4. In each case the fixed costs element of direct labour is £1000.
5. Tenders for each job have also been received by outside contractors; the best of these are:
   Job A   £90 000
   Job B   £100 000
6. The unit owns 20 units of plant of which 15 would be used on the Job A contract whilst all 20 will be used on Job B. If job A is accepted, 5 units will be hired out to other contractors at a rental of £500 each for the year 19X7/X8.

Required

A revised financial statement to show which job should be undertaken by the unit.

3.9   Tidy CC operates two landfill sites for refuse disposal and has three district councils in its area. These sites are becoming full and alternative arrangements are being considered. A large site for landfill could be made available but environmental pressures favour incineration at a more central site.

Present costs (£000):

	Refuse collection district			Refuse disposal site	
	East	West	South	A	B
Expenditure:					
Employees	400	180	670	80	120
Transport and plant	140	70	230	40	60
Other running costs	35	15	67	110	210
Debt charges	–	–	–	80	150
	575	265	967	310	540
Income	40	10	70	10	40
Net expenditure	£535	£255	£897	£300	£500
Tonnes collected/disposed (000s)	100	40	180	100	220
Proportion of time spent on:					
Collection of refuse	0.9	0.8	0.85		
Delivery to tip	0.1	0.2	0.15		

The revenue costs of the alternative arrangements now being considered are estimated as follows:

	New landfill site £000	Incinerator £000
Expenditure	1570	2380
Income	70	120
Net expenditure	£1500	£2260

The new arrangements would affect the time spent delivering refuse to the disposal site (affecting employee and transport costs) as follows:

District	New landfill site	Incinerator
East	+300%	+50%
West	+30%	+20%
South	–15%	–50%

A transfer station could be erected on the existing site used by East DC, thus eliminating its extra costs; the station would cost £300 000 per year to operate.

Separation of waste at the incinerator site could be achieved at an additional cost of £230 000 per annum, but income would increase to £350 000 per annum.

Required

Prepare a report setting out the effect on the various authorities concerned, recommending the most appropriate course of action.

3.10 Armstrong County Council Direct Service Organization has been invited to submit a quotation for a special order of 10 000 Chalmers for the Piltdown Water Authority. The Authority requires all tenders to be supported by a breakdown of costs and profit margins to justify the prices quoted. The accountant of the DSO has prepared the following estimate of total costs for this order, based on the organization's normal costing and pricing policies:

Direct Costs	£	£
Material A: 500 kgs at actual cost £3 per kg	1500	
Material B: 250 kgs at expected cost £1 per kg	250	
Material C: 400 kgs at actual cost £1.50 per kg	600	
Material D: 100 kgs at actual cost £1.50 per kg	150	
		2500
Labour: Grade I – 1000 hours @ £2.50 hour	2500	
Grade II – 500 hours @ £3.00 hour	1500	
Grade III – 200 hours @ £4.00 per hour	800	
		4800
Total direct costs		7300
Overhead: 30% of direct costs		2190
Total cost		9490
Add: Profit Margin: 10%		949
Suggested price		10 439

The following additional information is available:
1. 600 kgs of Material A have been ordered for another contract which has been cancelled; delivery is expected in a few days' time. Bloggs Ltd has no alternative use for the material. The current buying price is still £3 per kg but the material could be sold for only £2 per kg after deducting delivery costs.
2. Material B is not in stock or on order.
3. Material C is regularly used by the DSO. Because of a worldwide shortage of the material the current buying price has increased to £2.50 per kg, although the company could only realize £2 per kg from the sale of the material after deducting selling costs. The DSO's buyer foresaw the rise in price and purchased a large stock of the material six months ago; 3000 kgs are currently held by the company.
4. 50 kgs of Material D are left in stock from a minimum quantity which was purchased to carry out a contract four years ago. The organization has so far found no alternative use for the material and it is not used in the very near future it will become unusable, and will have to be scrapped at a cost of £1 per kg.
5. Grade I labour is in plentiful supply but only a certain number of that type are employed. If they are used on this contract then Grade II labour will have to replace them on existing contracts. Grade I labour is paid £2.00 per hour. For Grade II labour see (6) following.
6. Grade II labour has special skills. A considerable amount of the time of these employees is unused at present because of a fall in demand for the products which they manufacture. However, the DSO expects demand to revive next year, and has therefore decided not to dismiss any employees. The current wage for Grade II labour is £120 for a 40-hour week.

7. Grade III labour is in short supply; since it is highly specialized there is no possibility of using other grades of labour as a substitute. The current rate of pay is £4 per hour. If the proposed contract is accepted, other production yielding a net profit of £480 (based on normal pricing policy) would have to be abandoned.

8. The charge for overheads is made according to a standard formula used by the DSO and is intended to cover all variable and fixed overheads, including depreciation. The DSO would have to buy a special machine for use on this contract at a cost of £8000; the duration of the contract would be around three months. It is the DSO's policy to depreciate machinery at the rate of 10% per annum. On completion of the contract the DSO would have no further use for the machine and it is anticipated that it could be sold for £7000. It is estimated that one-third of overhead costs vary directly with production; the remainder are considered as fixed.

Required

(a) Calculate the minimum price at which the contract would be worthwhile to the DSO and for each item in your estimate which differs from the estimate made by the company's accountant. Clearly explain your reasoning for making the change.

(15 marks)

(b) Outline and briefly discuss the factors which the management of the DSO should take into consideration when deciding upon a price to quote for this contract.

(5 marks)

(c) Describe the problems associated with the post audit of this contract should the tender based on your figures be accepted.

(5 marks)
(Total 25 marks)

4 ▶ Budgeting

Key learning objectives

After reading this chapter you should be able to:

1. Explain the objectives of budget preparation in the public sector.
2. Discuss the strengths and weaknesses of different approaches to the budgeting process.
3. Prepare a probable out-turn statement and an estimate statement.
4. Explain the impact of the competitive environment on budgeting
5. Prepare budgeted cash flow and budgeted profit and loss statements.

Within the public sector, the annual budgeting process has a very considerable influence on the organization concerned; it tends to be very time consuming in preparation, and gives financial effect to political decisions on the raising and distribution of resources. It also severely constrains the manner in which the organization's resources may be disbursed over the forthcoming year.

Within central government, the annual budgeting process is concerned with an amalgam of capital and revenue items; within other parts of the public sector, revenue budgeting is clearly distinguished from capital budgeting. In this book, whereas revenue budgeting is covered in this chapter and the next, capital budgeting is dealt with in Chapters 8 and 9.

4.1 The objectives of annual budget preparation

The objectives of the annual budgetary process within the public sector are discussed below.

The establishment of required income levels

Levels of taxation, fees and charges will be established by examining current levels of income and by looking at the levels of expenditure planned for the forthcoming year. As will be seen, the desire to minimize tax increases, while increasing quality and quantity of services, provide the dynamics and stresses of the budgetary process.

Planning service expenditure levels

One of the most important objectives is to assist in the planning of service expenditure levels, and the levels of service provision. The total of service expenditures has to be accommodated within the total increases in income to be raised; but within this total, choices have to be made between expenditures on different services. Such choices are at the heart of political decision making and of the democratic process. In central and local government the decisions are taken by elected representatives, not by officers; they reflect the decisions that are arrived after political debate, pressure and negotiations. Ultimately those in power must account to the electorate for their stewardship while holding public office. Wildavsky (1974) has commented: 'If politics is regarded in part as conflict over whose preferences shall prevail in the determination of … policy, then the budget records the outcomes of this struggle.'

An illustration of the interaction of local authority members and officers within the budgetary process for 1993/94 for one local authority is contained in Figure 4.1.

In some parts of the public sector, this involvement of elected representatives does not occur at all levels. For example, once funds have been voted by Parliament to the National Health Service, the distribution of health funds at regional level is determined by formulae influenced by national political considerations but at district level is determined by those appointed to management boards and by health care professionals. Public corporations and universities, for example, also take decisions in an environment in which the elected representatives are absent, although central government determines the contributions to be made from public expenditure. Yet, in all of these, the determination of the annual budget is a political process which different individuals and factions will try to influence although, in a widening range of public sector organizations, the bottom line of profit is focusing attention in the budgetary process.

Authorization of expenditure

The budget authorizes the expenditure of public funds on those services, and to the total of those service expenditure levels, which are agreed in the budget. Indeed, money can only be spent on what has been authorized in the annual budget; and one guideline for subsequent decisions is to enquire whether an item of expenditure is included under a budget expenditure head. For this reason, the annual budget is a very detailed and very specific document, specifying service expenditures and also the breakdown in terms of subservice, wages, salaries, materials, transportation, and so on. As will be seen in the next

June 1992		
	Meeting of Special Policy Advisory Group	
	Group Executive	
	Full Labour Group	
		1. These meetings agreed a remit within which the Budget Advisory group and Project Appraisal Team could begin work a range of budget strategy options for 1993/94.
		2. The remit involved expenditure reductions of 3–4%.
		3. The additional revenue consequences of the 1993/94 capital programme were to be offset by revenue savings
June–October 1992		
	The Budget Advisory Group	
		The Budget Advisory Group interviewed Chief Officers together with their Chairmen and Vice Chairmen in order to produce a budget strategy in line with the remit.
October 1992		
	Special Policy Advisory Group	
	Group Executive	
	Full Labour Group	
		The Budget Advisory Group reported back to Members of the leading party on the range of options for meeting the reductions required. No decisions were taken at this stage.
December 1992		
	Special Policy Advisory Group	
	Group Executive	
	Full Labour Group	
		The Secretary of State for Wales announced provisonal SSAs and capping criteria. These showed that the Authority had to reduce expenditure by £15.2m.
December 1992/January 1993		
	Chief Officer Team	
		The Chief Officer team met to consider the required reductions in services arising out of the report of the Budget Advisory Group. They agreed a corporate programme of reductions to put before members.
January 1993		
	Special Policy Advisory Group	
	Group Executive	
	Full Labour Group	
		The majority party met to consider the proposed reductions put forward by Chief Officers. After due deliberations over three days they finally agreed the programme of budget reductions which they could reluctantly support.
January 1993		
	Programme Area Committee	
		Met to agree reductions for their individual services.
February 1993		
	Finance Committee	
		Met to make budget recomendations to the County Council.
February 1993		
	County Council	
		Agreed 1993/94 Budget and Council Tax levels.

Figure 4.1   *1993/94 Budget exercise.*

chapter, the opportunity for switching expenditure between budget heads (termed 'expenditure virement') is often very narrowly defined in practice. Within the National Health Service detailed budgets of the sort referred to here occur at sub-regional level only, that is at district level.

The control of expenditure

The budget provides a basis for control of expenditure. At its crudest, total annual expenditure should not exceed the budget. This philosophy can then be applied throughout the organization, to the expenditure of services and, within services, to expenditure on subservices and on detail heads. An *annual* control in itself is insufficient; the overall budget and its components need to be disaggregated into time periods, say monthly, to permit control at a much nearer point in time to when the expenditure is incurred.

A communication device

The budget serves as an excellent communication device; service managers are informed through the budget, not just of the annual expenditure allocation, but also of the service level proposed, as viewed from an input-orientated perspective.

The process focuses attention

The annual budget process focuses attention on the future; it thus forces a consideration by managers of the objectives, methods and costs of service delivery. This and the necessary consideration of inter-service and coordination issues is especially necessary within multi-service organizations. The multi-service characteristic is typical of many public sector organizations. For example, on one measure the health service provides hospital services for 472 diagnosis related groups (DRGs) and within each group patients differ according to degree of severity of condition.

Motivation of managers

The budget is said to motivate managers. However, in a situation where outputs are difficult to quantify and in which most measurements are input-orientated, this is likely to mean motivation to keep within the annual budget. As the following chapter indicates, the link between budgets and motivation is complex but it may be that managers are particularly well motivated, indeed form an attachment to the budget, when they have played a positive role in helping to formulate it.

4.2   Approaches to the budgetary process

Next we consider different models of the budgetary process within the public sector. We shall examine four models, which may be regarded as paradigms and may not accord with the specific budgeting processes in any one public sector organization. These four models are shown in Figure 4.2. Before examining the different approaches, the incremental/ departmental–rational/corporate continuum in Fig. 4.2 needs to be explained.

Incremental/departmental   Rational/corporate

◄───►

Bid system   Programme budgeting

    Financial planning   Zero-base budgeting

Figure 4.2   *Continuum of models of the budget process.*

Incremental/departmental

This end of the spectrum refers to budgeting systems which are incremental in nature; the budget for each year takes as its starting position the budget for the previous year and adds or subtracts marginally from that base. Budgeting processes within this grouping also tend to be dominated by the objectives of individual services and departments.

Rational/departmental

Towards this end of the spectrum we include budgeting systems which are rational: less concerned with the budget base, and the past, but more concerned with using resources to meet currently established objectives. Additionally, it includes those systems which foster a corporate or 'wide' view, taking account of interservice aspects, coordinating needs and giving pre-eminence to the objectives of the organization as a whole.

  Next we examine two models within the incremental/departmental grouping (bid and financial planning) and two models within the rational/corporate grouping (programme budgeting and zero base budgeting)

4.3   The bid system

This model is extremal, falling at the far left end of the spectrum. A summary of the budget cycle appropriate to this system is contained in Figure 4.3. In practice, it is infinitely varied in form but, for many organizations within the public sector, has formed the traditional approach to the budget process.

  The mechanics of the bid system are as follows.

Stage 1: separate estimate preparation

Separate departments or services prepare next year's estimate in isolation, adopting as a starting point the current year's expenditure and service levels (the 'base' budget).

Stage 2: aggregation and comparison

The separate estimates, or bids (as within an auction system), are then aggregated and the total is compared with what can be raised via taxation and charges. Invariably, total estimated expenditures will exceed total estimated income.

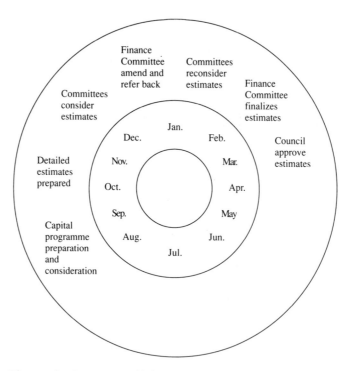

Figure 4.3 *The annual cycle – incremental bid system.* (*Source:* Financial Information Service, *Vol. 4, CIPFA.*)

Stage 3: reductions in estimated expenditure levels

Possibly estimated income may be increased marginally by a combination of higher taxes and higher fees and charges. However, the bulk of the necessary adjustment, in order to bring into equality budgeted income and budgeted expenditure, will come via reductions in estimated expenditure levels. The bid system tends to be characterized by a fairly short time scale; as Fig. 4.2 indicates, Stage 3 may occur at around December/January and the annual estimates may need to be finalized in February. In the face of time pressure, the practical guideline likely to be used to pare estimated expenditures back will be an extremely crude on e such as: departments' estimates are to be cut back to the current year's estimated expenditure + $x\%$.

Stage 4: detailed estimate reduction

Faced by the prospect of making cuts of a possibly severe nature in a short period of time, individual departments will tend to use the following two guidelines.

1. Projected starts on capital schemes are likely to be the first to be affected. This can result in cutting out new projects, delaying progress on part-completed projects by cutting funds, and postponing starts on projects to delay revenue consequences.
2. New services are likely to be cut before existing services because it may be easier to do so and because the current recipients of a service will not

then object. New services may be delayed (to give six months' instead of a year's expenditure, say), or the level of service may be reduced, by recruiting fewer staff, or a service may be deferred to another year, possibly never to reappear.

Criticisms of the bid system

The bid system has been criticized extensively as follows:

Little review of the base budget

Within the bid system there is little review of the base budget which contains, possibly, 99% of the final agreed budget. The increment to the budget is based substantially on past expenditure and this reinforces the statue quo. In reality, any public sector organization is faced with a complex network of changing needs and problems which the management will be struggling to anticipate and adapt to. It would not appear that the bid system outlined here would assist this practice.

A departmental orientation

The system views *departmental* estimates and allocations as the focus of the budgetary process. Of course, departments exist in order to further the object-ives of the community or nation vested in their elected representatives. However, interest groups are not solely the province of any one department: old people may require the services of health, personal social services and housing. The bid system, however, reinforces the professionalism which can exist in central and local government departments and in other public services. A clear example of professionalism at work may be seen in a county council's education department. In terms of the eventual budget document, this will be reflected in a budget which does not link the expenditures of different departments in working towards objectives.

Outcomes are ignored

The failure to specify objectives leads to a failure to establish a systematic review of the effectiveness of services in terms of their impact on the com-munity. Emphasis is placed, instead, on the financial control of inputs with little attempt to relate these to the outputs which emanate from the expend-iture. A department will be judged on its ability to keep within its expenditure limits. An increase in expenditure will be assumed to result in an increase in services to the community, although there may be no evidence to justify the assumption of a stable relationship between inputs and outcomes.

A single year emphasis

The system emphasizes the annual budget, yet one year is too short for effective planning. Present expenditure may commit the authority to future expenditures which limits the area of choice which will be available in the future. The short-term nature of the system may lead to the neglect of long-term objectives. Furthermore, as we have seen, the amount of time allowed for reconsideration of priorities, when cuts have to be made, is ridiculously short. Furthermore, in the version of the bid system which has been outlined, there has been no consideration of the impact of capital projects and their financial viability within the annual budget process.

Encourages a cynical approach

Finally, the system encourages its principal participants to behave in a cynical way; it encourages over-estimating by departments in situations where estimates will be cut back by $y\%$. The service which estimates honestly will suffer far more than one which pads out its bid in the expectation of a cut-back being required. The more that services inflate their bids, the greater the cut-back required and the more the innocent suffer. A second adverse behavioural outcome is to be found in the 'year end spending spree' which all those who have worked in the public sector will recognize. The insistence that the budget must not be overspent means that, every March, there will be unspent resources. However, no department will wish to reveal an underspend at year-end as this will certainly affect future years' budgets. There may also be a strong feeling that the money will be 'lost' to the department and possibly used to bail out other over-spending departments. In this situation, March will be categorized by the bringing forward of capital works, the maintenance of roads, the purchase of stationery, and the recarpeting of offices. That is, the money will be spent on relatively low-priority items in order to fully consume the year's allocation and to demonstrate that the finance was really needed by the service.

4.4 Financial planning systems

The term 'financial planning' also includes a spectrum of budgeting systems but all are characterized by being placed much nearer to the centre of the continuum than the extremal bid system which has been outlined above. A typical budget cycle for this system is contained in Figure 4.4. Features which distinguish financial planning systems from bid systems include:

1. their multi-year nature;
2. the issue of expenditure guidelines;
3. the joint consideration of capital and revenue budgets;
4. a more helpful specification and classification in the budget document.

The multi-year nature of financial planning systems means that medium term, say 2–3 years, commitments and forecasts are considered together with the annual budget under consideration. The annual budget may then be seen as the first year of a multi-year rolling programme in which, each year, one additional year is added on as the past year is dropped off. Such is the format of the government's expenditure plans as published in the annual Public Expenditure White Paper.

An expenditure guideline, a target growth percentage or even an expenditure limit is established for each service prior to the preparation of detailed estimates at departmental level. This avoids the waste of effort involved in paring estimates when they are referred back to departments. Such guidelines may be given for the next two years following the budget year, thereby encouraging a longer-term view of service development. However, during the 1980s,

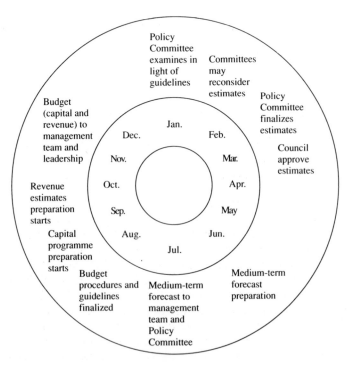

Figure 4.4 *The annual cycle – financial plan. (Source:* Financial Information Service, *Vol. 4,* CIPFA.)

local authorities within the United Kingdom were effectively hampered by the increasingly complex instruments used by central government to control the growth in expenditure in local authority services, ranging from grant penalties for over-spending against some arbitrary target, to the eventual introduction of rate capping, and in 1990/91, of community charge capping in its initial year of introduction in England and Wales.

There is simultaneous consideration of capital and revenue estimates. Figure 4.4 indicates that this is achieved by shifting forward the timing of the budget process. Thus, the revenue consequences of a multi-year capital programme (which is discussed in detail in Chapter 8) are considered in terms of a multi-year revenue programme. This clearly permits consideration of the future impact of current decisions and the extent to which current capital expenditure commits or frees future resources.

Much greater specificity is introduced into the budget process. In place of the bid system's Base Expenditure plus Increment, we now find, typically:

> Base Expenditure + Inflation – Reductions + Committed Growth + New Growth.

Committed growth includes the full year effect of capital schemes which had been completed in the previous financial year, but with part of one year's revenue consequences, for example, just six months running costs if it came on stream on 1 October. It also includes the full year effect of employees taken on in the past year and the increments in the salaries of employees. Finally, it includes the growth resulting from a past policy decision; for example, a past decision to provide state funded nursery education results in a pattern of future expenditure which will be significantly affected by demographic changes.

New Growth includes growth in service expenditure which is at the discretion of the organization; it can mean decisions to expand existing services or to introduce new services.

Financial planning systems have clear advantages as compared with bid systems and they do encourage the search for value for money in areas of growth and reduction. An illustration of one authority's use of this approach to examine expansion and contraction in expenditure is given by Armstrong (1992). He emphasizes the time constraint within which the budget was prepared and the benefits obtained by concentrating attention on the areas of reductions and growth.

However, financial planning systems, generally, have the following weaknesses:

1. Its focus is primarily incremental; it pays relatively little attention to justifying the base budget.
2. There are no explicit organizational objectives to which the budget can be reconciled; the emphasis contines to be a departmental one.
3. There is limited concern with monitoring efficiency and effectiveness; at best this is confined to the budget variations. Emphasis, as in the bid system is on inputs, with an absence of output measures.

Financial planning systems embrace a wide variety of approaches and, as we shall see later, some of these deficiencies can be addressed by supplementary additions to the financial planning framework.

4.5 Planning programming budgeting systems (PPBS)

This system is an extremal one, being fully rational and fully corporate in nature. It attempts to link together in a systematic fashion plans, objectives, the environment in which the organization is working and the feedback of control information. In 1965, PPBS was introduced into the Federal Government of the United States of America by President Johnson. Charles Schultze, then Director of the Bureau of the Budget, announced six goals of programme budgeting:

1. The careful identification and examination of goals and objectives in each area of government activity.
2. Analysis of the output of a given programme in terms of its objectives.
3. Measurement of the total costs of specific programmes, not just for one year but for several years into the future.
4. The formation of objectives and programmes extending beyond a single year to relate annual budgets to long-term objectives.
5. Analysis of alternatives to find the most efficient ways of reaching programme objectives for least cost.
6. The establishment of analytical procedures to serve as a systematic part of the budget review process.

Within PPBS a 'programme' is a set of activities which encompass all organizational efforts to achieve a specific objective. As has been indicated above, a programme such as Care of the Elderly will cross departmental boundaries.

The multi-year aspect, with a rolling plan, is similar to the process observed in Financial Planning systems and serves to highlight the constant trade-off between present action and future choice.

Programme structures

Each objective and major programme area is broken down into objectives and sub-objectives and activities. This taxonomy is intended to identify the activities within the authority which contribute to each objective; it will cross departmental boundaries and, by requiring inter-service cooperation, may weaken narrow departmentalism.

Programme analysis

Programme analysis has been defined as 'the total process of':

i) systematic identification and measurement of a community's needs and the systematic appraisal of existing resource allocations.
ii) identification of the alternative methods of achieving the objectives derived after consideration of the needs.
iii) comparative (quantitative and qualitative) evaluation of the total social and economic costs and benefits of those alternative methods (CIPFA, 1971).

Such analysis is an integral part of PPBS; the emphasis is on providing information which will aid government decision makers in making their choices. The analysis requires the measurement of achievement of the authority's objectives. This involves the construction of output measures which it may be difficult to make operational.

Feedback and review

The first year of the multi-stage plan lays down targets for those in the organization who must implement policies. Information on the achievements of the period must be generated and compared with the target and lessons learned. This will serve to update and extend the plans of the following period and act as a measure of the efficient and effective utilization of resources.

Limitations of PPBS approach

Despite being introduced into the United States Federal Government in 1965 and then picked up by states and by central and local government in the United Kingdom in the early 1970s, by the late 1970s its attraction had faded. The reasons for this decline, in spite of its coherent approach to budgeting and performance appraisal, are as follows:

The complexity of programme structures

Technical problems are encountered in constructing programme structures; one of the main reasons for adopting PPBS, the cross-over of activities, contributed to its decline. For example, the activities associated with a particular programme, such as care of the elderly, will fall to a number of departments. On the other hand, one activity such as the provision of school meals contributes to the programmes associated with health, education and social deprivation. Thus, there is a practical problem in allocating activities to programmes. This is further complicated when the financial information requirements are examined. Joint costs (the school meals example) will need to be allocated over programmes, yet there appears no rational basis for doing this. Furthermore, accounting systems normally generate information by departments rather than by programme. It might be possible to produce data by programme structure and organization structure respectively, with a cross-walk between the two. However, this leads to duplication and a preferred system would be rooted in a multi-functional database such as the Korner accounting system in the NHS which produces data for sites and for services. Finally, progress in measuring the outputs of programmes is essential for the type of activity analysis postulated; yet this is one area where progress has been remarkably slow.

The benefits of incremental policy making

Wildavsky (1974) has indicated that the budgetary process is an integral part of the political system. It is his contention that the incremental, fragmented and sequential procedures of the traditional budgetary system aid in securing agreement between participants and thus reduces conflict. It does this in two ways. First, it commences with incremental deviations from current year base expenditure; the base is generally not challenged and it is assumed by participants that departmental activity will be carried on at a level very close to that of the base expenditure. Secondly, the area open to dispute is limited to the incremental changes; and, of course, it is far easier to secure agreement on an increment than on a complete programme which brings into the arena conflict due to policy differences on priorities. An essential part of the political process is the negotiated bargain; incrementalism favours the consensus producing bargain by the trading of budgetary inducements without having to consider the ultimate desirability of programmes. Wildavsky (1974) comments: 'I am not saying that the traditional method of budgeting is good because it tends to reduce the amount of conflict ... What I am saying is that mitigation of conflict is a widely shared value in our society and we ought to realise that program budgeting is likely to affect that value.'

The pressure on participants in the process

In practice it requires its participants to adopt different roles within the organiz-ation; in the morning, a technical specialist within education, in the afternoon, playing a wider policy role in a multi-discipliniary group where departmental status can count for very little. Behaviourally, then, it is a technique which may well meet resistance from those required to implement it and who may well have to accept an additional workload consequent upon the additional inter-disciplinary focus.

Limited rationality

The presence of considerable uncertainty, the paucity of relevant information and the limited cognitive ability of human beings lead to a situation where a rational approach is severely limited. In such a situation, which may charac-terize much of organizational life, there may be an attempt to simplify reality and this may involve the technique of incremental decision making. Due to the inability to foresee the full implications of major changes of policy, movement towards goals will be made in small sequential steps. This reduces the possibility of major error from a root and branch change in policy and permits the decision maker to learn about the environment and the consequences of action by making small changes in a series of successive decisions.

Thus a number of reasons have been advanced for the failure of PPBS. However, although it may not be installed to any great degree, the ideas it contains are valuable, and can be used to help analyze the strengths and weaknesses of other budgeting systems. For example, as part of the whole central government Financial Management Initiative, the third report from the Treasury and Civil Service Committee, Session 1981–82, 'Efficiency and Effectiveness in the Civil Service', 8 March 1982, ended with recommendations which included:

1. The responsibility of Ministers and top management for the setting of objectives and targets in relation to departmental programmes.
2. The management of programmes with objectives/targets/resources/ outturn statements by programmes feeding directly into the Public Expenditure White Paper.
3. Devolution of responsibility for personnel and non-personnel costs coupled with greater accountability for objectives and targets set.

4.6   Zero-based budgeting (ZBB)

Zero-based budgeting (ZBB) is a technique whereby the total cost (base plus increment) of every item included in a proposed budget must be justified and approved. No base or minimum expenditure level should be acceptable for any activity. Resources are not necessarily to be allocated in accordance with the previous year's pattern. The approach is to require a re-evaluation of all expenditure and of all activity; all activities start from a zero base. Thus, ZBB focuses on the basic purposes of an organization. In reality many government organizations may retain functions or goals which have lost their usefulness as the environment has changed. ZBB seeks to expose all such expenditure.

Its advantages may be summarized as follows:

1. It allocates resources according to priorities, between the essential and the less essential.
2. It improves decision making because budgetary allocation is related to objectives.
3. It makes managers plan ahead and defend their budgets; thereby it creates a greater feeling of ownership of those budgets.

The idea is attractive in theory. However, a major problem is related to the time which is required to complete the exercise; it is physically impossible to appraise all activities each year. In addition, many departments are locked into expenditure programmes by long-standing legislation while some policies are carried out for compelling political reasons. Finally, it is likely to generate a mass of information which cannot be adequately assimilated by decision makers.

Although it may be impractical, in the majority of cases, to subject programmes to an annual ZBB review, there can be little doubt that there is a need to expose much of government expenditure to systematic scrutiny. Three methods of scrutinizing the base, possibly within a Financial Planning framework, involve the use of ad hoc efficiency studies, the use of a virement policy and the use of option budgets. These are discussed below.

Ad hoc efficiency and effectiveness studies

These may be the result of internal reviews, such as will be required of schools under the delegated financial management provisions. Alternatively, they may be sparked off by the activities of external review agents such as the Audit Commission, which has done much pioneering work in local government, its ambit now widened to include the NHS. Similar work in central government has been carried out by the National Audit Office.

Virement policy

Virement policy can also be used to encourage the search for savings in the base budget. This would involve allowing discretionary savings to be switched by service managers to expenditure heads according with departmental priorities. The big attraction of this approach is that there is an inducement for those closest to service delivery, who are most likely to be able to deliver efficiency savings, to search out those savings. If any savings are lost to the department there may be little incentive to search for them. It may be argued that the incentive increases as the total of 100% of savings retained by departments is reached. One could go further and introduce incentive schemes where employees share directly in the savings generated.

Where savings are accidental and not planned, it is doubtful whether the savings should remain with the department. For example, a fall in interest rates will feed through and reduce the charges to departments' budgets. However, it is highly unlikely that departments would be allowed to retain the savings as they are fortuitous and not planned, or worked for, by departments.

Option budgets

Systematically, organizations may test the priorities of departments by the use of option budgets. To illustrate their use, a specific service may be required to identify its response to a:

> 10% cut in expenditure
> 5% cut in expenditure
> 1% cut in expenditure
> 1% growth in expenditure
> 5% growth in expenditure

Such options force a service to consider policies and operating procedures. This can be made more acute by asking service managers to rank their responses to, say , a 10% cut in expenditure. If this is carried out over a period of time, cynicism (especially advancing of politically unacceptable options in response to cuts) can be squeezed out by the cumulative experience of a team of second-ranking officers who manage the options exercise, termed in a large Welsh local authority, the Budget Advisory Group (BAG). Pendlebury (1985) reports a readiness within local authorities to carry out systematic review of the base budget through the use of similar techniques. Morgan and Weaver (1993) report a recent approach to option budgets which emphasizes member/officer workshops and the use of facilitators and analysts to assist decision makers. They comment 'there was a commitment to a fundamental review of services. Muddling through via creeping incrementalism would not do. There was no sympathy for concepts of budgeting based on rough justice, across the board cuts or equal misery.' They emphasize the value for money aspects of the exercise and the enhanced understanding, commitment and ownership felt by participants in the process.

In summary, ZBB may be regarded as an essentially short-term and tactical technique whereas PPBS emphasizes long-term strategic and corporate planning. Some of the techniques of ZBB can usefully be allied with practically based budgeting approaches within the annual budget cycle to reveal information which may be used to formulate the budget and to provide an input of information into medium-term and long-term plans.

4.7 Formula funding

The 1988 Education Reform Act started the process whereby local education authorities (LEAS) delegated budgets to schools. Initially budgets were to be delegated to all secondary schools and primary schools with more than 200 pupils but now the legislation has extended delegation to all LEA schools. Schools which have 'opted out' of LEA control (grant-maintained schools) are funded directly by the Department of Education.

LEAs have been required to develop schemes for the delegation of the majority of the schools budget including:

1. the salary costs of staff employed to work in the schools;
2. schools' day-to-day premises costs including rent and rates;
3. books, equipment and other goods and service used by the schools concerned.

Mandatory exceptions to delegation

The Act originally excluded the following classes of expenditure from delegation:

1. capital expenditure and debt charges
2. central administration
3. inspectors and advisors
4. home to school transport

However, DES Circulars have eroded category 2 above leading to pressure on local authorities to delegate all service support costs to schools.

Discretionary exceptions to delegation

LEAs are free to propose excepting other items having regard to the principle of maximum delegation. The list of items is quite a long one and the following three examples indicate the type of reasoning which leads to discretionary exemptions:

1. *Child guidance and education welfare.* Some schools will wish to delegate this budget with schools being charged a cost for the services which they receive. However, the demand for these services is primarily client led and it would be impossible to predict via a formula exactly where need will arise. Therefore, other LEAs will consider that the needs of pupils can only be targeted effectively if schools do not have scope to redeploy resources meant for these services to other areas.
2. *Peripatetic and advisory teachers.* These services, such as music tuition, are provided directly to schools and there is a strong case for delegating the budget to schools via a formula which includes weightings for the special needs of pupils. However, in order to maintain a central team of a reasonable size and the ensure that specialist tuition continues, LEAs may wish to justify their exception from delegation.
3. *Structural repairs and maintenance.* Structural work is uneven in its incidence over time, and between schools, and may be included as part of a capital programme. LEAs as, effectively landlords may wish to except such expenditure from delegation. However, schemes should clearly define structural maintenance and both internal maintenance and grounds maintenance are excluded from the excepting category.

In each case the proposal for exemption has to be justified to the Secretary of State who will take into consideration issues such as in the examples given above in deciding whether to admit the exception.

The delegation budget

The amount appropriated by LEAs for the costs of school activities is termed the General Schools Budget. From this are deducted mandatory and approved discretionary exceptions. This results in the Aggregated Schools Budget which is the part of the General Schools Budget which is available for delegation to schools. The LEA must establish the basis for allocating resources to schools – the formula; a primary component of the formula will be the number and age of schoolchildren. The LEAs must also monitor the performance of schools and give advice to take corrective action if necessary. These various items are elements of a scheme of delegation which is submitted to the Secretary of State for approval.

The effect of delegation on the role of LEAs is significant. It results in a more strategic role. They are no longer able to exercise direct or detailed control over the bulk of spending in schools with delegated budgets. However, they have responsibility for schemes of delegation and for the quality of education which LEA schools deliver. LEAs lose control over schools which opt out; as stated above, such schools are funded directly by central government.

The financial link with local government is weakened considerably. Total exceptions (mandatory and discretionary) have an upper ceiling as percentage of the Aggregate Schools Budget and this has been increasingly squeezed, forcing LEAs to delegate to schools an increasing percentage of the Aggregate Schools Budget. LEA central staff must then make their services and the cost of those services sufficiently attractive for schools to purchase them from the LEA and local authority. This itself implies the use of service level agreements in the relationship between the authority and its schools. With the extension of competitive tendering to professional activities such as finance and information technology, the link between local authority employees and the LEAs schools is likely to be further weakened. The effect will be that LEA schools will behave increasingly like grant maintained schools, holding a budget which is almost fully delegated and purchasing services from a range of possible providers.

4.8   A practical approach to budgeting

This section considers the practical preparation of a budget for the financial year ended 31 March 19–2; it will assume that we are now in October 19x0. There are two practical steps with which we are concerned:

Step 1: To determine the 'probable' or 'estimated out-turn' for the current year: the year ended 31 March 19x1. This provides the budgetary base for the construction of the budget for the next year.
Step 2: To determine the estimate for the year ended 31 March, 19x2.

Determining the probable out-turn for the current financial year

Broadly, the process involved in calculating the probable for the current year is to:

Take: *Actual* expenditure to date
Add: *Estimated* expenditure for the remainder of the year.

In estimating the expenditure for the remainder of the year, we will need to take account of: the proportion of the year remaining; the anticipated inflation for the remainder of the year; the impact of pay awards on the employees expenditure for the rest of the year; the timing or phasing of expenditure on heating, employees and central administrative charges; and the start-up of any new activities authorized to commence during the year.

The scenario depicted in Table 4.1, relating to an old people's home, has been included so as to demonstrate this. It relates to the nine months to 31 December 19x0.

In order to convert the information contained in Table 4.1 to the estimated out-turn figure for the year ended 31 March 19–x1, the income and expenditure

Table 4.1   Home for the elderly: Expenditure for the 9 months to 31 December 19X0

	£
Income	18 900
Expenditures:	
Employee	18 360
Running expenses	54 500
Capital financing charges	7 500
Total expenditure	80 360
Net expenditure	£61 460

figures need to be uprated, taking into account the information from the budget file, a outlined below.

Income

Inflation will not affect this; income per resident will depend in part upon the weekly charge and the application of the assessment scales. Information on both of these is absent, so the annual income can be estimated at: income per month £18 900/0 = £2100. Income for 12 months = £2100 * 12 = £25 200.

Employees

Expenditure to date is £18360 over nine months. However, not all the months are of equal weight because employees received a pay increase of 4% with effect from the start of the third quarter. Thus, if an employee had received £100 for the first quarter's pay, then total pay to date would have been as follows:

Quarter 1	£100
Quarter 2	£100
Quarter 3	£104
Total	£304

The wage bill for the first three-quarters amounts to £18 360 and it is now clear that the figure of £18 360 was incurred in the proportions 100:100:104 over the three-quarters. Our individual employee would receive £104 for the fourth quarter as this is after the pay award. Therefore, because the first three-quarters cost a total of £18 360 (and our individual employee received 304), then the pay for the last quarter must amount to £18 360/304 * 104. This amounts to £6280 and gives a probable out-turn for the year of £18 360 plus £6280, amounting to £24 640.

Running expenses

First, it is necessary to disaggregate the figure:

		£
Non-heating: £54 500 − £9 000 =		45 500
Non-heating per quarter: (£45 500 − £500)/3 = £15 000		
Remaining non-heating expenditure		15 000
Annual non-heating expenditure		60 500
Heating: first 3 quarters		9 000
Heating per quarter	£3000	
Heating final quarter	£3000 * 2	6 000
Price increase for March: £2000 * 6%		120
Annual heating expenditure		£15 120

Financing charges

	£
Paid 30 September	7 500
Payable 31 March	7 500
	15 000

The statement of the estimated out-turn for the financial year is shown in Table 4.2.

Table 4.2 Home for the elderly: Estimated outturn expenditure for year ended 31 March 19X1

	£	£	£
Income			25 200
Expenditure			
Employees		24 640	
Running expenses:			
Non-heating	60 500		
Heating	15 120		
		75 620	
Debt charges		15 000	115 260
Net expenditure			£90 060

Determining the estimate for next year

The process involved in calculating the estimate for the next year is as follows:

1. Take the probable expenditure for the current year (Step 1).
2. Add the following:
   (a) The full year effect of any expenditure, notably employee costs, where a part-year effect in the current year is to be converted into a full year effect for next year; for example, the pay award in the Step 1 example for the last six months of 19x0/x1 will have to be paid for the whole of 19x1/x2 as it becomes consolidated into wages.
   (b) The part-year effect of next year's estimated pay award. Estimated price inflation for consumables, energy, transport, etc.
   (c) Any committed growth for next year, whether this be due to salary increments, the full year effect of completed schemes, and so on.
   (d) Finally, add in new or discretionary growth.
3. Deduct the following:
   (a) Any non-recurring expenditure in the current year which will not be repeated next year.
   (b) Any savings which are estimated to accrue in the next year.

With reference to the old people's home referred to above, the following items, referring to 19x1/x2, have also been extracted from the budget file.

Charges

Charges to residents are to increase by 10% with effect from 1 April 19x1; after taking account of assessment scales, this is likely to result in additional income of 6% overall for the year.

Employees

Due to increasing inflation, it is expected that a wage award of 6% will be made with effect from 1 October 19x1.

Running expenses

Non-heating costs are expected to increase by 7% year on year, with the exception of the non-recurring item of £500 incurred in 19x0/x1.

Heating costs are expected to increase by 7.5% with effect from 1 March 19–2.

Capital financing charges

For 19x1/x2 these are expected to amount to £12 000 for the year as a whole.

Using the information for the budget file, this can now be used to prepare the budget for next year.

	£
Income: £25 200 * 106%	26 712
Employees: 19x0/x1 Pay award, full year effect £6280 * 4	25 120
19x1/x2 Pay award, six months only £25 120/2 * 6%	754
	25 874
Non-heating: (£60 500 – £500) * 107%	64 200
Heating:	
Quarterly cost for the first 3 quarters:	
£3000 * 106% (6% increase on 1 March 19x1) * 3	9 540
Final Quarter:	
Twice the average £3180 * 2	6 360
Increase from 1 March 19x2 £2120 * 7.5%	159
	16 059

In practice it is usual to round estimates to the nearest £5 or £10; rounding to the nearest £10 will be followed as can be seen in the estimates for 19x1/x2 shown in Table 4.3.

Table 4.3 Home for the elderly: Estimated expenditure for year ended 31 March 19X2

	£	£	£
Income			26710
Expenditure			
Employees		25 870	
Running expenses:			
Non-heating	64 200		
Heating	16 060		
		80 260	
Debt charges		12 000	118 130
Net expenditure			£91 420

Re-pricing budgets and contingencies

In practice, an organization may make use of a November price base in assessing the probable expenditure for the year and also in preparing the estimate for next year. The reason for doing this is to allow a comparison in real terms (that is, at a constant price base between one year and another). If this is the case, then the following processes may be adopted:

1. The probable expenditure is stated at price levels extant at November and any known wage awards in 19x0 in this case; a contingency to out-turn prices is then stated, that is, a provision for estimated price increases over the period 31 November to 31 March. This provision is applied on a line-by-line basis, to permit control and on a total basis to ensure that overall net expenditure lies within the total finance available.
2. The budget for the year 19x1/x2 is also stated at November 19x0 price levels. The permits comparison with the probable for the previous year which is shown on the same price basis. In this case, however, the provision for estimated price increases most cover the period from 31 November 19x0 to 31 March 19x2. The out-turn net expenditure is that which has to be financed from tax revenues.

4.9 Budgeting in a competitive environment

The 1980 Planning and Land Act introduced the principle of compulsory competition for building work. The Local Government Act 1988 broadened this principle to all direct labour services. By 1991 the following services were subject to competition: refuse collection, building cleaning, other cleaning, school welfare catering, other catering, and vehicle maintenance and repair. The government now intends (1993) to extend this further to white-collar and professional activities such as architects, finance, legal and computing services. The council remains the client, specifying the type of services required, monitoring service delivery, purchasing services for its electorate. In the same way, following on from Working for Patients, a Health Authority is in the position of purchasing health care services for its client population. Those who contract with the clients to supply the services, whether they be in-house direct service organizations (DSOs), hospitals within the control of the Health Authority or hospital Trusts, will find that they will be in a competitive environment and will need to provide services efficiently and within budget.

In these organizations, the budgeting process is likely to change and become much more like the private sector with budgeted sales, budgeted costs, and a budgeted bottom-line which must be related to either breakeven or rate-of-return targets.

Business planning

A business plan is a written statement setting out how the unit making it intends to organize itself and its resources to meet the demands of its clients and thereby develop the business. Business plans were first used in the private sector, often in support of applications for loans or grants. In the public sector, the production of business plans has been a reaction to the pressure being placed on organizations; pressure which comes through a competitive environment and the necessity to win contracts, and constant pressure to cut costs and become increasingly efficient. In both of these situations, the plan demonstrates to the client or to higher authority the capacity of the unit to organize itself to deliver the planned service at a specified cost level. In the case of NHS trusts, for example, each trust is required to submit a business plan to the NHS Management Executive (NHSME) in March each year.

The plan would include:

1. an executive summary;
2. description of the main products and services provided by the unit;
3. an analysis of the current environment facing the unit and the unit's strengths, weaknesses, opportunities and threats;
4. details of the main markets available to the unit and the evidence of market analysis and research which has been carried out;
5. details of the planned changes to the business whether these are concerned with growth, or product differentiation;
6. an overview of the management and employees available to the unit, including any planned growth or reduction;
7. a list of key quality targets and indicators that will be used to measure performance against those targets. There should also be a description of plans to improve quality including arrangements for guaranteeing quality;
8. Finance:
    (a) Projected cash flow statements and profit and loss accounts over a three-year period.
    (b) Projected balance sheets over the same three-year period.
    (c) An explanation of the unit's financial strategy including capital expenditure, borrowing/investment strategy and the payments of any dividends.
    (d) Description of the approach to unplanned cost increases.
    (e) Description of plans for improving efficiency.
    (f) Description of plans for income generation.
    (g) An analysis of the sensitivity of the plan to changes in some of the key assumptions such as cost levels and income generation.

Projected profit and loss accounts

These will usually be required for a three year period. Organizations now will need to produce private sector type accounting statements, taking full account of the realization principle in recognising income and, for expenses, using the accruals basis. Some public sector organizations have used depreciation for many years, for example, the Post Office and the BBC. However, for the first time, many organizations will need to account for depreciation.

As well as producing an annual budgeted profit and loss account, monthly budgeted profit and loss accounts should also be produced. The monthly budgets will indicate the monthly income levels and maximum monthly expense levels that can be tolerated in order to achieve the target return for the year.

The monthly income levels will be derived from the terms of contracted services and the volumes of work specified to be carried out by the contract. The monthly costs will be related to workload and should be based upon standard costs for labour, transport, materials, overheads and so on. A full discussion of standard costs is contained in the next chapter. For the purposes of this chapter they can be regarded as costs which are held to represent efficient operation. In some services work study has calculated standard times for specific operations (for example, refuse collection) but in others average costs, or costs derived from regression analysis, will need to be used (for example, specialty costs). Such standards should, of course, be those that underpin the costing and pricing exercises used to formulate the tenders used to win the contracts.

The monthly budget is indispensable for control, permitting early detection of deviations from plans, and allowing time for management to take corrective action.

Projected cash flow statements

A cash budget for the year will be indispensable as it can be used to discover whether the organization's activities can be financed. As with the budgeted profit and loss account, the cash budget should be presented in a monthly format. This is especially important as the effects of terms related to the timing of the receipt of contract money and the payment of creditors can be seen in overall cash terms. For an organization which must have cash in order to pay wages and creditors it provides an opportunity to anticipate problems and make provision for loans, re-negotiation with creditors and so on.

Projected balance sheets

There is no reason to produce these on a monthly basis but the annual balance sheet (requiring asset valuations and depreciation) will be required. Aside from the legal requirement, it provides valuable information on liquidity, on gearing and provides a basis for the calculation of the organization's return on capital employed.

The contract specification

The competitive environment is one in which the organization gets paid for the work which it completes which is up to the contract specification. The organization must ensure that it completes this work to the required standard by the required date. However, any work which is not in the contract will not be paid for by the client and should not be undertaken. This will require discipline among employees who may well see themselves as operating professionally by fulfilling more than a set role. It also creates a major difficulty within the health service.

Assume that Health Authority X contracts for 1000 appendectomies at Hospital Y. How should Y's surgeons react when patients require more treatment than average because of the severity of the condition or because the patients have additional ailments or complications which, from a health viewpoint, should be treated at the time? Obviously, they will carry out the operation and the patient will receive whatever treatment is necessary. However, in budgetary terms, it is essential that the prices tendered must take account of the wide differences in case severity that will be experienced. Of course, tendering too high a price will not secure the contract, so realistic assumptions need to be made about case severity. Once the contract has been agreed, it is then a matter of hoping that a reasonably normal distribution of case severity results in practice.

This also highlights the importance of accurate costing systems. They assist accurate pricing of a tender and the preparation of more accurate budgets and, therefore, better decision making. They also allow managers to be far more confident in cost control when they know that the reported figures are accurate. In short, a good, accurate costing system gives a competitive advantage.

A refuse collection DSO

In order to examine these issues further, specimen budget statements for a competitive refuse collection DSO are presented.

Budgeted profit and loss accounts, and budgeted cash flow statements are shown in Table 4.4 and Table 4.5 respectively. The DSO has to achieve a return on assets employed of 5% for the year as a whole. The following notes refer to the numbers in the first column of both Tables 4.4 and Tables 4.5.

Note (i) refers to the contract value for refuse collection agreed with the local authority. The contract specifies standards of service, amounts to be paid, and dates of payment. In this case, as Table 4.5 shows, the payments are made one month in arrears.

Note (ii) refers to sales of refuse sacks and is based upon the DSO's estimates which is based upon past experience.

Note (iii) refers to wages figures which are based upon the same standard times used to prepare the tender and are based upon experience of what can be achieved. They also take account of the size of the labour force and of current wage rates.

Note (iv), wages on-cost, refers to specific wage related costs borne by the employer, such as Employers' National Insurance and Superannuation contributions; it also refers to employee related overheads such as supervision.

Note (v) refers to depreciation: all competitive legislation requires that depreciation be charged in the profit and loss account.

Note (vi) refers to the payment to the Central Departments for their services; these include financial services, computer services and legal services. As outlined in Chapter 3, such payments must now be negotiated and related to a level of service provision.

As Table 4.4 shows, a profit of £8088 is budgeted; this results in a return of 8.99% on the assets employed of £90 000. This is well in excess of the required return of 5%. However, turning to the cash flow statement in Table 4.5, it is evident that in the first year of operation there will be need for substantial loan or overdraft facilities. The revised cash flow statement in Table 4.6 includes under Note 7 a charge for interest on the overdrawn cash balances. The rate of interest which has been used is 12%. Table 4.7 shows that when interest is taken into account in the budgeted Profit and Loss Account, the return falls below the required 5%.

Therefore, management should seek some means of reducing the interest figure, or certain other costs, to give a return of 5% (or 6% if we were discussing the National Health Service, for example). One option which might be examined is the renegotiation of the timing of the payment of central support services to one month in arrears. The effect of this is shown in Table 4.8 and Table 4.9. As can be seen, this has the effect of increasing the return to above 5%.

Table 4.4 Refuse collection direct service organization. Budgeted monthly profit and loss accounts 19 – 1/– 2

Notes	Month:	Apr. £	May £	Jun. £	Jul. £	Aug. £	Sep. £	Oct. £	Nov. £	Dec. £	Jan. £	Feb. £	Mar. £	Year £
	Budgeted income													
(i)	Contract value	46 250	46 250	46 250	46 250	46 250	46 250	46 250	46 250	46 250	46 250	46 250	46 250	555 000
(ii)	Sale sacks	800	800	800	800	800	800	800	800	800	800	800	800	9 600
	Total income	47 050	47 050	47 050	47 050	47 050	47 050	47 050	47 050	47 050	47 050	47 050	47 050	564 600
	Budgeted expenses:													
(iii)	Wages – normal	11 267	11 267	11 267	11 267	11 267	11 267	11 267	11 267	11 267	11 267	11 267	11 267	135 200
	Wages – overtime	3 167	3 167	3 166	3 900	3 900	3 900	3 167	3 167	3 166	3 167	3 167	3 166	40 200
(iv)	Wages – oncost	5 847	5 847	5 847	5 847	5 847	5 847	5 847	5 847	5 847	5 847	5 847	5 847	70 160
	Salaries	1 251	1 251	1 251	1 251	1 251	1 251	1 251	1 251	1 251	1 251	1 251	1 251	15 012
	Transport related	13 272	13 272	13 272	13 272	13 272	13 272	13 272	13 272	13 272	13 272	13 272	13 272	159 260
	Materials	1 078	1 078	1 078	1 078	1 078	1 078	1 078	1 078	1 078	1 078	1 078	1 078	12 940
(v)	Depreciation	1 125	1 125	1 125	1 125	1 125	1 125	1 125	1 125	1 125	1 125	1 125	1 125	13 500
(vi)	Central support services	9 187	9 187	9 187	9 187	9 187	9 187	9 187	9 187	9 187	9 187	9 187	9 187	110 240
	Total expenditure	46 193	46 193	46 192	46 926	46 926	46 926	46 193	46 193	46 192	46 193	46 193	46 192	556 512
	Net profit/loss	857	857	858	124	124	124	857	857	858	857	857	858	8 088
	Assets employed													90 000
	Return on assets (%)													8.9

Table 4.5 Refuse collection direct service organization. Budgeted monthly cash flow statements 19 – 1/– 2

Notes	Month: Budgeted inflows	Apr. £	May £	Jun. £	Jul. £	Aug. £	Sep. £	Oct. £	Nov. £	Dec. £	Jan. £	Feb. £	Mar. £	Year £
(i)	Contract value	0	46 250	46 250	46 250	46 250	46 250	46 250	46 250	46 250	46 250	46 250	46 250	508 750
(ii)	Sale sacks	800	800	800	800	800	800	800	800	800	800	800	800	9 600
	Total income	800	47 050	47 050	47 050	47 050	47 050	47 050	47 050	47 050	47 050	47 050	47 050	518 350
	Budgeted outflows:													
(iii)	Wages – normal	11 267	11 267	11 267	11 267	11 267	11 267	11 267	11 267	11 267	11 267	11 267	11 267	135 200
	Wages – overtime	3 167	3 167	3 166	3 900	3 900	3 900	3 167	3 167	3 166	3 167	3 167	3 166	40 200
(iv)	Wages – oncost	5 847	5 847	5 847	5 847	5 847	5 847	5 847	5 847	5 847	5 847	5 847	5 847	70 160
	Salaries	1 251	1 251	1 251	1 251	1 251	1 251	1 251	1 251	1 251	1 251	1 251	1 251	15 012
	Transport related	13 272	13 272	13 272	13 272	13 272	13 272	13 272	13 272	13 272	13 272	13 272	13 272	159 260
	Materials	0	1 078	1 078	1 078	1 078	1 078	1 078	1 078	1 078	1 078	1 078	1 078	11 862
(vi)	Central support services	9 187	9 187	9 187	9 187	9 187	9 187	9 187	9 187	9 187	9 187	9 187	9 187	110 240
	Total expenditure	43 990	45 068	45 067	45 801	45 801	45 801	45 068	45 068	45 067	45 068	45 068	45 067	541 934
	Net cash flow	–43 190	1 982	1 983	1 249	1 249	1 249	1 982	1 982	1 983	1 982	1 982	1 983	–23 584
	Cumulative cash balance	–43 190	–41 208	–39 225	–37 976	–36 727	–35 478	–33 496	–31 514	–29 531	–27 549	–25 567	–23 584	

Table 4.6 Budgeted monthly cash flow statements 19X1/X2

Notes		Apr. £	May £	Jun. £	Jul. £	Aug. £	Sep. £	Oct. £	Nov. £	Dec. £	Jan. £	Feb. £	Mar. £	Year £
	Budgeted inflows:													
1	Contract value	0	46 250	46 250	46 250	46 250	46 250	46 250	46 250	46 250	46 250	46 250	46 250	508 750
2	Sale sacks	800	800	800	800	800	800	800	800	800	800	800	800	9 600
	Total income	800	47 050	47 050	47 050	47 050	47 050	47 050	47 050	47 050	47 050	47 050	47 050	518 350
	Budgeted outflows:													
3	Wages – normal	11 267	11 267	11 267	11 267	11 267	11 267	11 267	11 267	11 267	11 267	11 267	11 267	135 200
	Wages – overtime	3 167	3 167	3 166	3 900	3 900	3 900	3 167	3 167	3 166	3 167	3 167	3 166	40 200
4	Wages – on-cost	5 847	5 847	5 847	5 847	5 847	5 847	5 847	5 847	5 847	5 847	5 847	5 847	70 160
	Salaries	1 251	1 251	1 251	1 251	1 251	1 251	1 251	1 251	1 251	1 251	1 251	1 251	15 012
	Transport related	13 272	13 272	13 272	13 272	13 272	13 272	13 272	13 272	13 272	13 272	13 272	13 272	159 260
	Materials	0	1 078	1 078	1 078	1 078	1 078	1 078	1 078	1 078	1 078	1 078	1 078	11 862
	Central support services	9 187	9 187	9 187	9 187	9 187	9 187	9 187	9 187	9 187	9 187	9 187	9 187	110 240
7	Interest	216	434	419	403	394	386	377	361	345	329	312	295	4 272
	Total expenditure	44 206	45 502	45 486	46 204	46 196	46 187	45 445	45 429	45 412	45 397	45 380	45 362	546 206
	Net cash flow	–43 406	1 548	1 564	846	854	863	1 605	1 621	1 638	1 653	1 670	1 688	–27 856
	Cumulative cash balance	–43 406	–41 858	–40 293	–39 447	–38 593	–37 730	–36 125	–34 504	–32 866	–31 213	–29 543	–27 856	

Table 4.7 Budgeted monthly profit and loss accounts 19X1/X2

Notes		Apr. £	May £	Jun. £	Jul. £	Aug. £	Sep. £	Oct. £	Nov. £	Dec. £	Jan. £	Feb. £	Mar. £	Year £
	Budgeted income:													
1	Contract value	46 250	46 250	46 250	46 250	46 250	46 250	46 250	46 250	46 250	46 250	46 250	46 250	555 000
2	Sales sacks	800	800	800	800	800	800	800	800	800	800	800	800	9 600
	Total income	47 050	47 050	47 050	47 050	47 050	47 050	47 050	47 050	47 050	47 050	47 050	47 050	564 600
	Budgeted expenses:													
3	Wages – normal	11 267	11 267	11 267	11 267	11 267	11 267	11 267	11 267	11 267	11 267	11 267	11 267	135 200
	Wages – overtime	3 167	3 167	3 166	3 900	3 900	3 900	3 167	3 167	3 166	3 167	3 167	3 166	40 200
4	Wages – on-cost	5 847	5 847	5 847	5 847	5 847	5 847	5 847	5 847	5 847	5 847	5 847	5 847	70 160
	Salaries	1 251	1 251	1 251	1 251	1 251	1 251	1 251	1 251	1 251	1 251	1 251	1 251	15 012
	Transport related	13 272	13 272	13 272	13 272	13 272	13 272	13 272	13 272	13 272	13 272	13 272	13 272	159 260
	Materials	1 078	1 078	1 078	1 078	1 078	1 078	1 078	1 078	1 078	1 078	1 078	1 078	12 940
5	Depreciation	1 125	1 125	1 125	1 125	1 125	1 125	1 125	1 125	1 125	1 125	1 125	1 125	13 500
6	Central support services	9 187	9 187	9 187	9 187	9 187	9 187	9 187	9 187	9 187	9 187	9 187	9 187	110 240
7	Interest	216	434	419	403	394	386	377	361	345	329	312	296	4 272
	Total expenditure	46 409	46 627	46 611	47 329	47 320	47 312	46 570	46 554	46 537	46 522	46 505	46 488	560 784
	Net profit/loss	641	423	439	−279	−270	−262	480	496	513	528	545	562	3 816
	Assets employed													90 000
	Return on assets (%)													4.24

Table 4.8 Refused collection direct service organization. Budgeted monthly cash flow statements 19 – 1/- 2

Notes	Month: Budgeted inflows	Apr. £	May £	Jun. £	Jul. £	Aug. £	Sep. £	Oct. £	Nov. £	Dec. £	Jan. £	Feb. £	Mar. £	Year. £
(i)	Contract value	0	46 250	46 250	46 250	46 250	46 250	46 250	46 250	46 250	46 250	46 250	46 250	508 750
(ii)	Sale sacks	800	800	800	800	800	800	800	800	800	800	800	800	9 600
	Total income	800	47 050	47 050	47 050	47 050	47 050	47 050	47 050	47 050	47 050	47 050	47 050	518 350
	Budgeted outflows:													
(iii)	Wages – normal	11 267	11 267	11 267	11 267	11 267	11 267	11 267	11 257	11 267	11 267	11 267	11 267	135 200
	Wages – overtime	3 167	3 167	3 166	3 900	3 900	3 900	3 167	3 167	3 166	3 167	3 167	3 166	40 200
(iv)	Wages – oncost	5 847	5 847	5 847	5 847	5 847	5 847	5 847	5 847	5 847	5 847	5 847	5 847	70 160
	Salaries	1 251	1 251	1 251	1 251	1 251	1 251	1 251	1 251	1 251	1 251	1 251	1 251	15 012
	Transport related	13 272	13 727	13 272	13 272	13 272	13 272	13 272	13 272	13 272	13 272	13 272	13 272	159 260
	Materials	0	1 078	1 078	1 078	1 078	1 078	1 078	1 078	1 078	1 078	1 078	1 078	11 862
(vi)	Central support services	0	9 187	9 187	9 187	9 187	9 187	9 187	9 187	9 187	9 187	9 187	9 187	101 057
(vii)	Interest	170	342	325	309	299	290	280	263	246	229	211	193	3 158
	Total expenditure	34 973	45 410	45 393	46 110	46 101	46 091	45 349	45 332	45 313	45 297	45 280	45 261	535 909
	Net cash flow	–34 173	1 640	1 657	940	949	959	1 701	1 718	1 737	1 753	1 770	1 789	–17 559
	Cumulative cash balance	–34 173	–32 533	–30 876	–29 936	–28 987	–28 028	–26 327	–24 608	–22 872	–21 119	–19 348	–17 559	–17 559

Table 4.9 Budgeted monthly profit and loss accounts 19X1/X2

Notes		Apr. £	May £	Jun. £	Jul. £	Aug. £	Sep. £	Oct. £	Nov. £	Dec. £	Jan. £	Feb. £	Mar. £	Year £
	Budgeted income:													
1	Contract value	46 250	46 250	46 250	46 250	46 250	46 250	46 250	46 250	46 250	46 250	46 250	46 250	555 000
2	Sale sacks	800	800	800	800	800	800	800	800	800	800	800	800	9 600
	Total income	47 050	47 050	47 050	47 050	47 050	47 050	47 050	47 050	47 050	47 050	47 050	47 050	564 600
	Budgeted expenses:													
3	Wages – normal	11 267	11 267	11 267	11 267	11 267	11 267	11 267	11 267	11 267	11 267	11 267	11 267	135 200
	Wages – overtime	3 167	3 167	3 166	3 900	3 900	3 900	3 167	3 167	3 166	3 167	3 167	3 166	40 200
4	Wages – on-cost	5 847	5 847	5 847	5 847	5 847	5 847	5 847	5 847	5 847	5 847	5 847	5 847	70 160
	Salaries	1 251	1 251	1 251	1 251	1 251	1 251	1 251	1 251	1 251	1 251	1 251	1 251	15 012
	Transport related	13 272	13 272	13 272	13 272	13 272	13 272	13 272	13 272	13 272	13 272	13 272	13 272	159 260
	Materials	1 078	1 078	1 078	1 078	1 078	1 078	1 078	1 078	1 078	1 078	1 078	1 078	12 940
5	Depreciation	1 125	1 125	1 125	1 125	1 125	1 125	1 125	1 125	1 125	1 125	1 125	1 125	13 500
6	Central support services	9 187	9 187	9 187	9 187	9 187	9 187	9 187	9 187	9 187	9 187	9 187	9 187	110 240
7	Interest	170	342	325	309	299	290	280	263	246	229	211	194	3 158
	Total expenditure	46 363	46 535	46 517	47 235	47 225	47 216	46 473	46 456	46 438	46 422	46 404	46 386	559 670
	Net profit/loss	687	515	533	−185	−175	−166	577	594	612	628	646	664	4 930
	Assets employed													90 000
	Return on assets (%)													5.48

The budgeted figures included in Tables 4.4 to 4.9 were all prepared using a spreadsheet model. As can be seen, this is particularly suited to budget preparation as management can test the overall effect of changes in the underlying variables. In short, management can carry out 'what if' sensitivity analysis while paying particular attention to bottom line and financing issues.

Key points of chapter

1. There are many reasons why the budgeting process is so important in the public sector.
2. There is a range of budgeting systems ranging from the bid system to programme budgeting, with different strengths and weaknesses. Operational systems lie within these extremes.
3. The annual budget statement is prepared in two stages: the probable out-turn for the current year and the estimate for next year.
4. The competitive environment will require a business planning approach with budgeted monthly cash flow statements and budgeted monthly profit and loss accounts.

4.10   Summary

Traditionally the budgeting process in the public sector has been of crucial importance in planning and in allocating resources to different services. The crudest models are the incremental bid models which have a short time horizon and are limited by other weaknesses. The most sophisticated is programme budgeting but this appears to be non-operational. Financial planning allied with some of the more pragmatic versions of ZBB seems to offer an acceptable, operational middle way.

The mechanics of the budgeting process requires the involvement of service departments and is a two-stage process with the first stage being concerned with estimating the current years out-turn. This exercise requires the combination of estimated and of actual figures. The estimate for next year takes the current year as a base and then allows for changes in the levels of service and in price and wage inflation.

Finally, the emerging competitive environment shifts attention away from levels of service to income, to profits and to rates of return. Knowledge of costs will be important in order to tender correctly and to budget effectively. Monthly budgets should be prepared; any apparent difficulties can then be dealt with at an early stage. Two important factors mentioned in the chapter were the importance of a clear understanding of the terms of the contract by all service deliverers and the specific impact of the cash flow statement on the profit and loss account via overdraft interest.

4.1 The following information relates to a police authority for the six months to 30 September 19–9:

Eastern Criminal Records Office:

	£
Employees	235 500
Premises	48 000
Supplies and services	29 750
Transport	7 600
Central departmental and technical support services	35 300
Miscellaneous expenses	27 500
Financing charges	15 000
	£398 650

Note:

(a) Employees receives a pay award of 5% during the first half of the year and payable with effect from 30 June 19–9.

(b) Half of premises costs for the first half-year comprises space heating costs; space heating costs in the last 4 months of the year are expected to equal total costs for the first 8 months of the year.

(c) Financing charges are payable on 30 September and 31 March.

(d) Due to increase in the price of fuel, transport costs will be 2.5% higher in the second half than the first half of the year.

(e) Supplies and services includes a non-recurring payment of £5000 made in June 19–9.

Required

Prepare a statement giving the estimated outturn for the year ended 31 March 19X0.

4.2 Your local authority has agreed upon a policy of zero growth in real terms for the year 19X6/X7 and has instructed its Parks Committee that, provided their annual estimates for 19X6/X7 are prepared within a 'ceiling' calculated in accordance with this policy, they will be free to regulate their own spending on services within that 'ceiling'.

The following is a subjective analysis of the approved estimates for 19X5/X6 and the draft estimates for 19X6/X7 which have been received from the Director of Parks.

	19X5/X6 Approved estimates £	19X6/X7 Draft estimates £
Wages (inc. 50% oncost)	2 808 000	3 132 000
Premises expenses	480 000	660 000
Supplies and services	300 000	408 000
Transport	98 000	126 000
Central charges	420 000	576 000

		19X5/X6 Approved estimates			19X6/X7 Draft estimates
	£	£		£	£
Debt charges:					
Principal	56 400			67 200	
Interest	218 160			282 000	
		274 560			349 200
		4 380 960			5 251 200
Less: Income – fees and charges		120 960			121 200
		4 260 000			5 130 000
		(330 full-time staff)			(342 full-time staff)

Notes:

(i) Estimates are prepared using prices, etc. current at 31 October, except that the Wages estimates provide for known or anticipated national awards. Provision for other inflation is made centrally within a general contingency provision, which will also allow for price rises from October 19X5 to March 19X7.

(ii) The Wages estimates for 19x5/x6 assumed that wages would rise by 20% per annum from 1st November 19x5, but a national award caused a rise of £14.40 per employee per week from that date (assume 20 weeks to year end). It has been assumed that wages will rise by a further 10% per annum from 1 November 19X6.

(iii) An index of average prices is maintained which rose from 130 in October 19X4 to 175.5 in October 19X5.

(iv) Advances to finance capital expenditure are made from a Loans Fund, repayments being made in equal instalments over 40 years commencing in the year following that in which the advance is made. Interest is payable at the average Loans Fund rate on the debt outstanding at the commencement of the year plus 50% of the advances made during the year.

(v) New advances to finance capital projects in progress before 1 April 19X6 are estimated as follows:

	Original estimate Oct. 19X4 £	Revised estimate Oct. 19X5 £
19x4/x5	336 000	384 000
19x5/x6	–	285 000

The draft estimates for 19X6/X7 contain provision for capital expenditure of £480 000 in that year for a new depot (total cost £1 008 000).

(vi) The average Loans Fund rate of interest is estimated as follows:

	Original estimate Oct. 19X4	Revised estimate Oct. 19X5
19X5/X6	9%	9.35%
19X6/X7	-	9.5%

(vii) Central charges are allocated from the General Services Account, any variations in cost being reflected in the 'ceiling' of that account. The revised allocation for 19X5/X6 shows an overall increase of 15% on the original estimate.

Required

You are required to prepare the Parks Committee revised estimates for 19X5/X6 and a report indicating how their estimates for 19X6/X7 may be contained within the zero growth 'ceiling'.

Indicate how you have interpreted 'zero growth' in real terms and make whatever other assumptions you think reasonable.

4.3 The following information relates to the Careers Guidance Service of the Downshire Education Authority.

1. *Employees* (details at 1/10/X7):

Name	Salary Scale	Incr. point	Car engine	Monthly miles
M. Jones*	PO1	36	1600cc	300
H. Evans*	SO1–2	33	1215cc	400
E. Davies*	5	27	950cc	250
P. Brown	4	19		
L. Williams	4	21		
R. Lewis	3	15		
P. Smith	2	12		
J. Blake	1	5		
J. Edwards	1	1		
P. Jenkins	1	1		

Note: * signifies that travelling allowances are payable as detailed in Section 2 below.

Incremental progression takes place on 1 April for those staff who have been in post for more than six months.

A wage award of 4 % for all staff is expected from 1 July 19X8.

Staffing is normally very stable; however, L. Williams is to leave the service on 31 Dec. 19X7 and R. Lewis will be promoted to take her place on 1 January 19X8. He will be paid, initially, at salary point 20. His present job will be advertised and it is expected that a replacement member of staff will be in post by 1 April 19X8 at the bottom of Scale 3. (See Table 4.10 for salary scales.)

The Education Authority has recently decided to make an additional appointment at the bottom of scale 3 with effect from 1 June 19X8.

Employers' NI and superannuation amounting to 11% and 12% of salaries should also be taken into account.

2. *Travelling expenses:*

Employees are reimbursed for using their cars on official business in accordance with the following scales which will become effective on 1 January 19X8:

Car engine size (cc):	−999	1000–1199	1200+
Allowances payable:			
Annual lump sum	£342	£400	£430
Mileage allowances:			
<1100 miles per annum	−16.1p	−17.8p	−19.9p
11 000+ miles per annum	8.2p	9.2p	10.1p

When scales are revised next on 1 January 19X9, it is anticipated that allowances and mileage rates will be increased by 5%.

3. Computerization:

In 19X8/X9 the records of the CGS will be computerized and a microcomputer will be purchased for this purpose. Quotations for the necessary software and hardware have been in the region of £5000 but County Supplies expect to obtain a discount of 25% on this figure due to the fierce competition in this field.

In order to transcribe the records onto floppy disks, a temporary part-time clerk will be employed for 25 hours per week at £2.40 per hour for 20 weeks. Employers National Insurance contributions will be payable at 11%, but the post is not subject to superannuation contributions. The rate of pay will not be affected by the pay award on 1 July 19X8.

4. Other expenditure:

The cost of printing brochures in 19X7/X8 amounted to £3000. In 19X8/X9 the volume of brochures to be printed will increase by 12%. In addition the printer has announced a 6% increase in his charges with effect from 1 April 19X8. A further increase of 5% is forecast with effect from 1 January 19X9.

Required

Prepare the budget for the Service for 19X8/X9.

Salary points with effect from 1 July 19X7

	Salary scale point	1/7/X6 salary £	1/7/X7 salary £
	A1	2703	2 856
	A2	2 859	3 021
	1	2 976	3 144
	2	3 162	3 342
	3	3 414	3 606
	4	3 603	3 807
Scale 1	5	3 849	4 065
	6	4 200	4 437
	7	4 365	4 611
	8	4 485	4 737
	9	4 659	4 920
	10	4 788	5 058
	11	4 959	5 238

Salary points with effect from 1 July 19X7

	Salary scale point	1/7/X6 salary £	1/7/X7 salary £
Scale 2	12	5 139	5 397
	13	5 307	5 574
	14	5 493	5 769
Scale 3	15	5 640	5 922
	16	5 811	6 081
	17	5973	6 249
	18	6 135	6 420
Scale 4	19	6 264	6 555
	20	6 510	6 810
	21	6 753	7 065
	22/23	7 005	7 329
Scale 5	24	7 191	7 524
	25	7 404	7'746
	26	7 650	8 004
	27	7 896	8 262
Scale 6	28	8 154	8 532
	29	8 430	8 820
	30	8 712	9 114
SO1	31	9 060	9 477
	32	9 363	9 795
	33	9 660	10 107
SO2	34	9 945	10 404
	35	10 242	10 716
PO1 35–38	36	10 539	11 025
	37	10 761	11 259
PO2 37–40	38	11 052	11 562
	39	11 364	11 889
PO3 40–43	40	11 703	12 243
	41	12 087	12 645
	42	12 408	12 981
	43	12 738	13 326
PO4 43–46	44	13 065	13 668
	45	13 395	14 013
	46	13 725	14 358
PO5 46–49	47	14 034	14 682
	48	14 379	15 042
PO6 48–51	49	14 709	15 387
	50	15 033	15 726
	51	15 357	16 065

4.4 Glyn District Council maintains a leisure centre which is used jointly by the general public and the schools of Mega-Glynn County Council. For such use, the County Council contribute 30% of agreed estimated gross expenditure at November prices, plus an increase for inflation to out-turn prices measured by the Retail Price index (RPI).

The budget is formulated in November prices, largely based upon the probable for the current year, and then a contigency for inflation to out-turn prices is calculated.

(i) The original estimate for the leisure centre for 19X9/X0 (November 19X8 prices) is as follows:

	£000s	£000s
Employees		204.4
Premises		110.6
Supplies and services		53.5
Vehicles		1.5
Establish		50.0
Capital financing charges		115.0
		535.0
Income	295.0	
Sales and charges	160.5	
Estimated deficit		455.5
		79.5

The agreed contigency for inflation for 19X9/X0 is to be calculated by applying the following percentage increases to original estimates:

Employees 3%, Premises, Supplies and services, Establishment 4%, Vehicles 5%.

(ii) Most recent evidence and estimates of inflation are as follows:

Employees: a 4% pay award w.e.f. 1 September 19X9.
          a further 4.5% w.e.f. 1 September 19X0.
Price Indices:

	PRI	Premises, Supplies/services, and Establishment	Vehicles
Nov. 19X8	109.6	108	125
Mar. 19X9	112.3	110.6	127
Nov. 19X9	116.4	114.5	135
(Est) Mar. 19X0	121.3	119	140
(Est.) Nov. 19X0	124.5	123	143
(Est.) Mar. 19X1	127.1	126	145

(iii) Estimated capital financing in 19X9/X0 is made up as follows:

Principal	£70 000
Interest	£45 000

The loan was taken out in 19X7/X8 and is being repaid over six years on the basis of equal instalments of principal.

Expenditure of £25 000 for upgrade of the heating system is to be incurred in August 19X0; it is expected to be financed by loan, repayable over five years.

The estimated loans fund rate for 19X9/X0 was 11%: it increased to 11.5% w.e.f. 1 October 19X9 and is expected to increase by a further 0.5% w.e.f. 1 October 19X0.

Interest and principal repayments are made on 31 March, with no principal repayments in the year in which the loan is advanced.

(iv)   Actual expenditure and the usual expenditure profiles for the six months 1 April to 30 September are as follows:

	£	%
Employees	105 270	50
Premises	52 911	45
Supplies and services	27 265	50
Vehicles	790	50
Establishment	23 660	45
Income: Fees and charges	165 200	55

(v)   As compared with the 19X9/X0 estimates, use is likely to increase by 4% in 19X0/X1 despite proposed price increases of 10% w.e.f. April 19X0. This will result in a volume-related increase of 1% in Supplies and services and 6% in Employees. The improvements in the heating system are likely to reduce consumption in the second half of 19X0/X1 to 92% of consumption in the second half of 19X9/X0. Heating constitutes 70% of Premises expenditure in 19X9/X0.

(vi)   The District is aiming that the leisure centre should break even by the end of the financial year 19X1/X2.

Required:

(a)   Calculate the probable out-turn for 19X9/X0, compare the probable outturn with the original estimate plus contigency and comment on the implication of the variations for future budgeting.   (10 marks)

(b)   Calculate the 19X0/X1 original estimate and contigency.   (10 marks)

(c)   Comment upon the progress being made towards the objective laid down in note (vi) above, and identify the additional information which would assist financial planning to achieve that objective   (4 marks)

4.5   The following expenditure relates to a district laundry maintained by the Usk-Afan Health Authority for the 9 months to 31 December 19X7:

	£
Section manager	10 089
Assistant section manager	7 920
Superintendents	9 240
Laundry operatives	36 720
Administration and clerical	5 730
Engineering – pay	4 680
– parts and materials	3 930
Materials – washing	18 350
– dry cleaning	1 040
Water	4 230
Steam generation	8 160
Electricity	6 470
Rates	3 600
Transport	6 420

Miscellaneous	990
Domestic/cleaning staff	5 340

The laundry is organized into three flowlines. Statistics for the nine months to 31 December 19X7 are as follows:

Flow line processed	Articles standard		Productive water usage	Steam and consumption	Electricity
	No. 000s	Weight %	Hours	%	%
Large flatwork	1869	63	12 000	60	60
Small flatwork	453	31	9 000	40	35
Drycleaning	195	6	6 000	–	5

Expenditure is apportioned across the flowlines and, unless otherwise indicated, the pattern of expenditure and activity to 31 December 19X7 is expected to be typical of the pattern for the year as a whole.

The following information is available:

(a) Managers and superintendents received a pay award of 5% with effect from 1 November 19X7.

(b) All other employees were awarded an increase in pay in 6% with effect from 1 September 19X7.

(c) Rates are payable on 1 April and 1 October

(d) Washing materials are expected to increase in price by 6% for the financial year as a whole; the increase in price of dry-cleaning materials over the same period is expected to be 8%.

(e) An electricity bill of £2 500 is estimated for the quarter to 31 December 19X7; it is not included in the balances listed above. The bill for the January–March quarter is normally 50% higher than the average for the remainder of the year, and the Electricity Board have also indicated an increase of 5% in prices with effect from 1 January 19X8.

(f) All labour, managerial, administrative and transport costs are apportioned in proportion to productive standard hours.

(g) Engineering material costs are apportioned on the same basis as engineering pay.

(h) Washing materials, other than dry-cleaning materials, are related to processing activity by weight of articles processed.

(i) Rates and miscellaneous expenses are apportioned equally over all flowlines.

(j) The laundry is expected to fully recovery costs. To this end, the following rates for recovering costs were established in December 19X6 for the financial year 31 March 19X8:

	Pence per article
Large flatwork	4.5
Small flatwork	14.0
Drycleaning	16.0

Required:

(i) Prepare a statement showing estimated expenditure for the year to 31 March 19X8. (16 marks)

(ii) Comment upon the laundry's operating performance for the year to 31 march 19X8 (4 marks)

4.6 Supplies arrangements for several health authorities in the region are chanelled through a central stores administered by your authority, the following inform- ation is given for 19X9/X0 at outturn prices:

	X9/X0 Original estimate £000	X9/X0 Revised estimate £000
Issues	3600	3400
Opening stock	960	950
Purchases	2700	2800
	3660	3750
Closing stock	810	1060
Cost of issues	2850	2690
Surplus	750	710
Overheads:		
Salaries and wages	490	495
Running expenses	230	235
Surplus	30	−20

Investigations reveal the following:

(i) Stores issue prices are to be updated on 1 April 19X0 for 12 months by an average of 11.5%.

(ii) It is anticipated that in 19X0/ X1 the volume of issues will be 1% lower in volume terms than the latest forecast for 19X9/X0.

(iii) In 19X0/X1 it is planned to cash limit the sum available for purchases to that shown in the original 19X9/X0 budget. However, despite keen con- tract negotiation by the Purchasing departments, the anticipated year-on- year increase in purchase prices will amount to 5%.

(iv) Past experience shows that levels of stock at the year and normally amount to 30% of total purchases during the year.

(v) In 19X0/X1 it is estimated that salaries and wages of stores staff will increase by 13% on the revised out-turn for 19X9/X0. Running expenses are expected to increase year-on-year by 15%.

(vi) Discussions reveal that a large public authority in the area is interested in entering into the present supplies arrangement. If this new authority participates, issues are estimated to be 10% higher than currently pre- dicted after taking into account known factors affecting 19X0/X1. There would also be a corresponding increase in purchases. Initial calcuations show that, based on the present year's revised estimates, overheads would increase by £40 000 for salaries and wages and £8000 for running expenses. This is before the effect of any 19X0/X1 pay for price changes.

A sample investigation based on existing members has shown that a system of direct supply contracts would result in average prices some 10% less than the set stores issue prices at 1 April 19X0. Under these arrangement, prices would be held constant for three months and updated by 6% at the beginning of each quarter. Past records shown that 40% of the issues take place in the first quarter and the balance is spread evenly over the rest of the year. You estimate that there would need to be additional administrative and transport costs in the existing authorities amounting to £250 000 at 19X0/X1 outturn prices.

Required

(a) Estimate the financial position of the central stores in 19X0/X1 from the information given, and consider separatively the possibility of additional membership and the alternative offerred by direct supply contract arrangements.
(b) comment briefly on the position revealed by your findings.

4.7 The following information relates to the Department of Business Studies in a new University.

1. *Academic Salary Scales* (w.e.f. 1.4.X2)

Incremental Points	LII/SL Amount	LII/SL No. of Staff	PL Amount	PL No of Staff	HOD Amount	HOD No of Staff
	£	£			£	
1	16 600	–	21 400	–	25 000	
2	17 200	5	22 000	–	25 600	
3	17 800	–	22 600	–	26 200	1
4	18 400	–	23 200	–	26 800	
5	19 000	–	23 800	6		
6	19 600	5	24 400	3		
7	20 200	–				
8	20 800	7				
9	21 400	8				
10	22 000	10				
No. of Staff		35		9		1

Staff progress to the next incremental point on 1st September each year (unless at maximum of scale).

The following staff changes will take place during the year 1.4.X2–31.3.X3

(a) 1 SL retires on 31.8.X2   (currently on max. of scale)
(b) 1 PL retires on 31.12.X2 (currently on max. of scale)
(c) 1 SL (currently on max of scale) promoted to PL (salary point 3) on 1.1.X3
(d) 1 LII appointed a minimum of scale on 1.9.X2
(e) 1 SL appointed on incremental point No. 6 on 1.1.X3
(f) 1 new SL appointed to assist in teaching accounting on incremental point No. 7 on 1.9.X2

A pay award of 3% p.a. is to be implemented with effect from 1.4.X2.

2. *Clerical/Administrative Staff Salary Scale* (WEF 1. 7. X1)

	Incremental point (as at 1.4.X2)	Amount £
	1	8 200
	2	8 500
1 clerk/typist	3	8 800
	4	9 100
	5	9 400
1 clerk/typist	6	9 700
	7	10 000
	8	10 300
Departmental secretary	9	10 600
	10	10 900
Administrative assistant	11	11 200

A pay award of 1.5% with effect from 1.7.X2 is anticipated. Incremental progressive takes place on 1st April each year.

3. Provide for employer's National Insurance Contribution of 9.5% of staff salaries, and Superannuation contribution of 11 1/2% of staff salaries.

4. *Student Numbers* (19X2/X3)

Full time   850 (including 3rd year students on industrial training: 50 degree student and 150 HND students)

Part time   760

5. *Teaching Materials*

Current allowance is £10 per full time student (part time students' allowance is 80% of full time allowance)

6. *Travelling Expenses* (Staff)

Training: £80 per degree student) Full Time students only
£40 per HND student

Other: £70 per member of academic staff in post on 1.4.X2.

7. *Printing and Stationery*

Current allowance is £24 per full-time student
(part-time students' allowance is 75% of full-time allowance).

8. *Furniture and Equipment*

£12 000 allowances for 19X2/X3

9. *Inflation*

Provide for the following price increases in 19X2–X3 (where appropriate allowances will be increased in line with inflation).

	% p.a.
Teaching materials	4
Travelling expenses	2
Printing and stationery	2
Furniture and Equipment	1

Required

You are required to estimate the total cost of the Department for the year ended 31.3.X3.

5 ▶ Budgetary control

Key learning objectives

After reading this chapter you should be able to:

1. Understanding the importance of timely, relevant and accurate budgetary control information in a form suitable for managers.
2. Recognize the various techniques of budgetary control in respect of both capital and revenue expenditure
3. Be aware of the need to consider human aspects of budgetary control.

The previous chapter examined the process of budget preparation and also illustrated one measure of budgetary control by its reference to the calculation of the probable outturn for the year prior to that which the new budget relates. Clearly, once a budget has been established, it is necessary to set up controls and procedures which enable the budget to be monitored and for warnings of budget drift to be sounded as soon as possible. The calculation of a probable out-turn for the year at budget preparation time is but one element of this process. In many public sector organizations, also, the practice of holding a central contingency fund for unforeseen inflation or circumstance has been abandoned in favour of placing a cash limit on the appropriate managers thus restricting the ability to spend to the cash-limited figure. In the competitive tendering services this luxury is not possible in any case as all contracts must be completed in budget if the relevant profit is to be made. Any overspending in these circumstances will thus impact, in the first instance, on the resource available to the service manager and, in the second instance, on the overall profitability of the competitive unit. Failure to contain items within service department budgets will reduce the organization's working balances and could, depending on the circumstances of the public sector organization, result in government penalties being imposed, as with local government under the block grant system. These factors tend to place a premium on timely, accurate and relevant information. Control may be centered on detailed regulation as under

Standing Orders and Financial Regulations, both of which place emphasis on the regularity of the budgetary control process without measuring the performance of the budget-holder in carrying out the service function. This chapter examines the traditional methods of control in the public sector in the budgetary process and then considers how techniques developed in the private sector can have application to areas of the public sector.

5.1   Essentials of a system of budgetary control

Budgetary control can be defined as 'the establishment of budgets relating the responsibilities of executives to the requirements of a policy, and the continuous comparison of actual with budgeted results either to secure by individual action the objective of that policy or to provide a basis for its revision' (CIMA). It should be pointed out that there is no significant difference between the principles of budgetary control in either the public or private sector. The statement implies that, as budgets are established for various elements of the organization, managers are given responsibility for the management of budget resources in those areas. This has in part been illustrated by the mention of the cash limit system above but a recent example would include the changes made as a result of the introduction of local management in schools where the headteacher and governers assume responsibility for the delegated budget and its management. Clearly such a system requires information which has to be related to the delegated responsibilities within the organization. Thus the cost centres established to monitor and control expenditure must be related to responsibility centres and be sufficiently disaggregated to provide the information that is needed. Within these cost centres the financial coding system must not only provide maximum flexibility for the analysis of expenditure and income at the cost centre level, but must also provide the chief financial officer with information at the strategic level to take the overall global view on actual performance of the budget against estimate.

The basic principles underlying the budgetary control system should be as follows:

Timely, relevant, and accurate information

Line managers should not be reduced to maintaining 'little black books' to enable them to ascertain their budget position. The information system should be designed to meet the needs of the line manager and not just the convenience of the chief financial officer. Many public sector computer systems were designed around the need to produce the financial accounts and management information was almost a by-product of this process. Information needs to be accurate, but, on the other hand, it is no use providing 100% accurate information if the time for action has passed. There is also a need to avoid the provision of large computer tabulations which are beyond the ability of managers to assimilate. Information by exception is required. Increasingly, use is being made of on-line enquiry as in the LAFIS (Local Authority Financial Information System) system operated by local authorities. This system allows short programs to produce answers to straightforward preset questions under its

AIDA (programming language developed by ICL for on-line inquiry) system with more complex requests being processed usually overnight under a MERIT (modelling, enquiry, reporting interactive technique) program.

Clear divisions of responsibility

Levels of responsibility must be identified and set out in the appropriate regulations to avoid confusion and to speed up action. The basic rule is that the person certifying the expenditure for payment should be responsible for the budget, i.e. that expenditure being certified can be contained within his or her budget provision.

Consistency

It is essential that a consistent basis is used for comparison purposes. Thus if the budget is cash limited it will include an allowance for inflation. As expenditure is processed and appears in monitoring statements this will allow direct comparison with the original budget. This may be more difficult if a central contingency fund is maintained to cover inflation as, until it is allocated to individual budget heads, uncertainty will surround the sums of money that manages actually control.

5.2   Commitment accounting

One of the problems facing managers in trying to control expenditure and monitor income is to know, for example, what level of expenditure has been committed but, as yet, has not been reflected in the financial information that is available. This problem has resulted in the phenomenon of the 'little black book' (referred to earlier in this chapter) for recording this expenditure. A more formal method of recording this information is by way of a system of commitment accounting where the financial information system recognizes a transaction and its impact on the budget as soon as a purchase or other financial commitments are entered into. This clearly means that the information is more up to date and, as such, should be more meaningful to the manager, thus facilitating budgetary control.

A number of problems are, however, associated with the system and these include:

1. The difficulty of measuring the size of the commitment as an order may only be an estimate. If the commitment is entered on receipt of the invoice in the service department there can be duplication of effort if it is later submitted to the finance department for payment. This may even lead to a suggestion of distributed payment processing to save time in information processing rather than a commitment system.
2. There can be audit implications of allowing distributed data processing and direct access to the financial information system by departments outside the finance function.
3. The most significant areas of expenditure are salaries and wages in the public sector and these do not require a commitment system to aid control. Expenditure on central departmental support may be controlled

by a service level agreement which will specify the terms of payment and the total level of liability. Debt charges and debt management fees will be controlled by the finance department. Significant areas of expenditure can thus be controlled effectively without a commitment accounting system.

4. Additional complications are introduced as orders are cancelled or amended. There will be a need to adjust commitments at the year end in order to close the accounts to reflect the accruals position.

An alternative to a full commitment system developed by many public sector organizations is a memorandum note within the financial information system which records the commitment but does not amend the financial records.

5.3 Expenditure profiling

It is obvious that some expenditure that occurs during the year is highly predictable, the most obvious example being salaries and wages. This raises the concept of expenditure profiling (this idea is further developed when cash flow management is discussed in Chapter 6). The concept need not only be applied to expenditure as items of income are predictable, for example the receipt of government grants. Despite the difficulties, profiling should not be restricted only to the easier items like salaries and wages, and should be extended to the remaining budget heads. These can be built up by a historical analysis of expenditure and income, or through predictable payment as, for example, under a maintenance contract. Fuel bills can be studied and will indicate higher bills in the winter months. Income for a swimming pool is likely to be higher in the summer than the winter months. For an open-air swimming pool income is likely to be concentrated in June, July and August. The objective is not 100% accuracy but to provide managers with information on which to take decisions. At the end of each budget period the manager is able to compare actual with projected and calculate the variance. The key point is that the more significant the variance the greater the need for investigation. A projected out-turn for the year can also be calculated on the basis of actual expenditure to data and the consequent necessary action can be triggered. Such action may include reduction in planned expenditure on other heads to absorb any over-spend predicted as a result of the profile analysis. There is an obvious need for the manager to be concerned with the overall picture and not just the results on individual heads. Table 5.1 indicates a profiling exercise which has been carried out on fuel costs for a public sector organization. It also allows for inflation and changes as the result of virement, inflation and a supplementary estimate. The supplementary estimate illustrates the impact that the completion of a capital scheme can have on the revenue budget.

5.4 Virement

Virement is the transfer of funds from one budget head to another although the exact rules of virement will depend on the individual organization. One object of virement is to prevent the need for a supplementary estimate as an under-spending from one head may be transferred to another head which has an over-

Table 5.1 Energy profile

	Apr.	May	Jun.	Jul.	Aug.	Sep.	Oct.	Nov.	Dec.	Jan.	Feb.	Mar.	Year
Profile % expenditure	6	5	4	3	3	5	8	10	14	16	16	10	100
Cumulative % profile	6	11	15	18	21	26	34	44	58	74	90	100	100
Original estimate £	12 000	22 000	30 000	36 000	42 000	52 000	68 000	88 000	116 000	148 000	180 000	200 000	200 000
Inflation £						1 000	2 600	4 600	7 400	10 600	13 800	15 800	15 800
Virement £										1 000	2 500	3 000	3 000
Supplementary estimate* £												3 500	3 500
Control total £	12 000	22 000	30 000	36 000	42 000	53 000	70 600	92 600	123 400	159 600	196 300	222 300	222 300

*Capital scheme completed and operating ahead of schedule.

spending. A virement would not normally be allowed where, if it occurred, the organization would be involved in recurrent expenditure as this would represent a commitment of future resources.

It can be seen that virement allows some element of flexibility in the budgetary control process. One problem with unrestricted virement is that managers would inevitably spend all their budget allocation for fear of a budget reduction in the subsequent year. This is also linked to the problem of carry-over into the next financial year as treasurers may attempt to claw back under-spending. There is some evidence, however, of a more flexible attitude by some public sector organizations in allowing the carry forward of under-spendings on certain heads as an addition to the following year's budget. The converse, of course, is that any carry forward of over-spendings will result in a reduction in the following year's budget. Virement and carry forward may be allowed in an organization where the saving in the current year is a result of a conscious decision by the manager concerned. The percentage of the saving retained by the department will vary between organizations, but clearly it has to be sufficiently large to encourage such action. Savings arising as a result of good fortune will normally be prime candidates for return to central balances. It should be noted that the Health Service has the ability to vire automatically between capital and revenue, up to 1% from revenue to capital and up to 10% from capital to revenue. In addition carry forward is allowed of unspent monies from one year to the next of up to 1% of the combined capital and revenue allocation.

5.5   Supplementary estimates

Normally the budget process will be completed prior to the year to which the budget relates. During the year, however, items of income or expenditure may arise which are so large that they may require a supplementary estimate. In local government it was possible to levy a supplementary rate for unforeseen expenditure but this is now no longer possible. Clearly, if it is impossible for an item to be contained within an original budget, then action is required. This may take the form of providing a supplementary estimate by reducing balances and transferring them to the required budget head, or virement from within the overall department's budget, or even reducing another department's estimate to make funds available for transfer. The better the level of control and intelligence available the earlier this situation can be detected and more drastic action may be avoided. If it is decided that the budget is to be amended all changes should be built into the financial information system as soon as possible.

5.6   Reports

It has already been stated that reports should be timely accurate and relevant. H. A. Simon (1953, 1959) has commented that: 'Administrative man satisfices as he has not the wits to maximise', indicating that the cognitive ability of man is restricted. Thus reports should be restricted to the essential information appropriate to the level of the managers receiving the information. Exceptions should be reported and clearly flagged under ideally a priority system. To relate this discussion to the profiling above, any significant over- or under-spendings would receive priority indicators. This requires tolerance levels to the set for individual items of expenditure and income.

The monitoring cycle needs to be related to the needs of managers, although the normal reporting cycle is monthly. The competitive units may require weekly information on crucial contracts. Also, it should not be forgotten that on-line facilities may exist for day-to-day problems. In addition, it may be desirable that the computer information system contains both financial and non-financial information, including, for example, staff numbers and other physical units such as metres of road to be cleaned and patient bed-days. A form of budget report is shown for a theoretical new university in Table 5.2.

This illustrates the use of memorandum notes and the relationship between items within the budget, as, for example, the over-spending on lecturers has resulted in extra consultancy fees. Items of major significance have a marker attached.

5.7   Controlling central government expenditure

Within central government the Treasury monitors all expenditure by departments. As would be expected departments also monitor expenditure centrally with individual managers responsible for controlling their own expenditure programmes to the agreed level of spending on their own programme area. The way in which this is done is now explored in some detail in order to provide readers with an example of budgetary control in practice.

The main elements of the government's control system are:

1. *Reporting blocks*. The Treasury and departments agree early in the financial year the breakdown down of the vote into reporting blocks of expenditure of a manageable size. These then form the basic control units. Reporting blocks generally follow the subheads of the vote although where such subheads are too large they can be subdivided for better control. Subheads of minor items of expenditure are normally brought together into a single *de minimis* reporting block.

2. *Profiles* as discussed earlier in this chapter are then prepared for each reporting block to provide a planned flow of expenditure and income against which performance can be monitored. The forthcoming financial year is divided into quarters reflecting such factors as seasonal variation. These profiles are discussed and agreed between the Treasury and the departments to ensure realism as they represent the key control function in that they provide the bottom line. The Treasury must also be satisfied that when all blocks are combined they will not exceed the cash limit. As the year proceeds actual out-turn data can then be compared with the profile. A mid-year expenditure return showing likely results for the year is prepared showing the likely out-turn on each block for the year in question. This is discussed between the Treasury and the departments. If a department becomes aware that it will overspend at any time during the year it must notify the Treasury immediately. Supplementary estimates may be granted if considered appropriate by the Treasury and Parliament.

Table 5.2 Budget monitoring report (extract): A New University out-turn to month 8

| Subjective | Position to date | | | Projection to year end | | | Exception report and memorandum note |
	Planned expenditure £000	Expenditure to date £000	Variance £000	Approved budget £000	Projected out-turn £000	Variance £000	
Employee costs:							
Management staff	1 750	1 745	−5	2 800	2 820	20	Award higher than expected*
Principal lecturers	2 000	2 120	120	3 250	3 275	25	As above*
Lecturers	3 500	3 750	250	5 300	6 000	700	Vacant posts filled early – see income***
Administrative staff	2 300	2 300	0	3 500	3 500	0	
Manual workers	1 200	1 250	50	1 800	1 800	0	
Total salaries and wages	10 750	11 165	415	16 650	17 395	745	
Premises:							
Maintenance	800	800	0	1 200	1 200	0	
Energy	1 000	1 050	50	1 500	1 475	−25	Energy conservation scheme starts January
Rent and rates	750	750	0	1 125	1 125	0	
Cleaning	900	850	−50	1 350	1 100	−250	Cleaning made subject to competitive tender

Table 5.2 (cont'd)

Misc.	50	50	0	100	100	0	
Total premises	3 500	3 500	0	5 275	5 000	-275	Repair bills down**
Transport (detail)	904	975	71	1 356	1 300	-56	
Supplies and services (detail)	400	200	-200	800	450	-350	Savings on books***
Total polytechnic expenditure	15 554	15 840	286	24 081	24 145	64	
Income:							
Student fees	-18 000	-17 750	250	-22 000	-22 000	0	
Consultancy	-1 000	-1 050	-50	-2 000	-2 120	-120	Extra consultancy due to fewer vacancies***
Other	-50	-50	0	-100	-110	-10	Extra interest on investments
Total income	-19 050	-18 850	200	-24 100	-24 230	-130	
Net position	-3 496	-3 010	486	-19	-85	-66	

Note:
Capital expenditure charges and central administration controlled centrally.

Key:
*** Major variation from budget requires close monitoring.
** Keep under review.
* Minor over-spending predicted.

3. Receipts and expenditures are recorded by the APEX (Analysis of Public Expenditure) system controlled by the Paymaster General. Expenditure is included from departmental returns with receipts and adjustments notified separately. APEX data is sent to the Treasury weekly where it is transferred to the Treasury's financial information system which then provides the analysis as required for departmental monitoring.
4. Departmental monitoring is monthly with the computer system projecting the likely out-turn for the year based on the expenditure and income recorded to date. This highlights potential problem areas to enable cost centre managers to take remedial action if judged necessary. Clearly, as the year progresses and more information becomes available then the ability to predict the likely outcome for the year in question is more accurate.
5. Towards the end of the financial year as the Chancellor needs to prepare his budget departments need to prepare a forecast of their most accurate estimate of likely out-turn. This is particularly important for the demand led expenditures such as unemployment benefit due to the fact that they are not cash limited and have a major impact on the government's demand for finance. When the budget was in March this exercise was carried out in February, but with the move to a December budget this exercise will need to be done earlier.
6. At the end of the financial year the department must account for the sums spent. The final stage is the preparation of an Appropriation Account which shows for each vote the sums authorized and the sums spent and for ease of understanding normally follows the format of the supply estimates. Budget holders are responsible to line managers, who are responsible to the accounting officer (the permanent head of the department concerned). This individual in signing the appropriation account accepts responsibility for the propriety of expenditure and the accuracy of the account. Accounting officers are accountable to their Minister but may be called by the Public Accounts Committee to give evidence. The accounts are audited by the Comptroller and Auditor General (CAG). The Minister, the Public Accounts Committee and the CAG all report to Parliament. The control is thus complete in that Parliament voted the funds and has now received reports on how the money was spent.

The above reporting cycle has concentrated on the more traditional methods of budgetary control in central government. This is because it has been concerned with the monitoring of supply expenditure. For the new agencies there is a need to control not only cash but accruals as well. Under the 1990 Government Trading Act agencies operate in a trading fund environment. The trading fund gives powers to exist outside the normal votes system providing a financial framework which covers operating costs and receipts, the power to borrow and to establish reserves. The accounts will be published on the same basis as companies controlled by the Companies Acts and consequently the agencies will require budgetary control systems which relate to their published profit and loss accounts and take account therefore of accruals based transactions. The 1990 Act also gave the Treasury the power to extend these provisions to any suitable activities of departments irrespective of whether they are agencies or not (Hardcastle, 1990, p. 28).

5.8 Flexible budgeting and performance measurement

Having given an overview of the reporting framework and budgetary control process it is now necessary to examine the mechanism of control in action, and, at this stage, to attempt to couple the concept of budget performance in terms of outputs achieved with control. It is clearly nonsensical to suggest that because a budget has been controlled to achieve the planned spend that the objectives of that budget as originally perceived have been successfully met. There is a need therefore to relate the budget to some measure of outputs as these will identify the objectives that the spending pattern is meant to achieve. This reintroduces the concept of non-financial measures mentioned earlier in this chapter.

If we take, for example, a creditors payments team, the majority of any expenditure will be on those employed to deal with the payment of invoices received. This is a budget which it is relatively easy to achieve and control, especially if there is the minimum of staff turnover. Without some measure of performance the control process is almost meaningless as a budget spend may be achieved with little regard to the stated objectives. Financial control can be built into the process in that, when the budget is being set, target creditor processing figures should be built in. These could then be monitored alongside the actual spend. This process is effectively happening in terms of the service level agreements currently being negotiated with service departments by some finance departments. The estimated creditor payments will form the basis of the contract. It is therefore only a small step to introduce monitoring of the performance of the individual components of the service level agreement. This type of simple performance budgeting can be extended to such areas as the number of home help applications processed, the number of driving licence applications dealt with, and so on. Effectively it is attempting to measure and control against a performance standard those costs which are essentially fixed, as, for example, the bulk of salaries and wages in the public sector normally are.

This concept is obviously related to unit cost as the figures used invariably lend themselves to this type of analysis, but the important difference is that the budget has been based on target performance. If we now extend this concept of performance measurement to the catering budget for a hospital ward given in Table 5.3 its application to a variable cost can then be considered.

Table 5.3 Catering budget for a hospital ward

Performance measurement – catering costs Hospital Ward 10

Estimated patient days: 3 650
Estimated catering costs per patient day: £21.20
Estimated catering costs for year: £77 380
Actual patient days: 3 500
Actual cost per patient day: £22.00
Actual catering costs for year: £77 000
Estimated patient days based on 10 beds in an 11-bed ward occupied for 365 days (i.e. 90.9% occupancy rate)

Clearly, the first thing to note is that the catering cost is within budget in total but that the unit cost of catering is 80p above the estimate. If the estimated cost had been achieved then the total catering cost should have been £74 200 (a saving of £3 180 on the final cost or 4% of the original budget). The control question is not therefore did we achieve our budget but why did things go wrong and where. There are now a number of avenues of investigation opened up, including, first, did we pay more for food than anticipated or, secondly, was there a high level of waste and other inefficiencies in the preparation of the food? (It is obviously also possible to have a combination of the two.) At this stage we have identified a financial variance, and while further analysis may also question items such as quality at least questions are now being raised. In addition we might question the low bed occupancy rate achieved or, alternatively, the realism of the projected 90.9% occupancy rate. The skill lies in the interpretation of the data, not merely in its provision.

The key concepts to grasp at this stage are, first, that we have attempted to relate budget performance to the level of workload in that the budget was 'flexed' to compare with the actual results, secondly that we have introduced the idea of standard setting in terms of the workload required and the anticipated delivery of service (i.e. standard catering costs). The standard cost of the catering function used in the estimating process would be arrived at after suitable discussion with the appropriate staff. In addition the traditional approach of budgeting in the public sector would be to include in the analysis only those costs for which the catering manager would be directly responsible. The below-the-line costs such as central departmental support would be excluded.

Following on from this introduction into the principle of flexibility in budgeting it can be seen that we are attempting to measure output by comparison with the level of inputs that should have been committed to achieve the operation as it was actually performed. Table 5.4 illustrates this concept for a street sweeping and cleansing operation.

It can be seen from that the organization has cleaned more miles than intended under this contract in the first month of the financial year. If costs and income had been to budget net profit for April would have been £238. Under the actual result the organization appears to have made £361. However, it can be seen that when the budget is flexed the profit made on the actual road mileage cleaned is only £35. The reasons for the poor performance can be seen in the variance column. These areas could be further investigated as clearly this type of enterprise needs to perform efficiently if it is to achieve the required rate of return. It should also be pointed out that the control of additional work is essential to the survival of the organization. Traditionally public sector workers have undertaken extra work if requested by clients. This work will now only be paid for if a variation order is obtained.

Flexible budgeting is based on an adequate knowledge of cost patterns. In the above example costs have been assumed to be directly variable with mileage unless otherwise specified. The concept of a semi-variable cost was introduced in respect of the administration charge. This was because it was assumed that the basic monthly charge was fixed but that the extra wages costs triggered extra charges, possibly due to the need for more processing in the finance section. These terms would be stated in the service level agreement. The fixed cost of depreciation has not been flexed.

Table 5.4 Street sweeping and cleaning operation flexible budget exercise

	Contract 19–0/–1 £	Actual Apr. £	Flexed Apr. £	Variance £
Revenue billed:				
Contract fees	205 000	17 288	17 083	205
Misc. income	1 500	125	125	0
Total	206 500	17 413	17 208	205
Expenditure:				
Wages – ordinary	58 660	4 888	4 947	59
Wages – overtime	19 550	1 658	1 649	–9
Wages – on-cost	39 105	3 273	3 298	25
Salaries	6 520	543	550	7
Transport costs	41 220	3 480	3 476	–4
Materials	1 450	115	122	7
Depreciation – fixed	2 500	208	208	0
Administration – semi-variable	34 635	2 886	2 921	35
Total expenditure	203 640	17 051	17 171	120
Net profit	2 860	362	37	325
Assets at current cost	£31 000			
Return on current cost %	9.23	13.98	1.43	
Miles cleaned to standard	41.60	42.10	42.10	

Notes:
1. All revenue due was billed in April.
2. Additions to the contract mileage authorized for April were £205. (Anticipated income for April was £205 000/12. Actual is = £205 000/12 + £205 = £17 288.)

5.9 Control by standards

The concept of standard costs was introduced in the previous chapter and referred to in the previous section. It will now be examined in greater detail. The concept was originally developed in industry but has application in the public sector as this section will show. The most obvious direct application is in the competitive sections of public sector organizations but it has implications in other areas of the public sector, as will also be demonstrated. To establish the standard costs of an operation it is necessary to identify those costs which will be incurred as a result of the operation – labour, materials and overheads. These can only be established after detailed study.

The types of standard which can be developed are:

1. *Historic cost standards.* These are standards which remain unchanged over long periods and can be used as a base for comparison purposes, but often they do not represent currently achievable standards and thus have limited use.
2. *Ideal standards.* These costs would only be achieved under perfect conditions and clearly will have the potential to affect adversely the motivation of managers if it is perceived that the impossible is being asked.

3. *Currently achievable standards.* These are costs that can be achieved in an efficient organization. These targets provide a fair basis to measure performance against. These costs can be used in the planning process as they represent standards which should be achieved. In Table 5.3 the catering cost estimate should relate to an achievable standard.

Standard costing can ideally be applied where there is an activity which is primarily repetitive. In the public sector, for example, refuse collection is a standard function with repetitive runs and a measure of work in that the number of bins emptied is reasonably consistent. Street sweeping and cleaning activities fall into the same category. To apply the principle to these operations it is necessary to identify responsibility centres as it is pointless to establish standards and not hold individual managers to account.

Standard costs and results do not stand by themselves. It is necessary to undertake further analysis of the results to identify clear responsibilities and to take corrective action if required. It has already been indicated in discussing Table 5.3 that, having shown a variation between planned and actual catering costs, a number of avenues are open for exploration. The financial information system should indicate to managers where the problem lies. The fact that this process will take place may also work as an incentive to the individuals to perform better within the area of his or her responsibility. The analysis of events after they have occurred should also indicate ways in which performance might be improved in the future irrespective of whether or not problems exist at present.

Table 5.5   Blaenwent Street Sweeping and Cleaning Contract: Budget Period 1

	£	£
Budget for Period 1:		
Income: 10 000 miles of cleaning at £6 per mile		60 000
Direct materials: 500 kg at £10 per kg	5 000	
Direct labour: 3000 hrs at £8 per hr	24 000	
Variable overheads: 3000 hrs at £2 per DL hr	6 000	
Fixed overheads	15 000	
		50 000
Budgeted profits		£10 000
	£	£
Actual results for Period 1:		
Income: 9000 miles at £6		54 000
Direct materials: 510 kg at £9.90 per kg	5 049	
Direct labour: 2950 hrs at £8.10	23 895	
Variable overheads	5 750	
Fixed overheads	14 500	
		49 194
Actual profit		£4 806

Note:
Budgeted fixed overheads are charged on the basis of direct labour hours. This gives a fixed overhead rate of £5 per direct labour hour (£15 000/3000).

The concept of standard costs and variance analysis is now developed by of way Table 5.5 which applies the technique to a street sweeping and cleaning contract.

As street cleaning is subject to competitive tendering the contract price is fixed for any cleaning of street undertaken.

From Table 5.5 it is possible to calculate the following variances:

Materials

Total cost variance	= (Actual production × Standard cost per unit of production) – Actual materials cost
Price variance	= (Standard price per unit of material – Actual price) × Quantity purchased
Usage variance	= (Standard quantity of materials for Actual consumption – Actual quantity utilized) × Standard price

Labour:

Total cost variance	= (Standard quantity of labour hours for actual production – Actual labour hours worked) × Standard hourly rate
Rate variance	= (Standard wage rate per hour – Actual wage rate) × Actual hours worked
Efficiency variance	= (Standard quantity of labour hours for actual production – Actual hours worked) × Standard wage rate per hour

Variable overhead:

Expenditure variance	= Budgeted variable overheads for actual input volume – Actual variable overheads
Efficiency variance	= (Standard quantity of input hours for actual production – Actual input hours) × Standard variable overhead rate
Total variable overhead variance	= (Actual production × Standard variable overhead rate) – Actual variable overhead cost

Fixed overhead:

Expenditure variance	= Budgeted fixed overhead – Actual fixed overhead
Volume variance	= (Actual output – Budgeted output) × Standard fixed overhead rate
Efficiency variance	= (Standard quantity of input hours for actual production – Actual input hours) × Standard fixed overhead rate
Capacity variance	= (Actual hours of input – Budgeted hours of input) × Standard fixed overhead rate
Total fixed overhead variance	= (Actual production × Standard fixed overhead rate) – Actual fixed overhead

Income:

Total margin variance	= Total actual profit – Budgeted profit
Income margin price variance	= (Actual unit profit margin – Standard unit profit margin) × Actual sales volume
Income margin volume variance	= (Actual sales volume – budgeted sales volume) × Standard profit margin

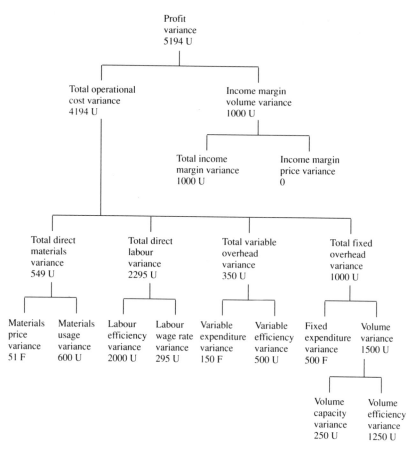

Figure 5.1 *Variance tree for Blaenwent Street Sweeping and Cleaning Contract: Budget Period 1.*

The relationship between these variances is shown in Fig. 5.1, together with the results of the calculations as given above. Before we analyse the variances, Table 5.6 reconciles the budgeted figures with the actual profit.

5.10 Examination of variances

Materials

1. *Price variances.* The purchase price of materials is clearly beyond the control of the operating department and will probably be based on a contract price negotiated by a central purchasing department. Price levels are thus the responsibility of this department unless an unauthorized supplier has been used. Quality should be borne in mind if the price variance is favourable, as should the effect of market forces beyond the control of the central supplies department.
2. *Usage variances.* Obvious causes of poor performance are excessive waste, poor quality and theft.

Table 5.6 Reconciliation of budget statement with actual results: Period 1

	£	£
Budgeted net profit		10 000
Income variances:		
Income margin	0	
Income margin volume	1 000 U	
Materials variances:		
Price	51 F	
Usage	600 U	
Labour variances:		
Rate	295 U	
Efficiency	2 000 U	
Variable overhead variances:		
Efficiency	500 U	
Expenditure	150 F	
Fixed overhead variances		
Expenditure variance	500 F	
Volume capacity	250 U	
Volume efficiency	1 250 U	5 194 U
Actual net profit		£4 806

Key:
F = favourable variance
U = unfavourable variance

Labour

1. *Rate variance.* Clearly the cost of labour is determined by the wage rate and, in the public sector, the rate is normally set nationally, although the recent trend is for local agreements. Wage rates will be beyond the control of the unit manager, although the use of higher skilled workers than necessary will raise the actual rate.
2. *Efficiency variance.* This factor is controlled by the unit manager and reasons should be sought from him or her for this variance. Factors may include breakdowns, inefficient working practices being allowed to develop or poor quality labour.

Overheads

When we examine overhead variances what is happening is that we are examining the difference between the actual amount of operational overhead incurred and the amount charged to operations through previously determined overhead absorption rates.

Fixed overheads

The fixed overhead expenditure variance is attempting to identify what proportion of the total fixed overhead variance is due to actual fixed overhead being different from budgeted fixed overhead. The volume variance seeks to identify the balance of the total fixed overhead variance which results from actual production differing from budgeted production. The volume variance can be further divided into the volume efficiency variance and the volume capacity variance which attempt to identify why actual operational performance was different from budgeted operational performance. The volume efficiency variance shows an inability to use capacity efficiently while the volume capacity variance indicates a failure to use capacity effectively (e.g. due to mechanical breakdowns).

Variable overheads

The total variable overhead variance is, as with the fixed overhead variance, broken down into two elements. The variable overhead expenditure variance measures the change between actual expenditure and the allowed overhead for actual labour hours (i.e. it allows for the current level of (in)efficiency). The variable overhead efficiency variance effectively in this case duplicates the labour efficiency variance and the reasons for this variance are the same.

Income variances

In this example the contract price was fixed and therefore there was no income margin price variance. The income margin volume variance arose due to the difference between budgeted operational mileage to be cleaned as against actual mileage cleaned.

Conclusions

This example of standard costing coupled with variance analysis and flexible budgeting has shown that a powerful tool is available to help service managers cope with the challenges of competition. The use of a computer would reduce the burden of calculation and the significant variances could be highlighted for managers by means of an exception report. This technique presents one of the challenges of change to the public sector manager.

In order to conclude this discussion of the technique of variance analysis and to show its versatility the example outlined in Table 5.7 looks at a typical grounds maintenance operation without the complication of the earlier overhead analysis.

The information in Table 5.7 is quite straightforward to calculate and would provide the manager with more information than is probably currently available. Reasons for the variances can now be investigated. The table has also concentrated on the costs and income which are directly under the control of the service manager. Variations in fixed overheads – for example, a variation in any central support charges – are not directly within the service manager's control. Any change in these charges, while relevant to the service department as a whole, are not directly relevant to this individual contract at this stage. The overall control of these costs lies at a higher level, though reasons for changes may be related to this individual contract, e.g. if a protracted legal dispute took place. Costs such as central support must be monitored at the higher level as they cross all internal boundaries in the service departments. Service managers need to be concerned with the costs they directly control.

Table 5.7 Ground improvement budget

	£
Estimated costs:	
Labour: 30 hrs at £3.85 (incl. overheads)	115.50
Materials: Soil – 24 sq. m at £21.5 per sq. m	516.00
Peat – 21 bags at £7.40 per bag	155.40
Transport	35.00
	821.90
Recharge to Service Dept.	900.00
Surplus	78.10

Actuals:
Labour: 32 hrs at a total cost of £126.40
Soil: 25 sq. m at a total cost of £525 (incl. delivery)
Peat: 20 bags at £7.45 bag
Transport: £35

Analysis of variances:

Costs	Actual £	Flexed £	Variance £	Price of rate £	Use or eff. £
Labour	126.4	115.5	10.9 U	3.20 U	7.70 U
Soil	525.0	516.0	9.0 U	12.50 F	21.50 U
Peat	149.0	155.4	6.4 F	1.00 U	7.40 F
Transport	35.0	35.0	0.0		
	835.4	821.9	13.5 U	8.30 F	21.80 U

5.11 Control of fixed overheads

One of the major fixed overheads incurred by service departments in the public sector is for the provision of central departmental support services such as legal and financial services. The allocation of central departmental support costs to service departments has been largely arbitrary leading to major fluctuations between the original estimate and the actual charge. This is no longer acceptable for the following reasons:

1. Compulsory competitive tendering for many services means central support must be easily, accurately and readily identifiable.
2. The emphasis on value for money requires central departments to be accountable for their costs and charges.
3. During the year service departments require accurate, timely and relevant information on charges. The year-end allocation of central support costs is inadequate for these purposes.
4. The accounting profession recommends full allocation which will only be correct if charges are made on a rotational basis.
5. The concept of devolved budgets requires the direct matching of all costs and revenues.

6. Arbitrary allocation of central support services effectively results in subsidies by some departments to others. Some services departments thus gain apparently 'free' services which distorts priorities.

These problems have led to the development of the concept of service level agreements where a contract is negotiated between the central department and the service department. This contract specifies the nature of the charges to be made for services in considerable detail and thus makes both sides fully aware of the implications of undertaking any activity. Any variations in the contract have to be agreed. The contract price effectively makes the central department a 'profit' centre with any non-approved over-spendings on the contract 'loses'. This arrangement gives the service department better control over one of its major fixed overheads both in terms of cost and the quality of service it can demand for the price that it is paying.

5.12 Control of capital programmes

The appraisal of capital schemes is discussed in subsequent chapters, but due to the relationship with the revenue account the control of capital expenditure is best dealt with here. Delayed completion in a capital scheme should result in savings on the revenue budget as provision for a scheme to come on stream should have been made in the revenue budgeting process. The opportunity for a virement would therefore exist. If the reverse situation applies then consideration will need to be made as to whether or not the scheme should go ahead early. Such a decision will depend on whether sufficient under-spendings already exist to absorb the running costs (i.e. the revenue consequences) of the capital scheme or if a supplementary estimate is to be provided. The change in the phasing of the capital programme as a result of the early or delayed completion of a capital scheme can have 'knock on' effects on the revenue profile. Cost overruns on capital schemes will also have revenue effects as other schemes, with planned revenue consequences, are deleted from the capital programme to stay within the overall capital budget. Reserve schemes may also be introduced to prevent any under-spending. Thus a complex web of interrelationships exist between the capital and revenue budgets. These interrelationships do not always result in increased revenue costs as some capital schemes such as energy conservation will result in reduced spending.

Slippage in capital programmes is always a major problem for public sector organizations so tight control needs to be kept of those factors which can cause delay. Detailed cash estimates with regular monitoring will indicate the build-up of slippage and any possible implications of rising inflation. Actual techniques of monitoring progress normally centre around network analysis with the critical path(s) identified. Any delay in critical activities will affect the overall completion time of the project. The network will also be used to provide an analysis of future cash flows as activities are either completed early or delayed.

While this chapter has concentrated on the single period revenue statement and its control, the existence of capital programmes stresses the importance of the need for a long-term revenue plan of three to five years, despite the difficulties to be faced and the assumptions needed to prepare it. This plan would range wider than just the implications of the capital programme of the particular public sector organization to include anticipated trends in revenue income and revenue costs. Control of the corporate revenue and capital programmes lies with senior management.

5.13 Human aspects of budgetary control

It is not possible to leave any discussion on budgets without considering the behavioural implications of accounting information. It can be argued that while budgets are about control they should also be about motivating people. Motivation can be defined as 'the need to achieve some selected goal and the resulting drive that influences action towards that goal' (Horngren, 1987). Argyris (1953) identified the budget as creating four areas for potential human conflict. These are discussed below in a public sector context.

The pressure device

The budget can be seen by managers and subordinates as a pressure device in an attempt to get individuals to work harder and more efficiently. Many public sector organizations are being forced to constrain budgets due to financial pressures. This creates additional pressure on staff as demand for the service may not be correspondingly reduced or it could even possibly increase. Pressure is imposed by management to achieve, say, higher case load levels per member of staff, resulting possibly in success from management's point of view but at the expense of increased resentment by staff and resistance to any further change.

Poor relationship with the finance department

The finance section is seen as the 'budget policeman', finding success in reporting poor performance. This effect is probably compounded in local government by the Treasurer having the section 151 responsibility for internal audit under the Local Government Act 1972. Success for the finance department in an adverse budget or audit report is the failure of the service manager. This can lead to loss of interest in budget reports and poor internal relationships. This effect may be enhanced where the service concerned is the subject of competitive tendering and jobs are at risk while the finance department has not been subject to the rigours of competition.

Disguishing of responsibility

Poor managers are able to blame the budget for failure to achieve, especially if participation was absent in the budget setting process, by stating that the budget was totally unrealistic. Subordinates, resentful of the managerial style adopted, also blame the budget for creating undue managerial pressure.

Departmentalism

The budget sets targets which in the public sector largely relate to the requirement for manager to spend only within strictly defined cash limits.

Departments spend to the cash limited figure for fear of losing funds next year. The needs of the department are thus put before the needs of the organization as a whole.

The way in which performance is reported would also appear to have an effect on aspiration levels and the cohesiveness of individuals and groups. This can be either positive or negative. Similarly the setting of standards for monitoring may have the same effect. It is suggested that one means of helping to create identification with the budget process is by participation both in the initial budget setting process and in subsequent revisions. This participation should, however, be real participation to be effective. Equally important is the receipt of adequate feedback as no one can maintain adequate motivation if they are kept in the dark on the results of their efforts.

Much of the work done on the human aspects of budgeting relates to the private sector but it is claimed that one aspect of the zero based budgeting process (discussed in the previous chapter) is that managers feel more closely involved in the decision-making process. Clearly there is more work to be done but the increasing demand by managers for financial management information means that any barriers which exist must be broken down if that information is to be used effectively. This implies an educational role for the accountant.

Key points of chapter

1. The importance of monitoring performance of the budget against the physical achievements of the budget was stressed.
2. The concepts of flexible budgeting, standard costing and variance analysis were introduced.
3. Emphasis was placed on the complex relationship between capital and revenue budgets and the need for a long-term revenue budget was stated.
4. The importance of budgets as a motivating factor was discussed.

5.14 Summary

This chapter has examined the process of control in the annual budget cycle but has also stressed the need for long-term planning and control of the long-term revenue and capital projections. Examination was made of the traditional method of budgetary control where expenditure is simply compared with estimate and the conclusion reached that this was inadequate and that some measure of workload needs to be built into the budget setting exercise. These measures should be related to the objectives of the budget and then be monitored as out-turn figures become available. It was stated that monitoring reports should be timely, accurate and relevant to the needs of the managers, with the computer system being used to highlight exceptions rather than produce bulky financial data beyond the cognitive ability of the individual manager to handle. Consideration was given to the part that standard costing could play, particularly in the competition services, and an illustration was given of the technique together with explanations of variances. Examination was also made of the relationship between the capital programme and the revenue budget. Finally human aspects of budgetary control were considered. Overall it was felt that the budgetary control process and the demands that it places on financial management skills represents the major challenge of change being faced by the public sector.

Questions

5.1 As a newly appointed management accountant at the Rossborough Health District you have been given the job of setting up and implementing a budgetary control/management accounting service for the Catering Department in the District's largest hospital. No system exists at present though the financial accounts record all expenditure and income subjectively for the hospital. The catering manager has been asking for some financial management information to be provided for him. Your terms of reference give you three months to set up the system and to put it into operation.

The following data is available to you:

(1) Name of Hospital – Getuwell General Hospital.
(2) Number of available beds – 700.
(3) Average bed occupancy – 90%.
(4) Number of catering staff employed – 100 (including management, clerical, cooks, kitchen and dining-room staff).
(5) A bonus scheme was introduced for catering staff three years ago.
(6) Total staff employed in the hospital – 3500 of which 1000 live on the site in accommodation that provides no facilities for self-catering.
(7) Number of staff meals provided – it is estimated that the numbers have stayed constant over the past two years. There is a requirement to provide three main meals a day for staff. Meal prices are altered periodically at the discretion of the catering manager in line with inflation.
(8) All meals (both for patients and staff) are provided from one central kitchen in the hospital and raw materials (food) are drawn in bulk weekly from the central store.
(9) The DHS has laid down the following cost limits:
  (a) The weekly allowable food cost per patient is £8.50.
  (b) Staff meal prices should be set so as to recover the cost of the food used plus 60%.

Outline the steps you would take to set up the system, indicating the type of information you would provide in order to assist the catering manager to control his expenditure.

5.2 'In the present economic climate, traditional negative financial control – primarily ensuring budgets are not overspent – is of great importance, but this should not devalue the need for developing positive financial control – the examination, review and re-direction of limited resources' (*Public Finance and Accountancy*).

In the light of this quotation critically examine the arguments for, and possible methods of, achieving flexibility in budgetary procedures and control.

5.3 Blaenwent BC owns and runs a leisure centre and is currently monitoring the likely expenditure on the complex to 31/3/X9. On the basis of expenditure to the end of November 19X8 the following position has been revealed:

Projected income and expenditure to 31/3/X9:

	Pool £	Hall £	Squash £	Catering £	Total £
Income:					
Charges	75 600	14 160	12 000	22 200	123 960
Expenditure:					
Employees:					
General	25 200	3 465	3 465	5 040	37 170
Man./Admin.	8 000	5 000	2 000	1 200	16 200
Cleaners	1 600	1 000	400	240	3 240
Premises:					
SP Supplies	13 800				13 800
Telephone	200	200	200	200	800
Printing	250	250	250		750
Sports mats		1 125	1 125		2 250
Catering				4 500	4 500
Debt charges	60 000	44 000	36 000	10 000	150 000
	109 050	55 040	43 440	21 180	228 710
Net expenditure	(33 450)	(40 880)	(31 440)	1 020	(104 750)

The Authority has set the following targets for 19X8/X9:

	£
Swimming pool	(33 000)
Sports hall	(33 650)
Squash courts	(30 000)
Catering (Surplus)	3 000
	£93 650

Under the Welsh Office Circular *Competition in the Management of Local Authority Sport and Leisure Facilities* the target set for the management of sport and leisure facilities is that expenditure should at least equal income. The authority having in mind this target for the future have agreed that the leisure centre be set this as a target for future years.

Required

Examine the above figures and with the target that has been set for 19X8/X9 consider what course of action can be taken and what further information is needed (if any).

What effect does the longer-term goal have on your strategy for the above?

5.4 It has been agreed by Curem Health Authority that, overall, the price of meals sold to staff and at functions should be based on a 50% mark up on the cost of provisions.

The following information refers to the out-turn for the year to 31 March 1981 of two hospitals within the Area, Hospital A, a large multi-specialist unit and Hospital B, a small neighbouring convalescent unit.

As Management Accountant, you are required to:
(a)   calculate whether the required target is being achieved at each hospital;
(b)   comment briefly on any reasons which you consider might affect the results.

		Hospital A £	Hospital B £
(i)	The following figures are extracted from the accounts for the year:		
	Provisions purchased (Zero Rated)	223 347	7 110
	Provisions purchased (inc. VAT at standard rate)	65 626	2 133
	Income from meals served	147 080	18 407
	Hospitality and other income	2 445	600

In addition the following points require to be taken into account:

(ii)	Stock of provisions as at 1/4/X0	34 205	1 315
	Stock of provisions as at 31/3/X1	29 874	734
(iii)	Outstanding invoices not yet paid (all Zero Rated)	4 915	308
(iv)	Meals Vouchers sold during the year	520	370
(v)	Hospital A provides meals for a local Meal on Wheels Service for which no bill has yet been charged	10 300	–
(vi)	There is outstanding income for hospitality provided	490	–
(vii)	Assume that all income figures are inclusive of VAT at the Standard Rate, except Meals on Wheels which is Zero Rated		
(viii)	At Hospital A, it is not possible to separately identify the cost of provisions for patients. For the purpose of this calculation this is assumed to be £8.15 per patient per week. In 19X0/X1 there were 21 340 such patient weeks.		

5.5   The following details have been extracted from the records of the Property Services Agency for the nine months ended 31 December 19–9. The information relates to the cleaning of three offices operated by the Agency. Details of the offices are as follows:

Office A is a medium-sized office complex built in the 1960s with a variety of administrative functions. The building was modified in the 1970s to operate on an open-plan basis within each administrative function.

Office B is a large office complex in the South East which houses the central functions of a main government ministry and has a major conference centre attached.

Office C is a small office based in a provincial town.

	Office A £	Office B £	Office C £
Cleaning materials	2 900	14 440	3 590
Equipment	890	1 780	453
Cleaning staff pay	9 500	48 300	14 000
Nl, etc.	950	490	1 400
travel	30	20	30
bonus	2 000	5 000	3 600
Contract services:			
Window cleaning	950	3 500	850
Supervisor (cont.)	4 000	4 000	4 000
Misc.	20	65	15
	21 240	77 595	27 938
Floor area	6 000 sq. m	16 000 sq. m	3 000 sq. m
Number of cleaners	3	18	4

Notes:
(a) The supervisor is responsible for the three offices and is paid an annual salary of £16 000.
(b) Stocks of cleaning materials at the following dates were:

	31/3/X9 £	12/12X9 £
A	230	500
B	900	3 000
C	90	80

(c) Wages owed to cleaning staff at Office C were £200 at 31 December 19X9.
(d) The budgeted cleaning costs for the year are £180 000.
(e) The window cleaning contract for the year is for £5800.

Required

Prepare a report for the director of cleaning services on the comparative costs of the service to 31 December 19X9 and the projected outcome to 31 March 19X0.

5.6 Derwent District Council owns and runs a leisure centre and is currently monitoring the likely expenditure on the complex for the year to 31 March 19X9.

 The following information relates to the eight month period 1 April 19X8 to 30 November 19X8:

Employees	£
Swimming pool staff	16 000
Sports hall and squash courts	4 400
Catering staff	3 200
Cleaning staff (private contractors)	2 160
Manager and administration staff	10 800

Premises

Running costs	32 400
Swimming pool supplies	9 200
Telephone (one quarterly account paid)	200
Printing tickets and stationery	500
Sports materials	1 500
Catering supplies	3 000

Income	
Squash courts	8,000
Sports hall lettings	9 440
Catering	14 800
Swimming pool	50 400

Debt charges (estimated annual charge)	150 000

Notes:

(a) Assume income and expenditure fall evenly throughout the year unless otherwise stated.

(b) Expenditure is allocated to facilities as follows:

In proportion to floor area	Cleaning staff
	Manager and administrative staff
	Premises
In proportion to capital costs	Debt charges
Equally to all facilities	Telephone
Equally to all facilities (except Catering)	Tickets/stationery
Equally to sports hall and squash courts	Sports materials and equipment
	Sports hall and squash court staff

(c) All employees except cleaners and the manager and administrative staff will receive a pay award in December backdated to 1 October. This will increase by 10% the cost of employees entitled to the award.

(d) Floor areas are:

Swimming pool	800 square metres
Sports hall	500 square metres
Squash courts	200 square metres
Catering area	120 square metres

(e) Capital costs are:

	£
Swimming pool	300 000
Sports hall	220 000
Squash courts	180 000
Catering area	50 000

(f) Anticipated deficits for the year are:

	£
Swimming pool	(33 000)
Sports hall	(33 650)
Squash courts	(30 000)
Catering (surplus)	1 000
	£95 650

Required

Prepare a statement showing the probable out-turn for 19X8/X9 together with a brief report on the results obtained.

5.7 The Northern District Health Authority operates a pharmacy which produces drugs which are sold to other districts within the region. The standard direct mix for a quantity of 1000 litres of the drug 'Keep Calm' is as follows:

			Standard price per litre
Chemical	A	500 litres	£0.50
	B	250 litres	£1.00
	C	300 litres	£0.75

The drug passes through three sections of the pharmacy and the following is the standard labour cost of 1000 litres 'Keep Calm':

Section	X	1.2 man hours @ £2.00 per hour
	Y	4 man hours @ £1.50 per hour
	Z	2 man hours @ £1.30 per hour

In the month of October 19X8, 20 200 litres of 'Keep Calm' were produced and the following costs were incurred:

Section	X	128 hours at a total cost of £259
	Y	360 hours at a total cost of £576
	Z	220 hours at a total cost of £264

	Materials consumed during October 19–8	Actual price per litre
A	11 800 litres	£0.45
B	4 900 litres	£1.10
C	6 100 litres	£0.70

As the management accountant responsible for the pharmacy **you are required to:**

(a) Prepare a statement that analyses the appropriate variances for the month.

(13 marks)

(b) Briefly outline possible reasons for the variances you have calculated in (a) above.

(3 marks)

(c) Outline the steps that are involved in calculating a standard cost and what is the role of a management accountant in this process.

(4 marks)
(Total 20 marks)

5.8 The following memorandum has been received from the Director of Social Services:

I have been notified by each of the six Divisional Offices that their quarterly expenditure tabulations appear to indicate overspendings on the home help employees (Code 483/711). The total of their expenditure on head at month 6 is £600 000; the annual budget is £1 000 000, presumably their expenditure should be only £500 000. Projected to the year end this given an overspend of £200 000.

(I say 'appear to indicate because in fact the manual records of number of hours' service provided, which is the record we use for determining how many home helps to employ, is, in the case of 3 Divisions, below the budgeted figure.)

We plan growth of £200 000 in our draft expenditure plans for next year, so this should cause no problems then. In the current year, fortunately present expenditure trends indicate that we are likely to underspend by an equivalent amount on the Elderly Persons Homes budget, and I suggest that we finance the home help overspend by virement form this head.

I thought I should bring this to your attention in view of your responsibility for budgetary control.

As principal accountant you examine the monthly expenditure tabulations in your Department and note that expenditure to month 3 was £200 000, which you see from past years' tabulations was normal at this stage, but that there has been a sharp rise since.

Your Chief Financial Officer asks you:

(a) To outline the points you would make in reply to the memorandum
(b) As part of imminent reviews of both the authority's computerised accounting system and its budgetary policies;
   (i) To outline the main requirements for computerized budgetary control information in respect of home help expenditure.
   (ii) To list the main issues to be considered in a review of the authority's policy on virement.

5.9 Managers are concerned to motivate staff yet budgets are concerned with controlling staff. How would you reconcile this conflict?

5.10 Discuss the extent to which the behavioural impact of financial information needs to be considered by those involved in the budgeting process in the public sector.

6 ▷ The management of working capital

Key learning objectives

After reading this chapter you should be able to:

1. Understand the importance of the management of working capital to the public sector.
2. Discuss the individual elements of working capital and the importance of each element in the overall working capital equation.
3. Understand the techniques available to manage working capital.

All businesses should be concerned to maximize the efficiency with which they manage both current assets and current liabilities. This is particularly important in the public sector because of the size of the organizations and the consequent value of these figures. To illustrate this point extracts from the published consolidated balance sheets of two local authorities showing the position with regard to current assets and current liabilities for the year ended the 31/3/93 are reproduced in Table 6.1.

Clearly these are large figures and, in addition, both authorities held substantial cash balances on their superannuation funds and various other funds (for example trust funds) at the year end which are not included. The superannuation fund balances, as will be imagined, are the major omission from the statement and amounted to £12 880 000 and £10 949 410 respectively at 31/3/93. It should be remembered that in the case of local authorities a funded scheme is operated for pension liabilities and an appropriate deduction is made from staff in addition to a contribution by the employing authority. It is normal for management of the fund to be undertaken by external consultants.

Such large figures are not only confined to local authorities and an additional examination of the accounts of a district health authority in Wales also revealed that in the year ended 31.3.90 it received a cash allocation for revenue

Table 6.1 Extracts from consolidated balance sheets

	Local authority A		Local authority B	
	£000	£000	£000	£000
Current assets:				
Temporary investment		28 100		–
Stocks		3 075		2 120
Debtors		26 940		25 540
Cash		–		210
		58 115		27 970
Current liabilities:				
Temporary loans	90		–	
Creditors	30 100		18 120	
Cash overdrawn	12 260		7 500	
		(42 450)		(25 620)
Working capital 31.3.93		15 665		2 350

expenses from the Welsh Office in excess of £145m, and a cash allocation for capital purposes of over £6m. It will be remembered from Chapter 1 that total general government expenditure planned for 1993–94 to 1995–96 rises from £286,600m to £316,400m. It is obvious that these figures imply a need for financial management.

Considerable attention in the public sector tends to be given to the management of capital expenditure but the thrust of this chapter is to argue that greater attention needs to be given to the management of working capital. This approach is one which includes concentrating on those resources which management outside of the finance function come into contact with most often and one which possibly may get overlooked in the financial planning process. The benefits of this approach are that proper management of these resources will generate additional revenue or reduce costs so that more funds will be available for services which are often under pressure. It may also make reduced bills possible for the taxpayer by the more efficient use of resources. It must also be pointed out that an overall policy on working capital management needs to be developed as, clearly, all items within the definition of working capital impact on each other.

6.1   Treasury management

The function of treasury management received considerable publicity following the collapse of the Bank of Credit and Commerce International (BCCI) and its closure on 5 July 1990. The Western Isle Council held over £20m with the bank at the date of collapse with a number of other local authorities also losing money. Other banks used by public sector bodies have also created problems for those organizations – Chancery Bank, and Edington Bank among others. In addition the hearings and report of the Treasury and Civil Service Committee into the collapse of BCCI were highly critical of the role of local authority finance officers in investment management (Banking Supervision and BCCI: The Role of Local Authorities and Money Brokers, Treasury and Civil Service Committee, 1992).

In the light of this and before examining in detail the mechanics of the control of the components of working capital a number of principles for the investment of cash balances are first examined. Lenders should:

1. Determine investment strategy in conjunction and parallel with their borrowing strategy. Cash balances should be invested where they achieve the best return commensurate with security.
2. Delegate legal authority to the investment manager to invest funds on behalf of the organization. This authority should clearly set out the duties and responsibilities of the investing officer acting under delegated powers.
3. Create separate responsibilities for deciding investment strategy, and supervising and controlling the day-to-day management of investments.
4. Regularly review the risks associated with particular investments and the range of investment opportunities. Risks should be spread by diversifying the portfolio.
5. Hold a list of authorized investments and regularly update it. This is particularly important with regard to the credit risks associated with all investments. Recourse should be made to credit rating agencies as appropriate although it must be remembered that at all times responsibility lies with the investor and not the agency.
6. Determine the maximum amount of cash (or percentage of available resources) that can be held in any particular investment and do not exceed any limits set.
7. Fully document all procedures and transactions.
8. Regularly report on performance at the appropriate level within the organization.

In 1992 the Bank of England published a new version of the London Code by which the conduct of banks, building societies and other financial institutions is governed. This code takes account of the recommendations made by the Treasury and Civil Service Committee and stresses that principals (the investors) have the responsibility to assess the credit worthiness of the counter-party whether dealing directly or via an agent when investing funds. It is also the decision of the principal as to what reliance is placed on statements made by brokers and other parties. The role of the brokers is to act as arrangers. The code even recommends that participants in the wholesale money market tape conversations which can be then used to resolve trading disputes.

6.2 Cash management

The cash management function will be undertaken in the finance department and is clearly concerned with forecasting the demands by the organization for such facilities as a bank overdraft with the objective of minimizing charges. The finance department will also attempt to maximize returns on any balances in hand. Where it is necessary to borrow to finance a capital programme then a strategy has to be devised which achieves this objective at minimum cost. In this context it is essential to at least develop an annual cash flow forecast, within the overall budget process, which can be continually rolled forward. It should, however, not be forgotten that where competitive units exist within the overall framework of an organization individual cash profiles should be prepared for them. This is because they will normally bear a charge for any overdraft facility they may require. Equally where they are in cash surplus they should receive an interest credit as a contribution to profit. It is also essential that such a cash flow forecast should take place within an overall business plan to enable the competition unit to manage its total resources to maximum effect in its attempts to achieve its profit targets.

Table 6.2 illustrates a cash flow forecast for 12 months for Cashshire County Council. The detail of this model may at first sight appear only to apply to those public sector bodies which have powers to raise overdrafts or make investments, for example local authorities and the public corporations. All organizations, however, need to plan their cash flow and with the increased emphasis being placed on business planning in the public sector greater emphasis is given to this aspect of working capital management.

It can be seen that a detailed breakdown of expenditure has been attempted but clearly in practice more information will be needed. This will include the preparation of separate cash flow projections for revenue and capital expenditure and income. These overall plans will represent the framework in which monthly, weekly and daily forecasting should take place.

Using Table 6.2 the following points may be made:

1. *Employee costs.* Employee costs will be available from the normal budget processes and will normally be incurred evenly over the year, although it is obviously possible to build in seasonal variations. In addition there will be a need to consider the impact of pay awards at the appropriate award date, although delays in settlement will affect day-to-day management and will be noted for the appropriate action.
2. *Premises expenses.* Premises costs such as those for repair and maintenance can be based either on a planned maintenance programme or, if these costs are consistent from year to year, on past performance. Many public sector organizations have agreements with the energy suppliers on payment and clearly the terms of these agreements can be built into the forward plan. Rates payments again should be known in advance.
3. *Agency payments.* Agency payments are the payments that Cashshire makes to agents such as district councils for services carried out on its behalf. These payments would normally be set out in the terms of the agency agreement.
4. *Precept dates.* Precept dates for those authorities percepting on the County Council would be known in advance and from past experience.
5. *Grants.* Grants from central government and precept income from district councils would be known before the year began and can thus be fed into the plan with a considerable degree of confidence.
6. *Capital cash flows.* Capital cash flows can be forecast from the capital programme with any major changes – for example, as a result of action by the capital contracts auditor – which affect payment modifying the forecast as it occurs. The forecast would obviously only include payments to outside contractors as many in-house direct service organizations are paid by internal transfer.

A detailed analysis needs to be made of all the items in the forecast to establish as far as possible any trends. Clearly, however, there will be some items

Table 6.2 Cashshire County Council cash flow forecast

	Apr. £000	May £000	Jun. £000	Jul. £000	Aug. £000	Sep. £000	Oct. £000	Nov. £000	Dec. £000	Jan. £000	Feb. £000	Mar. £000	Total £000
Expenditure:													
Employees:													
Teachers	15 124	15 124	15 124	15 124	15 124	15 124	15 124	15 124	15 124	15 124	15 124	15 124	181 488
APT & C	4 600	4 600	4 600	4 600	4 600	4 600	4 600	4 600	4 600	4 600	4 600	4 600	55 200
Manual workers	3 800	3 800	3 800	3 800	3 800	3 800	3 800	3 800	3 800	3 800	3 800	3 800	45 600
Premises:													
Repairs and maintenance	1 200	1 200	1 200	1 200	1 200	1 200	1 200	1 200	1 200	1 200	1 200	1 200	14 400
Fuel and light	500	490	300	300	300	475	475	550	750	800	800	800	6 540
Rent and rates	90	90	90	90	90	90	90	90	90	90	90	90	1 080
Miscellaneous	45	45	45	45	45	45	45	45	45	45	45	45	540
Transport	980	980	980	980	980	980	1 090	1 090	1 090	1 090	1 090	1 090	12 420
Supplies and services	4 000	4 000	4 000	4 000	4 000	4 000	4 000	4 000	4 000	4 000	4 000	4 000	48 000
Agency services	1 200	450	650	1 200	450	650	1 200	450	650	1 200	450	650	9 200
Precepts	1 200	1 200	1 850	1 200	1 200	1 850	1 200	1 200	1 850	1 200	1 200	1 850	17 000
Pay awards	850	850	850	1 210	1 210	1 410	1 410	1 410	1 410	1 410	1 410	1 410	14 840
Net capital payments	2 540	− 510	− 80	2 300	500	− 100	1 950	2 000	2 250	3 700	4 100	14 950	33 600
Total expenditure	36 129	32 319	33 409	36 049	33 499	34 124	36 184	35 559	36 859	38 259	37 909	49 609	439 908
Income:													
Sales and services	7 500	7 690	5 000	8 300	3 500	3 500	3 500	7 500	9 000	9 000	8 500	7 300	80 290
Revenue Support Grant	22 000	22 000	22 000	22 000	22 000	22 000	22 000	22 000	22 000	22 000	22 000	22 000	264 000
Precepts	0	9 750	9 750	9 750	9 750	9 750	0	9 750	9 750	9 750	9 750	9 750	97 500
Total income	29 500	39 440	36 750	40 050	35 250	35 250	25 500	39 250	40 750	40 750	40 250	39 050	441 790
Total net expenditure	− 6 629	7 121	3 341	4 001	1 751	1 126	− 10 684	3 691	3 891	2 491	2 341	− 10 559	1 882
Balance b/f	10 500	3 871	10 992	14 333	18 334	20 085	21 211	10 527	14 218	18 109	20 600	22 941	10 500
Balance c/f	3 871	10 992	14 333	18 334	20 085	21 211	10 527	14 218	18 109	20 600	22 941	12 382	12 382

where it will be necessary to make assumptions if no set pattern can be identified. The key point is that the 12 months rolling forecast provides the framework for the organization to manage its cash resources effectively. Proper monitoring of actual receipts and payments is essential to maintain the detailed control necessary for the ongoing monthly, weekly and daily forecasting on which management decisions will be made.

Daily cash forecasting

It has just been stated that the yearly forecast provides the framework within which monthly, weekly and daily forecasting takes place. A brief examination now follows of a possible procedure for daily cash forecasting for a typical public sector organization:

1. obtain actual balance for previous day from the bank;
2. estimate cheques clearing and credits due for the day;
3. check direct debits;
4. contact cashier for any income still held;
5. calculate investments or borrowings to be repaid including principal and interest and any loans and interest due;
6. calculate estimated balance at the end of the day deducting any likely uncleared income leaving the cleared balance available for investment or the borrowing needs identified.

On completion of the above process a decision can be made on the size, and period, of any loan (borrowing) that it will be possible to make (to arrange). In taking the decision it will be necessary to consider the following factors:

1. future availability or otherwise of cash as indicated by the weekly, monthly and amended long-term cash flow forecasts;
2. interested rates on loans and borrowings;
3. predicted interest movements;
4. borrowing/lending instruments.

Clearly, it is necessary to consider making arrangements to ensure that there is always sufficient funds available to meet any future demands. It may be sensible, therefore, to establish call accounts into which cash may be deposited pending demands but which still earn interest. Interest rates and their relationship are obviously important and will be a major factor in deciding on the size and period of any investment. The rates for overnight money, call accounts and longer-term investments will vary between the type of investment, the length of the investment and as relative rates change between investments opportunities. It is also important to consider predicted movements in interest rates as the organization would clearly not wish to tie itself into long-term lending if interest rates were anticipated to rise. An extra 1/4% on a loan of £3 000 000 would produce additional interest of £3750 over six months.

6.3   Bank reconciliation

A complement to the process of cash flow planning is the need to reconcile the organization's cleared bank balance with the balance shown in the cash book. This process is known as bank reconciliation and acts both as a check against fraud and error and as a check on the assumptions regarding cheque clearance and income receipts built into the cash flow projection. The primary task is to perform an analysis of the cheques presented and the cheques outstanding with the balance at the bank and the cash book balance. In theory the exercise is relatively simple but the complexity of the exercise in practice will depend on the extent to which the organization has computerized the system.

6.4   Transfer of money

The traditional method for payment of sums due has been by cheque and cash. Today, however, numerous methods of payment exist and each method will have an impact on the cash flow management of the organization. These methods of payment are therefore examined below:

Standing orders

Under this system a debtor will instruct the bank to pay a set sum on a specific day at regular intervals to the organization to which the sum is due. Any alteration to the sum due and the date payable must receive the authorization of the debtor. Payment details are provided by the organization and this reduces the possibility of error.

Direct debits

As with standing orders the debtors will authorize the organization to remove an agreed sum from the debtor's account. The main advantage is that for changes in the amount due no further authorization is needed.

Credit transfers

The debtor full details of the bank account numbers and sort codes of each of any numbers of creditors to be paid can effect transfers to those creditors' banks of the payments due by means of a single cheque if the relevant information is attached. This method might be used by a public sector organization to pay its monthly salaries bill.

Bankers automated clearing services (BACS)

The main purpose of this system is to process payments quickly by transferring payment details using electronic communication devices such as magnetic tapes and direct communication links.

Bank giro credits

The bank giro system operates by providing the debtor with the necessary payment details on a giro form. This is then taken to an appropriate payment point with the cash or cheque needed to pay the account. The amount is then credited to the organization's bank account. Examples of its use in the public sector include where there are regular weekly or monthly sums due, as for community charge payers and council house tenants, and for which pre-printed payment forms are provided.

In any organization it is likely that all these payment methods may be used. It will be essential therefore that the most appropriate method is used in relation to the sums collected. All methods have a cost of collection and this must be balanced against the advantages gained. Under a housing rents collection system, for example, it may be decided to employ rent collectors. This will have the direct costs of employment plus overheads but it might be considered that the rent collector maintains contact with the tenant and may be in the best position to identify and chase up arrears.

6.5 Alternative investment instruments

Having identified the cash that is available for investment it is necessary to consider the types of alternative investment instrument that are available. With public sector bodies it may not be possible to invest in the full range of instruments that are available to the private sector. In the case of local government, for example, regulations under the Local Government Act 1989 restrict the approved investments open to a local authority. Superannuation funds, operated by county councils, are also controlled separately, their operations being covered by the Local Government Superannuation Regulations 1986.

Government bonds

These are stocks issued by the government and are default free. This can be seen as a major attraction. The yield may, however, not be viewed as being particularly attractive unless an investment is made at the peak of an interest rate cycle, in which case there is the opportunity for the capital gain. With government stocks a rise in price effectively means a fall in the interest rate while the reverse applies when the price falls.

Local authority debt

This is similar to government bonds and can take a variety of forms. While some writers argue that it is not as secure as government debt it is secured on the council tax and as such the risk of default is low.

Certificates of deposit

These are certificates issued by banks and building societies for deposits received. They can be held long term but the period is decided by the investor. There is the additional advantage that they can be sold in the money market. The investor is therefore able to realize funds if unforeseen problems arise. In return for this advantage interest rates can be lower than available elsewhere. The advantage to the bank is that the deposit period is fixed and the funds deposited are not refundable until the term matures.

Call and notice money

Call money is money invested with no fixed date of repayment in contrast to notice money which, as the title suggests, requires due notice of withdrawal.

Eligible bank bills

Eligible bank bills are certificates for debt issued by private companies but which are guaranteed by an eligible accepting house (i.e. merchant bank). The process of accepting means that in exchange for a commission the merchant bank guarantees repayment on maturity. Eligible bank bills can be sold on the market.

Treasury bills

Treasury bills are pure discount instruments and are issued by the government and local authorities. They are a marketable and safe investment for the investing organization but the yield may be low due to their high creditworthiness.

In summary, a wide range of potential investment opportunities exist varying from overnight lending to Eurodollar deposits denominated in sterling or a foreign currency. The ability of a public sector organization to invest will depend on government controls, alternative interest rates, brokerage and commission charges and the amount of money available. Finally, targets should be set for returns on investments which should be closely monitored to measure success. (A more detailed analysis of the type of investments open to public sector organizations can be acquired from the Financial Information Service of the Chartered Institute of Public Finance and Accountancy, 3 Robert Street, London WC2N 6BH.)

6.6 Borrowing

Clearly, the opposite to the ability to lend is the need to borrow. This may take the form of a bank overdraft or a long-term loan to finance capital expenditure. The need to enter this area of cash management will again be indicated by the cash projection that the organization has prepared. In the case of some public sector organizations such as the Health Service there is no borrowing. Local authorities, however, are heavily involved in these transactions and in very specialized areas such as the interest rate swaps (see Chapter 7). The financing of capital expenditure is dealt with in a subsequent chapter where such interest rate swaps are also examined.

6.7 The practice of investment management

In order to set the above discussion in a practical context the investment practices of a number of public sector bodies are examined. The procedures adopted by each body clearly depends on the circumstances facing those bodies. The more funds that are available to invest the more sophisticated the procedures necessary to ensure the proper management of surplus funds.

The overall objective of the Severn Trent plc in investing surplus funds is 'to secure adequate operating funds at least cost, to invest surplus funds to best advantage (subject to an acceptable level of risk) and maintain a good financial reputation for the Company at all times'. Treasury policy is approved by the board of directors and there is a strong reporting chain with the treasury set up as a separate cost centre. Investments are diversified to minimise risk and a monetary limit is set for each investment. Investments are concentrated in areas in which the investment team has expertise and specialist investments such as foreign exchange are avoided. The counter-party list is regularly updated and contains, for example, the major UK clearing banks, Swiss banks and sterling commercial paper. Dealing procedures are clearly laid down in a detailed written manual. Appropriate targets are set and performance monitored (Cargill, pp. 10–12, 1991).

Local authority investment is constrained as mentioned earlier by regulations issued under the Local Government Act 1989 (the Local Authorities (Capital Finance) (Approved Investments) Regulations 1990). At Kingston Local Borough Council the effect of these regulations was to bring cash management in-house and restrict investments. The council was able in 1989/90 to borrow £23.5m from the Public Works Loan Board at fixed rates and given its large internal cash balances was able to lend this money at higher rates. The authority has a small team under the treasurer which meets regularly to plan investment strategy which is to maximize returns at minimum risk. This is within the context of maintaining short-term liquidity and the council's need to borrow funds. Performance is measured by comparing actual results against the returns which could have been earned from the seven-day rate of interest. The authority uses brokers who are members of the Sterling Brokers Association as well as dealing directly with a limited number of borrowers (Knights, pp. 12–14, 1991).

Smaller bodies may well adopt a more passive approach to investment management, investing only in the major clearing banks or a limited number of building societies. Others have appointed external advisors. Test Valley District Council has used the services of external companies offering a cash management service. The primary objective of this strategy were to provide secure longer-term returns than could otherwise be achieved by investing internally. Investment was restricted to high quality longer dated securities in the narrow range of investments as defined under the Trustee (Investment) Act 1961. The composition of the portfolio was to be the subject of discussion but the movements of securities within a particular market was left to the external consultants. The treasurer comments that the authority has achieved a higher return than if the investment policy had been decided in-house, although it is recognized that ultimate responsibility for the credit-worthiness of borrowers lies with the authority (Giddings, pp. 14–15, 1991).

6.8 Management and debtors

Any public sector organization must be concerned with the proper control of its debtors. This applies not only to those services which are provided to clients on a voluntary basis and may be withdrawn if a bad payment record exists, but also to clients who are already in possession of a service such as council housing. As the Audit Commission points out: 'The prevention of arrears is by far the most effective strategy.' A significant problem which has been created under the community charge system for financing local government is the difficulty of collecting income from debtors. This creates extra pressure on cash flow and may result in a need to borrow resulting in extra interest charges on the revenue account.

In its debt collection system a public sector organization needs:

1. a close working relationship between the service departments and the recovery department or section to ensure that problem cases are identified as soon as possible;
2. accurate, complete and timely information available to all staff involved in the arrears process;
3. a standard recovery procedure to be in place which is an automatic system and is regularly reviewed. Due to the politically sensitive nature of some of its services and its public image it needs to have provision to identify special cases;
4. to ensure that any action should be quick and effective;
5. firm action to be taken against poor payers (subject to point 3 above) to demonstrate that the organization is prepared to apply sanctions;
6. consideration to be taken of the costs of recovery as once legal action is started the process is expensive;
7. to avoid giving credit if the service is one where cash can be collected on delivery.

The granting of credit involves the organization in a cost as interest could be earned on the outstanding balances, or interest could be saved on any overdraft which finances the credit granted. Some public sector organizations offer incentives for lump sum payments of due amounts or for specific payment methods. Exhibit 6.1 illustrates the cost of credit granted for a competitive arm of a public sector organization where there is a choice in respect of its client base and trading terms.

While it is assumed that in dealing with other public sector tax-financed bodies they will be financially secure, where legislation allows trading with private sector organizations this is not necessarily the case and the possibility of bad debts must be considered. It may be felt that by offering a discount for prompt payment this risk may be reduced. Similarly credit references may be taken up and this would certainly apply with large contracts. (In the case of capital contracts public sector organizations operate an approved list of contractors. In order to be placed on this list it would be normal for the accounts of an applicant for inclusion on the list to be appraised.) As trade credit is an institution in the market-place the allowance of credit is almost a prerequisite to increasing business and profitability. Risk is thus inevitable, but as with all risks it must be managed.

Exhibit 6.1

Transplant is a public sector organization which undertakes vehicle maintenance for other public sector organizations. It has been approached by a potential customer for a vehicle repair which it estimates will cost £1500. The standard mark-up on this type of contract is 15%, but Transplant is considering offering 30 days credit or, alternatively, a 5% discount for payment within 15 days. The cost of borrowing to the organization is 10%. The cash implications of these methods of payment are set out in Table 6.3.

Transplant is now in a position to examine the cost of these alternative strategies and decide which may prove most attractive to winning the business. As the organization is a new customer the incremental cost of the transaction is the £1500 cost price and this has been used as the basis of the transaction.

Where 6.3 indicates that the profit is £132.59 Transplant now has the use of these funds for an additional 15 days and as such is in a position to consider either investing them or reducing its borrowing. Assuming that borrowing is at the higher rate then this would increase the profit to £139.33 (10% x 1638.75 for 15 days).

Clearly, both parties have to weigh up the costs and opportunities of the transaction as any saving Transplant makes will represent costs to the other organization. In a competitive situation, Transplant must also consider the likely terms and conditions of contracts on offer by its competitors.

Table 6.3   The cost and credit to transplant

Payment strategy	Cost price £	Contract price £	Profit £	Profit %
Cash sale	1 500	1 725	225	15
30-day credit (cost of credit £1 500 at 10% = £12.33)	1 500	1 725	212.67	14.2
5% discount (cost of credit 15 days at 10% = £6.16)	1 500	1 638.75	132.59	8.8

Alternative methods of debt collection

It has been assumed up to now that the organization is undertaking its own debt recovery procedures but possible alternatives include the following:

1. A debt collection agency could be employed which would charge a commission on the value of debts successfully recovered. The organization inevitably loses some control of the recovery process and would have to specify the terms of the contract carefully.
2. Debts could be factored which will generate cash flow but there will obviously be a charge. In addition a factor would only be interested in 'good' debts and it is difficult to imagine factoring the individual debts that many public sector organizations have.
3. Credit insurance involves the insurer in covering risks which cause a significant loss to the organization if the client becomes insolvent. Normally there is a risk limit with the insured bearing the balance. Clearly, this method is unsuitable for covering the many small debts that, for example, a district council may build up in terms of rent arrears.

6.9   Management of creditors

It was reported in Hansard (2.2.90) in the debate on the Interest on Debt Bill that certain government departments do not consider for payment any account unless it is at least 30 days late. In the same debate it was also pointed out that a health board in Scotland had gone on public record as saying that due to a cash crisis it would not get to the end of the financial year unless it did not pay any bills. Clearly this type of action could place suppliers in severe difficulties and could present major difficulties over future supply. Politically, this exploitation of credit from small suppliers may not prove acceptable.

In many ways this process is the reverse of that considered earlier in relation to debtors. Now the 'boot is on the other foot' and the public sector organization is consequently in the position of judging whether or not it is to its advantage to pay early and claim any discounts. If there are no discounts then there is no advantage to paying early unless there is a desire to impress creditors with speed of payment. This is illustrated in Exhibit 6.2.

Exhibit 6.2

A public sector organization has received a bill for £10 000 with the receipt of goods. Payment is to be with the supplier in 30 days. The cost of capital to the organization is 15%. If payment is delayed the supplier charges a penalty of 3% monthly on the uncleared balance.

It can be seen from Table 6.4 that for up to 50 days the public sector organization still has an advantage in delaying payment. This is a financial advantage only and could result in the loss of supplier goodwill. Moreover, if it is a call-off contract negotiated by a central supplies department, it could result in the loss of discounts. It is the possibility of gaining a poor reputation for payment that is the major control on delaying payment as interest charges for delay can be difficult to sustain.

Most public sector organizations are normally large bodies with centralized payment functions. The delay in processing that this involves may result in the loss of discounts (if these are considered desirable) and – equally significantly from the manager's point of view – the loss of flexibility which results from the financial information provided for them to control cost centres, especially if a commitment system of accounting (Chapter 5) is not in operation.

There is a need to assess the impact that the creditor system has on the financial information available. It is suggested that 'typical' system might be:

1. invoice received in service department, matched with goods received note and original order, arithmetically checked, contract price examined, certified for payment, coded and checked for possible discounts;
2. batched for payment with other invoices and forwarded to finance department for payment on appropriate dates as per notification from finance department;
3. received in finance department batched for computer input and control totals recorded;

Table 6.4 Financial implications of delaying payment

Time period	Credit £	Cost	Saving £
30 days	10 000	0%	123.29
40 days (no penalty)	10 000	0%	164.38
40 days (with penalty)	10 000	36% p.a.	65.74
50 days (no penalty)	10 000	0%	205.47
50 days (with penalty)	10 000	36% p.a.	8.21

Note:
This example assumes that the cheque has been cleared by the end of the credit period.

4. keyed in to computer for subsequent preparation of cheques and update of financial information system and bank reconciliation;
5. rejected invoices will be subsequently resubmitted;
6. distribute financial information to service departments (on-line enquiry may be possible).

While special procedures will exist for urgent payments and capital contracts it can be seen that the above system inevitably builds in delay, especially if an invoice misses a deadline. Similarly, the system may not be flexible enough to cope with discount deadlines. An alternative is decentralized payment procedures where departments enter invoices directly leaving the finance department to process the cheques and concentrate on internal controls and audit trails. The main advantage is that the financial information is updated more quickly which should lead to improvements in budgetary control. In addition the service departments will be aware of discounts and prompt processing can lead to these being claimed. In this case the policy of discounts against the cost of early payment will need to be considered.

6.10 Management of stock

The application of inventory control is of particular importance to those units of the public sector which are subject to competitive tendering. This is particularly true for those businesses which are required to make a return calculated on the current cost of assets as the stock adjustment under current cost accounting (CCA) affects the profit and loss account and also the level of capital employed. It is obvious that any loss of stock from whatever cause will be a charge to the profit and loss account. To this end many direct service organizations have made a conscious effort to reduce or remove stocks and stores (buildings are also part of capital employed). Stock-holding is important, however, in normal service activities as the traditional end of year spending spree to utilize the remainder of the budget can lead to large increases in stocks of materials which would not otherwise be ordered. Cash is thus tied up in materials and not earning interest. There is also a danger of deterioration if stocks are not kept in adequate storage conditions.

There is a need in any activity for adequate sources of supply to complete the task in hand. In the case of the competition activities this may take the form of holding items in stock as this will reduce the uncertainty of supply. The holding of stocks in sufficient quantity may also result in attracting discounts. Clearly, this strategy has to be set against the cost of operating stores. The alternative is to direct purchase supplies to the site on the just-in-time (JIT), principle but then there is the danger of late delivery and the costs of idle time, and so on. In any case the public sector may require emergency stocks to be held and a stores building will need to be maintained. Thus only the marginal costs will be relevant to the organization. It is probably true to say that for a DSO activity that a balance of combining direct purchase and a stores system will achieve the optimum policy. This will require a detailed study to tailor need to the individual organization but the following factors would need to be considered:

1. transportation costs;
2. idle time in waiting for materials;

3. price differentials between stores items and contracted direct suppliers;
4. stores running costs;
5. levels of emergency items;
6. stock-holding costs;
7. capital costs of buildings;
8. the general nature of the work, e.g. construction contracts would involve forward planning to enable materials to be pre-ordered for delivery direct to site.

In respect of emergency items it might be possible to operate an imprest system with vehicles carrying a basic stock of materials regularly used, which is reimbursed after any use either from stores or direct suppliers.

Once a decision has been taken to operate a stores it is necessary to ensure that it is operated efficiently in terms of the levels of stock carried. Maximum and minimum stock levels should thus be set and regularly reviewed. In terms of ordering stock the following formula has been devised for economic order quantities:

$$\text{Economic order quantity} = \sqrt{\frac{2 \times AD}{S}}$$

where:

A is the annual cost of placing an order;
D is the annual demand;
S is the annual cost of holding one unit of stock.

The recorder point is the quantity level of the stock that triggers a new order to placed and is simplest to calculate when there is certainty about demand and lead time (i.e. time for delivery). This is given by the formula:

Recorded point = Demand per unit of time × Lead time

Where, however, there is uncertainty about demand or supply there is a need to provide a safety stock which will be the minimum level necessary to meet unexpected demand. The computation of safety stocks hinges on the ability to forecast demand which is based on past experience. The major relevant costs will be the costs of holding stock and the stock-out costs. The optimum exists where the costs of carrying an extra unit are exactly counter-balanced by the expected stock-out costs. Exhibit 6.3 provides a brief example of the calculations required.

Key points of chapter

1. The importance of the management of working capital in the public sector has been stressed.
2. The need to develop policies for each element of working capital is important.
3. It is an area in which managers in service departments are able to play a vital role.

6.11   Summary

Working capital management has a key role to play in the public sector but its importance may be overlooked due to the distributed management of financial resources operated in public sector organizations. Substantial policy benefits are available if this importance is recognized and communicated within the organization. By the creation of a stated policy and objectives for the management of working capital the organization has the opportunity to speed up or slow down the flow of cash. This will have major implications, due to the size of working capital balances, for the returns available to the organization and its ability to maintain services.

Exhibit 6.3

Transplant, the competitive vehicle repair workshop of a public sector organization, competes with other public sector organizations for work. One fleet that it services regularly has just replaced its 3-ton lorries with a new vehicle specification and these lorries will require a new type of brakeshoe. The daily demand for brakeshoes it is estimated will be 12 pairs and the purchase price of each set is £25.

The cost associated with placing orders and maintaining a stock of brakeshoes are estimated as follows:

1. The total costs incurred in the purchasing department over the last year are £18 800 and the number of orders placed were 4000. It is expected that costs will rise by 5% over the next year.
2. Shipping costs are £10 per order.
3. A storeman will receive and inspect the brakeshoes as they arrive and it is estimated that this will require one hour per order. The storeman is paid £3.50 per hour and variable overheads are allocated at the rate of £5 per hour in this department.
4. The desired rate of return on stock is 20%.
5. The management operate the workshops on a 260 day year.
6. Six working days are required to receive delivery from when the order is placed.

Required:
Calculate the economic order point and the recorder point in units together with the minimum annual cost at the economic order point.
The first step is to calculate the cost of placing an order:

	£
Estimated order costs (£18 000 1.05%)/4000	4 935
Shipping costs	10 000
Labour costs per order	8 500
	£23 435

Estimated cost of placing an order

The value of the carrying cost is composed of the required rate of return on stock which is £24 x 20% or £5. The annual quantity required is 260 working days multiplied by the number per day which is 10:

$$EOQ = \sqrt{\frac{2(260 \times 10) \times 23.435}{5}}$$

= 156 pairs per order

Recorder point = Usage per day × Lead time
= 10 × 6
= 60

Recorder point is when 60 pairs of brakeshoes are in stock.

Minimum annual cost is calculated by:

$$C = \frac{A \times P}{E} + \frac{E \times S}{2}$$

$$= \frac{2600 \times 23.475}{156} + \frac{156 \times 5}{2}$$

$$= £781.25$$

Questions

6.1 A local authority DSO uses 5000 units of raw materials on a continuous basis in a year. The DSO estimates that the cost of carrying one unit in inventory is £0.20 per year. Placing and processing an order for additional inventory cost an estimated £225 per order.

   (a) What are the annual ordering costs, carrying costs and total costs of inventory, if the DSO orders in quantities of 1500, 2000, 2500, 3000, 3500 and 4000 units, respectively?
   (b) Graph the ordering and carrying costs (y-axis) relative to order quantity (x-axis) and comment on the results achieved.
   (c) Calculate the economic order quantity using the appropriate formula.
   (d) Discuss the value of establishing a sound policy of inventory management to any public sector organization.

6.2 The Central Purchasing Department of a large government department places orders for various items of stationery at monthly intervals. In respect of one particular item (Code Z400) the relevant data is:

   Annual usage 40 000 boxes
   Minimum order quantity 2500 boxes
   Cost per box £2.75

   Usage of material is regular and on average 40% of the amount purchased is held in stock. The cost of storage is 60% of the value of stock held. The average cost of placing an order is £140.
   A value for money exercise is currently being carried out in the purchasing department and as part of this exercise the above item has been selected for review.

   You are required to:
   (a) Explain what is meant by the term 'economic order quantity', supporting your explanation with an appropriate graph.
   (b) For item Z400 tabulate the costs of storage and ordering the item for each level of orders from five to twenty.
   (c) Calculate the economic order quantity using an appropriate formula. Compare the results achieved with (b).
   (d) Discuss the advantages and disadvantages to the purchasing department of using the results of your calculations.

6.3   Transplant is a vehicle maintenance department of a public sector organization. It has been approached by a local health organization to undertake some repair work on one of its fleet of ambulances. The estimates cost of the repair work is £2000. The standard mark-up on this type of contract is 10% with Transplant considering offering 30 days credit or alternatively a 5% discount for the receipt of payment in full within 20 days. The cost of borrowing to Transplant is 13%.

(a)   Calculate which option is the most appropriate for Transplant.
(b)   It is understood by Transplant that the local health organization is considering contracting out all its present in-house maintenance. Assess any implications of this to Transplant in deciding its policy in (a).
(c)   Discuss what is meant by an organization's credit terms and what they determine.

6.4   A public sector organization has received a bill for £15 900 with the receipt of goods. Payment can be made in three days for a 5% discount. Payment in full is due within 30 days. If payment is delayed a penalty of 4% monthly is payable under the terms of the contract to the supplier. The cost of capital to the public sector organization is 14%.

(a)   Which policy on payment should the public sector organization adopt?
(b)   What effect would a rise in the cost of capital to 15% have on this policy?
(c)   What effect would a fall in the cost of capital to 10% on your advice in (a)?
(d)   Discuss who pays the cost of credit – the supplier or the buyer – and in what way.

6.5   A District Health Authority is to consider the building of a health centre in an expanding town at one end of the District. Two sites have been proposed; site A is in the centre of the town and can be developed immediately, whereas site B is on the edge of town and progress can only be made in 18 months' time when the access road is improved. The Planning Department has prepared the following information for the authority:

	Site A	Site B
Cost of land	£50 000	£15 000
Works contract	£240 000	£260 000
Contract start	April 19X8	August 19X9
Contract period	8 months	7 months
Fitting out costs	£25 000	£25 000
Running costs p.a.	£92 000	£94 000

You may assume that the contractor will be paid in equal monthly instalments for the contract period, except for the 5% retention which is paid 6 months after completion. You may make any other reasonable assumptions about the timing of cash flows, but they should be stated in your answer.

(a)   Carry out a financial appraisal of the two options and interpret your results.
                                                                    (15 marks)
(b)   Comment on any other information that ought to be presented to the Members at the same time as the financial appraisal in part (a).
                                                                    (15 marks)

6.6 The customers of a public sector organization pay their accounts in the following ways:

	Number of annual transactions
Cheques banked centrally	1 200 000
Cash at shops (value – £40 million)	1 100 000
Bank giro credits	300 000
National Girobank credits	100 000

The following cost are incurred in processing the income:

	£000s
Shop salaries	590
Central cheque handling salaries	40
Central cash balancing and control salaries	30
Collection of cash by security firms	62

The organization pays bank charges as follows:

Cheques paid in	5p each
Cash paid in	9p per £100

Notes:
(i)   20% of shop staff time is spent on cashiering.
(ii)   Employer's superannuation, etc. amounts to 20% of salary.
(iii)   Balancing and control of cash items costs twice as much as cheques. Giro items involve no cost.
(iv)   20% of customers using bank giro pay in cash.
(v)   Customers are charged 30p by National Girobank for the payment for an account at a post office.
(vi)   Cheques received in shops are banked centrally.

The bank proposes to introduce a charge to the organization of 20p for each bank giro payment. **You are required** to prepare a report for the Board indicating whether the facility should continue to be offered.

6.7 A public authority is currently examining methods of payments of its weekly paid 'manual' workforce which numbers 260 employees.

Details of the current payment system are as follows:

(a)   180 employees are paid in cash. The payroll is run on Wednesday, the day before pay day; the payslips, coin analysis and a cheque for the total cash payment are collected by a security firm. The security firm cashs the cheques on the Wednesday, makes up the wages and pays out at four pay points on Thursday morning. Employees attend the pay points in work time and this takes, on average, 20 minutes per employee. Pay packets not collected are returned to the wages office which acts as a fifth pay point. In the case of employees at distant locations, the pay packets are normally collected from the wages office by the appropriate supervisors and delivered to the workforce, thereby averting 'Lost Time'. Total cash payments amount to £15 120 per week; of the 180 employees, on average, 135 attend the pay parades.

(b)   80 employees are paid by open cheques, sent either to homes or banks by first class mail to arrive on pay day. Open cheque payments amount to

£6900 per week and analysis of the time at which these cheques are debited to the authority's bank account reveals the following pattern:

	No. of days after pay day					
	0	1	2	3	4	5+
% Debited	15	5	0	0	75	5

Two alternative systems have been proposed:

Alternative 1:

All employees would be paid by crossed cheques sent directly to bank accounts; this would necessitate all manual employees having bank accounts. The stationery required, cheques, is expected to cost £180 per year. It is estimated that, on average, cheques would be cleared three days after pay day. The authority's bankers have indicated that the current charge of 22 pence per cheque cleared would apply under this option.

Alternative 2:

All employees would be paid by BACS transfer. As with Alternative 1, this option would require all employees to have bank accounts. Costs involved amount to:

Weekly tape delivery to BACS processing centre	£11
BACS cost per transaction	3.5 pence
Magnetic tapes (initial cost only)	£25

Under this option the total wage bill would be debited to the authority's bank account on pay day. This will necessitate some reorganization of internal payroll procedures and require the employment of one additional person in the wages office for one half-day per week, at an appropriate proportion of an annual cost of salary and overheads amounting to £5800 per year.

Other information:
(a) The security firm charges £3450 per annum for its services.
(b) Manual employees work a 38-hour week.
(c) The wages office currently employs 2.5 people at an average total weekly cost of £130 per person; it has been estimated that about 2% of their total time is devoted to holding and reissuing pay packets not collected at designated pay points.
(d) Discussions with unions representing the manual workforce indicate that a one-off *ex gratia* payment of £50 per employee would be sufficient to encourage all employees to open bank accounts.
(e) Current short-term borrowing rates are 10% per annum.

Required

You are the auditor investigating this issue as part of a more general investigation of BACS. Prepare a report to the Senior Assistant Treasurer detailing your findings and making appropriate recommendations.

Your report should concentrate on analysis and interpretation rather than description.

(24 marks)

6.8 Wondershire County Council operates a workshop for the disabled which produces and sells a single product – Ali Baba linen baskets. In order to train the disabled in all aspects of commerce the workshop is run as a separate entity. The following information relates to the workshop:

(a) Each basket sells for £10 and has a variable cost element of £6.50 made up as follows:

	£
Materials	1.50
Labour	4.00
Overhead	1.00
	£6.50

(b) Fixed costs of £2500 per month are paid on the 28th of each month.
(c) Anticipated credit sales are as follows:

1986			1987					
Oct.	Nov.	Dec.	Jan.	Feb.	Mar.	Apr.	May	Jun.
650	700	700	600	620	640	640	640	660

(d) Cash sales are expected to be 5% of credit sales and are at a discount of 5%.
(e) Production quantities are forecast as follows:

Oct.	Nov.	Dec.	Jan.	Feb.	Mar.	Apr.	May	Jun
750	800	750	610	630	650	660	670	680

(f) Customers are invoiced at the end of each month and payments are received:

    60% by the end of the month following the month of the invoice
    35% by the end of the next subsequent month
    5% one further month later

(g) Suppliers of material are paid one month after the material has been used in production.
(h) Wages are paid in the same month as they are incurred.
(i) 60% of the variable overhead is paid in the month of production, the remainder in the following month.
(j) The workshop manager anticipates that the workshop will be £2000 over-drawn at the bank on 31 December 1986.

Required

(i) A month by month cash budget for the 1st six months of 1987.

(14 marks)

(ii) The manager considers that cash flow may be improved if customers paid their bills earlier. Briefly outline the advantages and disadvantages of offering discounts.
  Market research suggests that by offering a 5% discount 75% of credit sales will be received by the end of the month after the customer is invoiced. Assume the remainder pay one month later at full price. What effect would this have an cashflow? (6 marks)

6.9 A public body expects the following cash receipts and payments in the financial year beginning 1 April 19X7:

1. Opening cash balance at 1 April 19X7 of £500 000 credit.
2. Annual revenue receipts of £13 500 000. Two-thirds is receivable bi-annually on 1 April and 1 October. Normally 50% is collected in the due month, 40% in the next month, and 10% in the third month. The remaining one-third is receivable in 10 equal instalments, May to February.
3. Annual revenue grant of £13 120 000, receivable in two equal instalments in September and March.
4. Monthly employee payments of £1 600 000.
5. A pay award of 5%, operative from 1 July, although delays in the bargaining process are expected to result in actual agreement and implementation three months after the operative date.
6. Annual material purchases of £3 000 000. 40% of the purchases occur in the first six months. Creditors are paid 60% in the month of purchase, 40% in the following month. Purchases in March 19X7 total £250 000.
7. Other expenses of £204 000 incurred evenly throughout the year.
8. Capital payments of £800 000 in June and £610 000 in December.
9. Bank charges of £250 000, payable in advance. The bank has offered a further option for consideration, namely, one-half of 1% of turnover (gross annual receipts plus gross annual payments), payable in arrears.
10. Cost of capital is 10%.

You are required
(a) to prepare the 19X7/X8 cash budget;   (12 marks)
(b) to decide the best method for paying bank charges;   (4 marks)
(c) to outline briefly the main functions of cash budgets in the public sector.
                                                                  (4 marks)

6.10 Gwent CC have been experiencing severe problems recently in the collection of trade debts in terms of payments to Gwent DSO being delayed.

It has asked you, (a representative of a public sector advisory agency) for advice on ways to reduce the effect of these problems on its liquidity position.

One of the alternatives which you have identified for Gwent DSO is to enter an agreement with a factor which has the following features:

1. The factor would forward 90% of Gwent DSO's invoice values on receiving a copy of these. Remaining amounts would be remitted to Gwent DSO, by the factor, as received from customers.
2. All sales invoice raising and debt collection duties would be undertaken by the factor for which it would charge a fee of 5% p.a. of the gross annual invoice value, payable in 12 equal monthly instalments.
   This will lead of a saving in fixed sales ledger costs of £4000 per month.
3. Amounts advanced to Gwent DSO would attract an interest charge, payable to the factor of 15% p.a. payable on a simple, monthly basis.
   Gwent DSO's sales are currently at a level of £500 000 per month, all on credit, and these are expected to increase at 3% per month for the next 3 months and then to remain at that level.
   Gwent DSO's credit terms are 30 days net, but most of its customers are currently paying after 90 days. It is estimated that the factor will reduce this payment period to, at most, 60 days.
   Gwent DSO's cost of short-term borrowing is 14% p.a.

Required

(i)   Calculate whether it is likely to be to Gwent DSO's advantage to enter
       the factoring agreement.   (14 marks)
(ii)   Identify and discuss other possible alternative methods of overcoming
       Gwent DSO's debt collection problems, if its entire sales are made within
       the UK.
                                                                   (5 marks)
(iii) Explain the ways in which debt collection problems might be increased
       should Gwent DSO decide to commence exporting and describe three
       ways of reducing these problems' effects.   (6 marks)
                                                            Total 25 marks

7 ▷ The financing of capital expenditure

Key learning objectives

After reading this chapter you should be able to:

1. Discuss the relative advantages of the different methods of capital fiance.
2. Distinguish between the capital finance of central government departments (including the NHS) and local authorities.
3. Explain the capital expenditure controls operating in the different parts of the public sector.
4. Identify the key issues in a borrowing strategy, a leaseback deal, and the use of derivative instruments.

The strict definitions of capital expenditure within different parts of the public sector are provided in Chapter 8. This chapter will be concerned with the objectives, policies and constraints relating to the financing of such expenditure, and specifically will consider the following:

1. The different approaches to the finance of capital expenditure, and the implications of these diverse approaches.
2. The impact of various controls and constraints which have been imposed by legislation or by agreement between parties.
3. An examination of the dynamics of three important and changing areas of capital finance, namely, borrowing strategy, lease finance and derivatives.

7.1   The central objective in capital financing

The central objective in the financing of capital expenditure is to ensure that all calls on the organization for money to support expenditure on fixed assets, and the refinancing of loans which fall due for repayment, can be met. Consider a simple example such as is shown in Table 7.1.

Table 7.1 Projected financing needs

Year:	Current £m	Current +1 £m	Current +2 £m
Capital expenditure	27	29	19
Refinancing	6	11	4
Finance required	33	40	23

In the situation depicted in Table 7.1 over the three year period the Treasurer or Director of Finance has to ensure that a total of £96m is available to support planned capital expenditure of £75m and to re-finance borrowing used to finance past capital expenditure, amounting to £21m. This finance will need to be provided in the required pattern which is shown in Table 7.1. with £33m in this year, £40m next year and £23m in the year after.

In looking for ways of securing this finance, the responsible officer will be seeking funds which minimize the cost to the organization; furthermore, that finance is raised only when it is required so as to minimize the time period over which it is held and, therefore, the time period over which it has to be paid for. We next consider, in broad terms, the approaches to the sourcing of capital finance which are employed in the public sector.

Approaches to the financing of capital expenditure

Broadly, there are four different approaches employed within the public sector, as follows:

1. financing from revenue;
2. financing by borrowing;
3. financing from reserves;
4. financing by leasing.

7.2 Financing from revenue

If an organization pays for capital expenditure, as it occurs, out of its recurring revenue resources, this has been termed 'pay as you go'. It involves using the revenues from current taxation, fees and charges, asset sales and privatization proceeds. It avoids financing assets by borrowing. Local authorities may choose to indulge in this approach to the finance of capital expenditure, financing expenditure on assets from income from fees, local taxation and the government block grant.

There are five advantages of pay-as-you-go. First, it saves the organization concerned interest charges, it also avoids the not inconsiderable costs associated with managing debt, as would certainly be involved with borrowing. Secondly, it is said to foster accountability; a decision made now to extend the town hall will be reflected in current taxation. Thus, the expenditure may be felt quite sharply by current taxpayers, and the accountability link between expenditure and impact on the taxpayer, made immediate. Thirdly, it avoids

Table 7.2 Pay-as-you-go and borrowing compared

Year:	Now	+1	+2	+3	+4	+5	+6	+7	+8	+9
Capital expenditure £m	10	10	10	10	10	10	10	10	10	10
Finance Pay-as-you-go	10	10	10	10	10	10	10	10	10	10
Borrowing Annual borrowing	10	10	10	10	10	10	10	10		
Repayments Principal	1	2	3	4	5	6	7	8	9	10
Interest	.5	.95	1.35	1.7	2	2.25	2.45	2.6	2.7	2.75
Total	1.5	2.95	4.35	5.7	7	8.25	9.45	10.6	11.7	12.75

committing future generations of taxpayers, who will have their own burdens to carry; and it prevents current politicians from deferring to the future the financing impact of their decisions. Fourthly, in the case of direct service organizations (DSOs) the current regulations specify that revenue-financed assets are to be excluded from an organization's asset base when the return on capital employed is being calculated. This results in a doubly positive impact in the return on capital employed in the years following the acquisition of the asset: there are no annual financing charges to be borne by the revenue account and the asset base within the return on capital employed calculation is reduced. Finally, in the long run it can be shown that, with regular and recurring capital expenditure, pay-as-you-go will eventually work out more cheaply than borrowing. This is illustrated in Table 7.2; as can be seen, in seven years time the revenue consequences of borrowing start to exceed those of pay as you go.

In Figure 7.2 it is assumed that the loan is repaid in 10 equal instalments so that in the first year the repayment is simply one-tenth of the first year borrowing. In the second year it is one-tenth of the first year borrowing and one-tenth of the second year borrowing and so on. It is also assumed that repayments are made at the end of the year.

The interest calculation is based upon a rate of interest of 5%, which is estimated to remove from current interest rates the allowance for estimated inflation. It is also assumed that the annual interest is repaid annually. The calculation of the interest payment is shown in Figure 7.1.

However, the pay-as-you-go approach can be criticized. First, given that the expenditure is being incurred for capital purposes future generations of taxpayers will have the benefit of the asset at no capital cost to them. The present generation is effectively subsidizing the future.

It may also have the major disadvantage, as the White Paper 'Working for Patients' (Department of Health, 1989) supports, that capital is seen as a free good by service managers. This applies particularly to a situation where there is no annual charge for capital consumption in the annual revenue accounts although such a charge does not necessarily have to relate to the method of financing. After all, it is possible to have a system of depreciation accounting which is entirely independent of the method by which an asset is financed; for

Year 1: 5% * 10

Year 2: 5% * (10 + 9) (10 being the second-year loan, and 9 being the amount outstanding relating to the first-year loan).

Year 3: 5% * (10 + 9 + 8) [10 being the third-year loan, 9 being the second-year loan, and 8 being the first-year loan]

This is then applied to the remaining years of the loan using the simple formula for the sum of an arithmentic progression:

$$Sum = \frac{(first\ number + last\ number)}{2} * Number\ of\ items\ in\ the\ series$$

thus,

Year 4	=	(10 + 7)/2 * 4	=	34 * 5%
Year 5	=	(10 + 6)/2 * 5	=	40 * 5%
Year 6	=	(10 + 5)/2 * 6	=	45 * 5%
Year 7	=	(10 + 4)/2 * 7	=	49 * 5%
Year 8	=	(10 + 3)/2 * 8	=	52 * 5%
Year 9	=	(10 + 2)/2 * 9	=	54 * 5%
Year 10	=	(10 + 1)/2 * 10	=	55 * 5%

Figure 7.1   *The calculation of interest charges in Table 7.2.*

evidence of this, one has to look no further than the accounting principles employed throughout the private sector in the construction of accruals-based profit and loss accounts.

Thirdly, if a 'pay as you go' policy is adopted it may be difficult to achieve a reasonable level of stability in tax rates and council tax levels from year to year. In addition this will be further complicated by the gearing effect for local government as the central government has indicated that it will only increase grants and the uniform business rate by no more than the rate of inflation. Consequently, a 'pay-as-you-go' policy may significantly affect council tax levels from year to year. Table 7.3 illustrates this quite clearly.

In this figure inflation is assumed to be 6% and revenue expenditure and government grant are both increased in the second year in line with this. As can be seen, the increase in gross expenditure of 25% is wholly attributable to financing capital expenditure out of revenue. However, government grant is

Table 7.3   Pay-as-you-go and council tax levels

Year:	19–1 £m	19–2 £m
Revenue Expenditure	50	53
Capital Charged to revenue	2	12
Gross Expenditure	52	65
Less Grant	20	21
Raised from Council Tax	32	44
Increased in Tax		37.5%

assumed to increase only in line with inflation and this results in a 37.5% increase in council tax. The assumption that government grants increase in line with inflation is likely to be over-generous if declining levels of grant in real terms are used to squeeze increasing levels efficiency out of the local authorities. Furthermore, the stringent capping of local authority expenditure by central government would render impractical any policy which results in such a significant potential increase in revenue expenditure.

7.3 Finance from borrowing

The advantages of using borrowing to finance capital expenditure are, obviously, a mirror image of the disadvantages of pay-as-you-go. In practice, the main philosophical argument is that assets such as schools have long lives and, within existing legislation, borrowing serves as one method of spreading the capital cost over several generations of taxpayers; that is, relating benefits received to taxes paid in a fairly crude way. In addition there has been a strong practical argument, which is that many assets can only be afforded because payment for them is deferred via borrowing. Table 7.3 indicates that in the long term pay-as-you-go is cheaper than debt finance. However, there can be no doubt that borrowing allows the provision of a greater volume of asset-related services in the short run than pay-as-you-go can ever provide. Also, with pay-as-you-go, the costs of borrowing are effectively shifted from the government to the taxpayer, who must bear higher taxes, or reduced services, because of annual expenditure on fixed assets.

Inflation provides an argument in favour of borrowing. When the loan is repaid inflation reduces the real cost of the money repayments and, therefore, the real cost to the taxpayer. If the organization has a choice the balance of advantage must be decided by factors such as the interest rate, repayment periods and government controls.

There are significant differences in approaches to borrowing within the public sector, and it is important to make a clear distinction between central government borrowing and local government borrowing. The case of central government borrowing is dealt with first.

Central government and the NHS

All borrowing for central government departments and the NHS is carried out by central government at Treasury level and it must be stressed that borrowing is not available to individual central government departments or to the NHS other than the hospital trusts.

The NHS receives from central government an allocation of capital and revenue funds each year and all capital expenditure in that year is charged against its capital allocation for that year; none is defrayed by borrowing. Thus, it may appear that the NHS is following a pay-as-you-go-policy for capital expenditure. However, as has been stated, the funds to finance that expenditure come from central government. These in turn come from either the taxpayer, the money markets, in the form of government borrowing, or from sales of public sector assets under the privatization policy. No attempt is made by the Treasury to identify the specific source of finance which is tied to a specific expenditure.

The Public Sector Borrowing Requirement (PSBR) indicates the extent that the public sector borrows from other sectors of the economy and overseas and covers borrowing by central government, the nationalized industries and local authorities. It is closely related to another concept, particularly in the framework of national accounting, the public sector financial deficit (PSFD). The PSFD is the balance of public sector current and capital transactions combined and represents the net acquisition (positive or negative) of financial assets by the public sector.

PSBR forecasts are prepared by the Treasury and are built up from detailed assessments of receipts and payments provided from other sources by, for example, the Inland Revenue, Customs and Excise, and The Department of Social Security. While an attempt is made to build in all the information available the forecasts can go wrong for a number of reasons. Economic developments may be forecast incorrectly as certain elements of public sector expenditure and income are sensitive to upturns or downturns in the economy. These elements would include taxes on income, expenditure taxes and social security payments. Even if aggregate economic development may be predicted accurately there may be a failure at a lower level to translate this information correctly by sector. A changing pattern of consumption might affect VAT receipts for example. Another problem is concerned with the timing of the receipt of income and the payment of bills which can represent unpredictable variations. Finally, unforeseen receipts and payments, which may be large and are clearly unpredictable, may result in forecasting errors.

If the Health Service is taken as a specific receiver of funds the authority will receive its capital allocation and draw down funds as needed from the Department of Health. Bank balances are required to be kept to a minimum (while avoiding overdrafts). There is no question of investing money received in advance of requirements although this is permitted for self-governing trusts within the NHS.

Local authority borrowing

Here we are explicitly concerned with raising long-term loans to finance capital expenditure. As has been seen, in the case of some public sector organizations, such as the NHS, there is currently no borrowing. Local authorities, however, are heavily involved in these transactions which require fairly considerable skills in debt management.

General powers that permit local authorities to borrow for capital purposes are contained within Schedule 13 of the Local Government Act 1972. It is no exaggeration to state that the controls on borrowing by local authorities have effectively determined the accounting system employed since the ability to hold permanent debt is denied to them. Under Schedule 13 all loans are secured on the revenues of the authority and each year the authority must raise sufficient in local taxation to cover repayments of principal and interest which must then be charged to the annual revenue account.

7.4   Finance from reserves

Financing from reserves involves using sources of finance that have been built up in the past. The reserves may have been built up from a variety of sources such as contributions from revenue, the sale of assets, or charitable contributions and bequests. The advantage of such reserves is that they isolate the organization from a harsh outside world which may be characterized by high interest rates. In addition, they avoid the costs associated with servicing and managing debt.

They may also be useful as a means of adding to the volume of capital required to support a capital expenditure programme. At one time local authorities used them in this fashion, although this is now barred to them. Indeed, the Local Government and Housing Act 1989 repealed the general power to set up separate funds such as a capital fund. In their place, local authorities adopted commercial practice of setting up reserves and provisions. Apart from relatively insignificant charitable trust funds, they are not currently found in the NHS or in central government generally. Capital reserves are found in the private sector. If such reserves are represented by funds, then pending investment, it is usual to invest such reserves, the interest and dividends from the investments accruing to the reserve fund, such as happens with a superannuation fund.

There is one other specific instance where reserves may be established to provide for future capital expenditure; this is where outgoing are irregular, but it is desired to regularize their impact on the organization. For example, in a programme of vehicle replacement, one way of smoothing the impact of irregular purchases of vehicles is to charge the expenditure to a designated renewals provision, the revenue account making regular transfers to the provision. Of course, there will be other ways of smoothing the expenditure, notably by a planned replacement programme which avoids peaks and troughs in replacement or via a programme of leasing vehicles.

Finally, when the reserve is an organization-wide reserve and not built up for a specific purpose, a policy has to be determined regarding repayment of advances from reserves. The advantage of repayments is that the value of reserves is maintained. Additionally, in order that no one service benefits at the expense of others, it would seem essential that interest is paid to the reserve fund. Then, it would be necessary to determine what rate of interest to prescribe; in order to preserve the neutrality of the reserve, it would seem appropriate to select a rate of interest close to that which other new non-reserve loans are paying. By doing this, the organization as a whole may benefit, as no outside borrowing takes place (although the opportunity to invest outside is lost!), but no one service benefits compared with another.

7.5   Financing by leasing

Leasing involves use of an asset, under agreed terms and with agreed payments, but without ownership. It is extensive within the private sector, having enjoyed a boom in the 1980s, initially the result of favourable tax treatment of lessors, following from a much longer term development in the United States. However, its use is significantly limited within the wider public sector within the United Kingdom; although prevalent within local authorities, until recently its use was proscribed within the National Health Service and it enjoys very limited use within Central Government generally. As far as local authorities are concerned, there is no specific statutory authority for leasing but these transactions are a well-established method of finance and are *intra vires*, although the government has stepped in to regulate certain aspects of leasing arrangements entered into by local authorities with particular reference to land and property.

The principal advantages of leases are twofold:

1. They can provide a source of finance, when others are limited at very competitive rates.
2. They are very flexible and can provide levels of service at the lessees specification, with low or no risk.

The basic types of lease agreement are discussed below.

Land and property leasing

There are three types of lease. The first is *lease/leaseback*. Under this type of scheme the public authority first requires a site and then develops it with money provided by the investor. The investor leases the land from the authority at a peppercorn (minimal) rent, and then subleases the development back to the authority at an agreed economic rent.

The second type is *sale/leaseback*. Again, the public authority acquires a site, sells the site to the investor or developer who then leases the complete development back to the authority.

The third type is *deferred purchase*. In this type of transaction the organization enters into an agreement to buy a development over a period of time and reimburses the investor the funding costs. Title remains with the investor until the final payment.

In each of the above cases, a public authority has access to a developer or investor who provides the required development, at the authority's specification, when the authority's ability to enter the conventional lending market may be curtailed by, for example, constraints imposed by central government. To finance from revenue would be prohibitive, in terms of the impact on local taxation, and property leasing deals offer a way forward.

They have been in use for over 20 years in the United Kingdom, but during the 1980s gained a poor reputation as they because associated with 'creative financing'. Thus, for example, one local authority sold assets such as bus shelters and public conveniences to an investor; the investor paid up-front cash for the assets, which the authority could designate as capital receipts, and use to finance much needed capital development elsewhere. In return, the local authority agreed to lease back its former assets from the developer over a period of time. This was regarded as a classic piece of 'live now, pay later' financial chicanery, and from 1988 the use of such financing vehicles required the approval of the Secretary of State.

However, the general property leaseback idea does have a noteworthy track record an may represent a source of finance for self-governing hospital trusts within the competitive structure now found in the NHS.

Equipment leasing

There are basically three types of equipment lease available. These are finance leases, contract hire and operating leases.

Under a finance lease the substantial risks and rewards of ownership are transferred to the lessee for the life of the asset. The lessor covers his finance charges and capital costs in the initial primary period. The lessee bears all maintenance charges. At the end of the lease the asset is sold to a third party with any income as a lease rebate to the lessee. A secondary period may be available normally at a nominal percentage of original purchase price.

The lessee's payments are rental in nature but the purchase price of the asset counts against the government's capital controls on local authorities.

Under an operating lease the lessee pays an economic rent to the lessor who takes all the risks and benefits of ownership. Operating leases do not count against capital controls on local authorities as it is felt that they effectively represent revenue expenditure. There are, however, specific requirements for local authorities and these include:

1. the residual value does not accrue to the local authority;
2. the property of the asset does not transfer to the authority at the end of the lease;
3. a renewal or extension of the lease is not made at materially less than the market rent.

Contract hire agreements are a straightforward rental agreement whereby the user agrees to rent the asset for a fixed period at a fixed sum. Ownership and all the ongoing risks remain with the lessor and, while the terms of each agreement vary, the lessor assumes responsibility for running costs (excluding fuels and oils) and arranging replacements in the event of breakdown. If supported by an operating lease contract hire agreements do not count against capital expenditure controls on local authorities.

For direct service organizations, and for any organization within the public sector needing to obtain a specified return on capital employed within the new competitive environment, a major advantage is that leased assets do not form part of capital employed as ownership remains with the lessor.

Consider the example in Figure 7.2. The organization concerned must obtain a return of 5% on assets employed. As can be seen from the 'Assets owned' column, it is highly marginal with a return of just 4.6%, which could endanger its continued existence. Faced with this problem, and encouraged by central government wishing to see sales of public sector surplus assets, the plant is leased under an operating lease, it no longer forms part of the organization's capital and return on capital increases to 27.5%.

Indeed, faced with competitive legislation, many local authorities have separated direct service organization (DSOs) from plant ownership, locating

	Assets owned £m	Assets owned and leased £m
Assets employed		
Buildings	0.2	0.2
Plant	1.0	
Totals	1.2	0.2
Operating income	2.955	2.955
Operating costs		
Operating expenditure	2.7	2.7
Depreciation (20% Plant)	0.2	
Lease charge (20% Plant)		0.2
	2.9	2.9
Net Profit	0.055	0.055
Return on assets	0.055/1.2 = 4.6%	0.055/0.2 = 27.5%

Figure 7.2 *Effect of leasing on return of assets.*

the latter as a separate commercial unit, leasing out its vehicles and plant to those DSOs wishing to make use of them; reinforcing the commercial principle, the lessor unit is itself required to make a specified 5% return on capital employed.

7.6 Capital expenditure controls and local authorities

It will be apparent from what has been said above that local authorities are subject to particularly tight central government controls on their capital expenditure and its financing.

Prior to April 1990, the system of control in operation had been introduced under the Local Government Planning and Land Act 1980, which came into force on 1 April 1981. These controls specified that for each authority the Secretary of State would detail 'prescribed' capital expenditure and the amount which each authority could spend on capital expenditure, termed its capital allocation. Capital expenditure had to be contained within the total capital allocation for each authority, subject to a tolerance of 10%; any further under-spend would be lost. The capital allocation could also be enhance by using capital receipts (cash raised by selling assets). In most cases, 50% of the capital receipt could be spent in the year of receipt with 50% of the remaining balance in teach successive year – termed the 'cascade effect'.

The pre-1990 system was criticized on a variety of grounds, and to give a flavour of these, the following are included:

1. It operated on a short one-year planning cycle with no commitment to future years and fostered uncertainty when long-term planning was needed.
2. It had contributed to a decline in the quality of capital stock, especially in education, with insufficient allocations for adequate replacement and maintenance.
3. The system was extremely costly and complex to implement.

The Local Government and Housing Act 1989 introduced a revised system of control with effect from 1 April 1990. The new system has the following features:

Credit approvals

The Act states that local authorities will be given 'credit approvals' which will limit, to the value of the credit approval, the amount of capital expenditure which can be met from borrowing or other credit arrangements such as leases. There are two types of credit approval: a basic credit approval (BCA) which can be used at the discretion of the authority, and a specified credit approval (SCA) which may be used for projects specified by the Secretary of State. There is no provision for tolerance between years; if an authority under-spends, it loses that spending power.

The credit approval may be supplemented by a proportion of capital receipts, and by meeting capital expenditure from revenue. Revenue financing is limited by capping and, politically, by the amount which the council tax payer will agree to pay.

Capital receipts

In determining the BCA, the Secretary of State will take into account his assessment of available capital receipts. However, a proportion of capital receipts received must be set aside for redemption of debt (currently 75% of receipts regarding the sale of council dwellings, and 50% of other capital receipts). The non-reserved part of capital receipts, for example the 25% part of the amount received from the sale of council dwellings, can be used to finance capital expenditure over and above that covered by credit approvals. The cascade interpretation applied to the previous legislation is now prohibited so that the initial discretionary 25% (say) is fixed and none of the balance can subsequently be converted to discretionary use.

It is possible, as occurred in 1992 and 1993, that the Secretary of State may announce a temporary moratorium on the prescribed use of new capital receipts.

Leases

Operating leases relating to vehicles, plant and equipment are not charged against the credit approvals. However, new property leases will count against the credit approvals based upon the capitalized value of the payments to be made under the lease approval.

The 1989 legislation represents a change from that imposed under the Local Government Planning and Land Act 1980 when the nature of the expenditure itself was controlled rather than the source of finance.

7.7 Capital expenditure controls and the National Health Service

Capital expenditure in the National Health Service (NHS) is a small proportion of total expenditure, and it is initially distributed by central government to regional health authorities; the regions retain a proportion for the funding of regional schemes and distribute the balance to the (district) health authorities and any non-trust hospitals. Trusts are outside this system. Health authorities are purchasers within the competitive framework, and the hospitals are the providers. By 31 March 1994 all providers will have become hospital trusts. Thus, regions and health authorities are given a capital allocation for the year; unlike the local authority case, this actually represents cash to be spent.

There are certain tolerances allowed on the capital expenditure which is allocated to regions and health authorities:

1. Up to 10% of the allocation may be carried forward from one year to the next.
2. Up to 10% of the capital allocation may be transferred to the Revenue allocation, and up to 1% of the revenue allocation may be transferred to capital.

In addition to these tolerances, there is one further important element of flexibility. Perrin, in Henley et al. (1992), explains that health authority treasurers operate a capital 'brokerage' system coordinated by the regional treasurers. A authority may be unable to use all its capital allocation because of project slippage. Alternatively, it may have to slow down capital development because it cannot cope with the revenue consequences as soon as was originally planned. In either case, it can waive part of its capital allocation back into the regional pool of capital for 'brokerage' to some other authority that can use the capital in the current year. In return, the first authority will receive favourable consideration at some later date if it needs some extra capital. In effect, this is a form of inter-authority loan scheme, interest free.

NHS trusts

The controls on trusts are fairly stringent. Every March each trust must submit a business plan to the NHS Management Executive (NHSME). The trust must include within the business plan justification for capital expenditure and include plans for its financing. Trusts must normally fund capital expenditure from their own resources or by borrowing, which is subject to constraint. Thus a trust's capital authorizations are obtained through this project appraisal process and the amount of borrowing available in total is determined by the outcome of the Public Expenditure Survey process. Until trusts have access to private capital, their capital expenditure proposals will be subject to similar constraints as operated in the pre-trust era. Additionally, the trusts are subject to two further constraints which have a connection with capital expenditure:

1. They must earn a 6% rate of return on capital employed. Depreciation is charged in their accounts and their income must cover all costs, including depreciation, and earn the rate of return. The income of Trusts is obtained by contracting with the purchasing health authorities and general practitioner fundholders within the competitive health environment.
2. Each trust is subject to an annual External Financial Limit (EFL). This control limits the total externally generated finance available to a trust; therefore, it acts as a constraint on a trust's ability to borrow. In total EFLs derive from the annual public expenditure round and if EFLs for individual trusts become increasingly tight, trusts must look at their own internal resources to reduce calls on external finance and examine factors such as increased efficiency, reductions in inventories, and sale of assets such as surplus land. It is possible to have a zero EFL which implies that all capital expenditure must be financed from internal sources. A trust's ability to keep within its EFL while continuing to provide value for money is keenly monitored by the NHSME.

7.8 Special topic 1: Setting a borrowing strategy

In this section we examine some of the key variables in the establishment of a borrowing strategy; the organization chosen as a vehicle for demonstrating this is a local authority because, currently, they are one of the few types of public sector organizations which take an active role in debt management.

First, we look at the types of borrowing, or the range of borrowing instruments, that are available to the local authority treasurer. The types of borrowing that a local authority may undertake include:

Short-term (less than 12 months)

Short-term borrowing for capital purposes is termed 'temporary borrowing' and includes the range from borrowing overnight to borrowing for up to a year. The money is usually cheaper than longer term finance because it is at risk for a shorter period of time, and provides an important source of finance when long-term interest rates are high. If interest rates high, borrowing short-term is very advantageous because it does not commit the organization to high interest rates over a long period. Regular short-term borrowing provides an entree to contacts in the money markets which will permit the lending of temporary surpluses of cash.

However, it is volatile, in that some forms of temporary money are repayable on demand, and temporary borrowing may require refinancing when interest rates are high. Finally, the amount of temporary borrowing that an organization can take is limited by legislation.

Medium term (one to five years)

Local bonds

These are usually sold to the general public and the amounts involved are often relatively small in capital financing terms; they are deliberately flexible in structure with a flexibility over term, dates for interest payments, and a relationship between interest rates offered and the size of the loan. A register is maintained by the local authority and, as with building societies, interest is paid net of standard rate income tax except in the case of investors on a low income to whom interest may be paid gross.

Negotiable bonds

These are concerned with larger sums than local bonds and are sold in large tranches on the money market; they offer same-day transferability, and this advantage confers lower rates of interest. However, an issue is an expensive exercise.

Long-term (over five years)

Public Works Loans Board

Local authorities have access to borrowing from the Public Works Loans Board (PWLB), which allows access to funds raised by central government. The money is usually very long term with a minimum period of 10 years and, in theory a marginally attractive rate of interest is available on loans that do not exceed an authority's given quota.

Stock

This is issued, and traded on the London Stock exchange, in common with government and corporate stock. The amounts involved are very substantial, as are the fixed costs of issue, which mean that organizations may form into consortia in order to secure the cost advantages of a large-scale issue. There is a queuing system for issue, and a considerable amount of time is required to organize a stock issue.

Apart from these, there are a variety of other loans available from the market, and among the most popular are variable or floating rate bonds; these are medium and long-term loans with the interest rate tied to underlying short-term interest rates (the London Inter-Bank Offer Rate – LIBOR) but adjusted by previous agreement. Thus, the interest rate may be adjusted annually or more frequently.

The variety of loan packages on offer means that discounted cash flow (DCF) techniques need to be employed to identify the true interest rate that a loan carries. DCF is discussed in Chapter 9.

Constraints on borrowing

As has been indicated above, the volume of temporary borrowing available to an authority is subject to control by legislation. We have also seen that total annual borrowing is subject to the ceiling imposed in the BAC.

Additionally, for some years, following Treasury pressure, local authorities have agreed to organize their borrowing in excess of one year to meet certain *minima* within the Voluntary Code of Borrowing; the overall effect of these *minima* is that authorities must have an average loan period on borrowing of seven years.

In summary, the position is highly complex with a range of borrowing instruments, costs of administration and rates of interest, with constant changes in overall rates of interest, with financing required for both new capital expenditure and for refinancing of debt. To compound it all, there are the three constraining factors noted immediately above.

We now examine the application of the above to a problem of borrowing policy within a local authority.

Scenario

At the 30 December, 19–0 the Assistant Director of Finance of the Loanshire County Council is considering the borrowing policy for the remainder of the financial year. The position on interest rates is that they have fallen by about 2% since April 19–0, but are now expected to increase in view of the inflationary outlook. The composition of current outstanding debt is shown in Table 7.4. The estimated borrowing requirement, excluding the refinancing of temporary debt, is shown in Table 7.5. The loans which are expected to be

Table 7.4 The composition of current debt

	£m
Stock	15.00
Fixed rate bonds	24.08
Variable rate bonds	21.00
PWLB loans	73.60
Temporary loans (£28.5m repayable by 31.3.19–1)	31.50
Total (average rate of interest 10.8%)	165.18

Table 7.5 Estimated borrowing requirements

Jan/March	19–1	–1/–2	–2/–3	–3/–4	–4/–5	–5/–6
£m	5.4	14.5	38.7	13.4	25.9	33.0

available during the next three months are as summarised in Figure 7.3. The authority's temporary loan debt is limited to £25m at 31 March 19–1.

The authority also aim for an average of seven years on all debt raised in a year to maintain the overall average loan period of outstanding debt. The long-term debt raised during 19–0/–1 thus far has been as follows:

£17.5m PWLB 10-year instalment
£1.0m Fixed interest rate bonds for two years
£1.0m Fixed interest rate bonds for three years

Type of loan	Amount	Terms		
PWLB	£2.5M	12% 10 year 12.5% 25 year		
Fixed and variable rate bonds	Unlimited	Interest rates		
		Years	Fixed	Variable 3-month + rate
			%	%
		1	11.5	
		2	11.75	.75
		3	12	1
		4	12.125	1 1/16
		5	12.25	1.124
		6	12.375	1.25
		7	12.5	1.5
		8	12.5	1.5
Temporary Loans	Unlimited	< 3 months		11.25%
		3 months +		11.375%

Figure 7.3 *Loans available during the next three months.*

Discussion

Faced with this scenario, the matters which the Assistant Treasurer is likely to be concerned with are discussed below.

Increasing interest rates

Interest rates have been declining but are expected to increase. In itself this would lead to long-term borrowing, but this is mitigated by the fact that at 11/12% long-term interest rates are still relatively high. Presumably then, one would advocate borrowing for a period of, say, three years, allowing time for interest rates to rise and then fall, hopefully to below today's levels.

Future borrowing needs

The previous recommendation is reinforced by the need to borrow £38.7m in two years time which would lead one to avoid any further borrowing for refinancing of debt during that financial year. On the other hand, the estimate for 19–3/19–4 shows a much lower level of borrowing. Later years shown an increase in borrowing well above the 19–3/19–4 level.

The next three months

£28.5m of the temporary loans will need to be refinanced by 31 March 19–1. However, the temporary loan ceiling is £25m; this means that after allowing for £3m re the loans which do not require refinancing (£31.5m–£28.5m), there is £22m of temporary loans available. This leaves £6.5m which must be found from non-temporary sources.

Non-temporary borrowing will amount to £11.9m for the next three months, made up of £6.5m from the temporary shortfall plus £5.4m of new borrowing.

The average loan period

The debt raised so far this year provides an average loan period of 18.7 years. The calculations underlying this are contained in Figure 7.4.

```
                          Loans
                          £
                          17.5m   *   10 years  =   175m  loan years
                          1m      *   1 year    =   1m    loan years
                          1m      *   2 years   =   2m    loan years
                          ─────                      ─────
    Totals                19.5m                      178m  loan years
                          ─────                      ─────
    Weighted average loan years = 178/9.5 = 18.7 years
```

Figure 7.4 *The calculation of the average loan period.*

The authority is aiming for a minimum average of seven loan years on current borrowing; with an additional £11.9m of non-temporary money required, all of that borrowing can be over three years without pulling the overall average below seven years.

Variable and fixed rate bonds

The choice between variable and fixed rate bonds is a difficult one but if the whole spectrum of interest rates are going to increase, they will probably stay above current levels for at least a year which may push the future variable rate up above the current fixed term rate. However, if interest rates fall, the future variable rate may fall to below the current fixed rate. There is no correct answer to this problem; it depends on economic forecasts and one's attitude to risk.

Conclusion

In conclusion, the following policy represents one way forward:

1. replace 'temporary' with 'temporary up to the ceiling of £25m',
2. fund the remaining requirement with three year fixed interest rate bonds.

7.9 Special topic 2: A property leaseback deal

The bare bones of a leaseback deal have been outlined above. In this section we look more deeply into the dynamics of such an arrangement. A summary of the steps involved in such a deal is contained in Figure 7.5.

```
Public Body                              Developer

  1.  Acquires site

  2.  Commissions a design
                                 3.  Finances the development

  4.  Leases the site to the
      developer, at a peppercorn
                                 5.  Subleases the site back to the public body
```

Figure 7.5 *The main steps in a lease-leaseback deal.*

As may be seen in Fig. 7.5, it is the public authority's responsibility to acquire the site in the first place and then to commission a design for the scheme that it wants. The developer provides sufficient finance to construct the development, including the original costs of site acquisition and design, if necessary. When the site is fully developed, the public authority leases the site to the developer at a nominal rent termed a 'peppercorn'. The developer than subleases the scheme to the public authority at a rental which is initially related to the amount of finance advanced by the developer. This final step gives it the term lease-leaseback.

Usually, the finance required to construct the development is advanced in stages by the developer, often with floors and ceilings relating to the amounts to be advanced, so that the funding company can manage its own cash flows efficiently. Any drawings outside these limits may be subject to a penalty clause. Such advances normally accrue or 'roll up' compound interest which is added to the total of monies advanced.

The payments to the developer will commence on completion of the project and will be established, as a minimum, at $x\%$ of the total of the amount advanced plus rolled up interest. The initial total annual payment is known as the 'finance rent'.

The finance rent is usually subject to review at regular intervals and may well be tied to the growth in rental value of the actual development. The sub-lease may specify that the developer may have a share in the equity of the development with the 'equity sharing ratio' accruing to the developer being set at:

$$\frac{\text{Finance rent}}{\text{Initial market rental value for the development}}$$

Therefore, subject to the floor set by the finance rent, the developer can expect to see income rising with rental values.

The advantages to a public sector organization of this type of agreement is that the management and control of the organization rests with them, as do any risks associated with the development. The financier is shielded by the finance rent from a downturn in returns.

Of course, if the public sector body wants to share more equally in the fruits of its own commercial management, it should strive to minimize the amounts advanced by the financier and, therefore, the equity-sharing ratio. This would require the contribution of finance from its own internal resources.

In the past, such deals have been arranged for the purpose of financing buildings such as civic and commercial centres and, in the future, could be used to finance a variety of greenfield areas such as, for example, car parking and luxury private bed provision at hospitals.

7.10   Special topic 3: Derivatives

The term 'derivatives' refers to financial instruments which derive from primary instruments such as loans. Here three types of derivative are examined:

1. interest rate swaps;
2. financial futures;
3. options.

Interest rate swaps

During the 1980s interest rate swaps were a rapidly growing activity in the United States, and were used by several local authorities in the United Kingdom during the latter half of the 1980s. Swaps have largely arisen as a means by which organizations can gain access to borrowing on more favourable terms than could be achieved with direct borrowing.

Basically, a swap may be defined as a transaction in which two borrowers agree to borrow equal amounts of principal, from different lenders, and then make interest payments which are unrelated to the direct borrowing of each.

Swaps exist because different organizations can borrow at different rates of interest in different markets. They frequently involve swaps between fixed interest rate loans and floating rate loans, where the interest is tied to an underlying short-term rate such as the London Inter Bank Offer Rate (LIBOR).

There are many variations on the swap idea, but for illustration, the simple or orthodox swap is as follows. Suppose that one borrower is local authority X which can borrow fixed interest rate money fairly cheaply but wants access to floating rate loans because it feels that interest rates will fall. Borrower Y is a company which is able to raise floating rate funds very cheaply but wants to raise fixed rate loans and secure itself to the current interest rate for a long period.

The current situation is shown in Figure 7.6. Next we shall consider how each party may benefit from the relative advantage obtained by the other.

Considering Figure 7.6, X and Y make an agreement with each other; X will borrow £10m fixed for five years at 10%, Y will borrow £10m floating five years at 8%. Each also agrees to pay the interest due on the loan raised by the other: X pays floating rate interest at 8%, Y pays fixed rate interest at 10%. Each gains as follows:

X: annual gain (9% – 8%) * £10m = £100 000
Y: annual gain (11% – 10%) * £10m = £100 000.

Thus, each organization borrows in the manner that it desires and in each case at 1% below the interest rate available to it.

A public authority	A company
Borrower X	Borrower Y
Available:	Available:
£10m, fixed 5 year, 10%	£10m, fixed 5 year, 11%
£10m, floating 5 year, 9%	£10m, floating 5 year, 8%

Figure 7.6 *The initial position.*

Local authorities have used swaps as a method of reducing the interest cost of debt or in order to hedge against a fall in interest rates which also serves to reduce interest costs.

However, the case of Hammersmith and Fulham had a significant effect on the dealings of local authorities with the banks and other financial institutions in relation to interest rate swaps. The Court of Appeal decided that interest rate swap transactions were capable of being in the power of local authorities as long as they were undertaken for the purposes of interest risk management and not for trading purposes. Thus under the swap principle local authorities would be able to swap fixed rate debt for variable rate debt as long as they are able to show that the transaction is to further normal investment management. The judgement in the Hammersmith and Fulham case was that the council's transactions between 1983 and July 1988 were illegal in that they were entered into for trading purposes and contravened section 19 of the Local Government Act 1972. The House of Lords subsequently ruled that swaps were *ultra vires* and therefore unavailable to local authorities. This ruling meant that local authorities were precluded from getting the best out of prevailing interest rates which must increase the overall costs of borrowing. This ruling had important implications for the banks as transactions which they had entered into with local authorities were now deemed illegal and several banks made significant provisions for losses within their accounts following the House of Lords ruling.

Financial futures

Financial futures are contracts to buy or sell a standard quantity of a financial instrument at a predetermined future date but at a price agreed now. The financial instrument may be an interest rate on a five year loan or a stock market index, for example. Within the United Kingdom the heart of the market in financial futures is the London International Financial Futures and Options Exchange (LIFFE). Local authority superannuation funds have power to use these under the Local Government Superannuation Regulations 1986.

The main function of futures is to protect the fund and reduce risk. One illustration of this is the use of futures to guarantee the purchaser of a specific interest rate at some predetermined future date. If a financial manager expects interest rates to increase but this sentiment is not shared by the market then a future can be used to ensure that funds are available in the future at current market rates of interest.

Future contracts must be completed and a pension fund, say, must be able to fulfil the contract. In practice, completion is assured by both buyer and seller depositing a small initial margin as a form of security. Then, each day the gain or loss on the futures contract is calculated within the clearing system and is settled up by whichever party needs to make the payment.

Options

These are financial instruments which give the buyer the right but not the obligation to buy or sell the underlying asset at an agreed price (termed the exercise or strike price) and within a specified time period. The underlying assets might be a quantity of shares in a company, an amount of a loan at a future interest rate or a quantity of an underlying market index such as the *Financial Times* stock exchange list of the top 100 firms on the London Stock Exchange known as (FTSE100). Thus, options differ from futures on one very important respect; with a future the buyer has to complete the deal whereas with an option the buyer is not obligated to complete the deal. However, the seller of the option does have an obligation to complete the transaction if the buyer wishes to exercise the right to complete.

Options are of two types:

1. Call options which give the buyer the right to buy the underlying asset.
2. Put options which give the buyer the right to sell the underlying asset.

The buyer of the option pays a small premium to the seller or writer of the option contract. This premium is retained by the writer of the option and is used to defray expenses and compensate for the risk involved in writing options.

There is a traded market for options which is regulated by LIFFE but options have existed for considerably longer than the organized market. Options which are bought and sold on the organized LIFFE market are termed traded options; they offer standardization in terms of quantity represented by one option contract (for example, 1000 shares) and in terms of duration of the contract. Standardization provides for an organized market and it is possible for the purchaser of an option to resell the option. Premium prices and exercise prices for traded options are quoted on a daily basis in the press. The risks and rewards for traded options differ as between the different parties. The risk of buyers is limited to the premium price which has been paid. The gain to writers of options is limited to the premium received but potential losses can be substantial because the writer has an obligation to complete the contract if called upon to do so by the buyer.

As with futures, call options may be purchased in order to protect the fund against anticipated price rises. A fund manager should not consider writing call options unless it holds the underlying asset so that the fund can settle the option from existing resources if the option is exercised.

It is important that fund managers have adequate understanding and experience if they are going to take advantage of the opportunities offered by options. It is also essential that there are sound control systems in place.

7.11 Summary

Local authorities can finance capital expenditure in a number of ways although the use of capital funds has recently been withdrawn from them. The latest method of central government control constrains the total of annual capital expenditure via the system of credit approvals. The total can be enhanced by a defined proportion of capital receipts and by financing from revenue. In local authorities the management of loans and the use of leases are well developed.

Central government uses a combination of borrowing, revenue (taxation primarily) and the receipts from asset sales and privatizations. Leasing plays a very minor role.

The NHS currently receives a capital allocation from central government; this allocation is effectively cash for capital expenditure. No borrowing is permitted. There is some flexibility at the margin via the capital/revenue and inter-year tolerances and this is increased by the brokerage system implemented by NHS treasurers. Currently, trusts have little flexibility in the area of capital finance. However, in future we may see them looking at borrowing strategies, leaseback and derivatives. As we have seen, these represent ways of reducing the costs of borrowing while leaseback is a way of bringing private sector funds into the public sector in a joint financing approach.

Questions

7.1 You are the loans officer for a small district council responsible, under the Treasurer, for managing the borrowing and lending activities of the authority. Your Treasurer has recently been appointed after a career in the Health Services.

  (i)   Write a note to the Treasurer about your job.

                                                          (13 marks)

        Include in your answer:
        (a) The objectives your are seeking to achieve.
        (b) An outline of the constraints under which you work.
        (c) A summary of the information you require at various stages to do your job.

(ii) How would your recommend that your performance should be evaluated; for example, who should receive reports on your activities and what should be the contents of these reports?

(5 marks)
(Total 18 marks)

7.2 Contrast the methods of capital finance available to a health authority and a local authority.

7.3 Prepare a reply to the following letter:

16 Bramble Villas
Goodtown
25 September 19X0

The Treasurer
Good Health Authority

Dear Sir

Annual Accounts

I have just seen a copy of your annual accounts for 19X9/X0 and I feel that you and your staff have made some elementary errors.
These are as follows:

(a) I have myself visited the Good Health General Hospital recently, and I note from a plaque that it was opened in 19X8. Yet you seem, somehow, to have forgotten to include this asset in your balance sheet.
(b) As far as I can see, you have neglected to provide for depreciation in your accounts.

I look forward to your explanation.

Yours faithfully

Ian M Expert

7.4 Set out the principal arguments for a policy of pay-as-you-go rather than a policy of financing through borrowing.

7.5 Contrast the capital controls on health authorities with those on local authorities.

7.6 Prepare a short memorandum setting out the principal factors to be considered in establishing a borrowing policy at the current time.

7.7 A developer is financing a project via a leaseback deal. The developer makes the following advances of cash:

1 April 19X1	£500 000
1 October 19X1	£500 000

The project is completed on 31 March 19X2. It is agreed that the developer is to be credited with interest on advances at the rate of 20%, compounded each six months, and added to the total advanced on 31 March 19X2.

Required

Calculate the developer's total financial interest in the project at 31 March 19X2.

7.8   Indicate how interest rate swaps may be of value to both the following parties:

Authority A	*Company B*
Funds available:	*Funds available:*
£25m fixed ten-year 11%	£25m fixed ten-year 12%
£25m floating ten-year 10.5%	£25m floating ten-year 9%
Funds required:	*Funds required:*
£25m floating	£25m fixed

7.9   Glamshire (Cars) Ltd a subsidiary company of Glamshire Council are considering the correct method of financing their car fleet.

Michael Morris, the Group Accountant, has narrowed the choices down to two.

1. Purchase the fleet outright.
2. Lease the fleet on contract hire (with maintenance) basis – an operating fleet.

He had spent some time gathering information which he felt was relevant to the decision in hand:

General information

(i)   Cost of capital – 15%.
(ii)   Corporation Tax – 35%.
(iii)   Capital Allowances on fleet purchase to be 25% reducing balance.
(iv)   Corporation Tax to be payable one year from end of accounting year to which it relates.
(v)   There are six major costs of acquiring and operating a fleet, finance, insurance, maintenance, fuel, incidentals and management.
(vi)   The fleet of vehicles to be acquired would be 17 Ford cars ranging from the Sierra 2.0i Ghia to the Escort 1.3L 5 door estate.
(vii)   Useful life of fleet three years before replacement. Straight Line Depreciation is used for the outright purchase option.
(viii) Costs relate to best quotes obtained for each option.
(ix)   Cash flows deemed to arise as follows:
Initial Purchase price – year 0.
Lease Payments – at *beginning* of each year in which they occur. All other payments – at end of each year which they occur.
(x)   Ignore inflation.

Company	Evans Hailshaw	Lease Plan
Method of Finance	Purchase	Contract Hire
	£	£
Purchase Price (*Total*)	141 132	N/A
Monthly Lease/Hire Payments	N/A	6052
Residual Value after 3 years	58 343	N/A
Insurance per *vehicle* per *year*	1000	inclusive
Total maintenance over 3 years	21 219	inclusive
Total petrol over 3 years	47 850	inclusive
Total incidentals over 3 years	16 173	51 000
Total management charge over 3 years	9750	1950

Note: that the management charge is calculated as follows:

Number of hours required × fully absorbed cost per hour.

The fully absorbed cost per hour is £13, made up as follows:

	£
wages of fleet manager(ess)	5
pension and wages cost	2
admin. overhead	5
provision of car	1
	£13

*These figures are based on a manager(ess) having to spend 1/3 of their time (1/15 in the case of contract hire) managing the car fleet.

Required

(a) Evaluate the options open to management, taking taxation into account but ignoring inflation, and carefully explaining your treatment of the management charge.

(b) Which would you recommend, taking into account the advantages and disadvantages of each method of financing?

(c) One advantage of contract hire is that more of your costs are certain. How would it be possible to put some sort of monetary value on this? (You are not required to do any calculations).

8 ▷ Capital budgets and capital programmes

Key learning objectives

After reading this chapter you should be able to:

1. Identify the problems of defining capital expenditure in the public sector.
2. Prepare a capital programme and demonstrate its benefits to managers.
3. Explain, critically, how projects are screened and selected.
4. Calculate the revenue consequences of a project.
5. Explain one way in which financial and non-financial factors may be combined in project appraisal.

Capital expenditure by Central Government, the NHS and the Local Authority sector runs currently at about £30bn per annum. Within the different sectors, there must exist systems for appraising, organizing, financing and controlling such investment. It is important that the correct capital investment decision is taken as poor decisions can have the following consequences:

1. They can lead to investments in assets which give no productive benefit and, due to the large scale, and sometimes specialist nature of some projects, may have no alternative use. The resale value, if any, may bear little relationship to actual cost.
2. In those areas of the public sector subject to competitive tendering, incorrect investment will increase costs with no obvious improvements in efficiency or output, leading to reduced profits or even losses which, if sufficiently large, could ultimately close the operation down.
3. In the more traditional service areas of the public sector such as health, social services and education, the incorrect investment decision will place increased costs on the taxpayer. This could prove particularly important in local authorities given the potential impact of the council tax, in that the commitment of the government is to increase the business rate and revenue support grants by no more than the retail price

index. This will inevitably place a greater burden on the local taxpayer resulting from specific local authority inflation or local authority service increases that are not in line with central government's expectations. The relationship between local increases in expenditure and the resulting disproportionate increase in local taxation is termed the gearing effect.

All capital investment decisions should be taken within a framework which identifies a specific need for a project within the stated objectives of the organization. In the private sector the objective of all projects is usually the maximization of profit. Within the competitive arms of the public sector any investment decision must contribute towards the stated target rate of return. For example, in a capital works unit of a local authority where the return is expressed as a 5% return on the current cost of capital employed the selected project must achieve at least this return. A similar requirement would apply to NHS trusts which have to achieve a return of 6%. Where the target is expressed in terms of income equalling expenditure at a minimum the project should be at least self-financing. Where no stated target exists any project should contribute to maximizing service delivery by improving economy, efficiency and effectiveness.

8.1 The definition of capital expenditure

Within the private sector, a fixed asset is defined according to the nature of the expenditure, its materiality and whether it confers benefits beyond the current accounting period. In the case of local government, a similar approach is taken, with capital expenditure being regarded as any outlay which is of value to the authority in the provision of its services beyond the end of the year of account. It is then recorded as a capital asset provided there are no legal constraints. Capital outlays which are very small in relation to the general magnitude of such outlays may be recorded in an aggregate minor capital assets account. Capital outlays which are not material to the size and nature of the local authority or which could be consumed in the following accounting period are disregarded in the asset accounts. Within the NHS and other sections of central government, rules are specified as to the type and scale of the expenditure. Thus, at the time of writing, capital expenditure the NHS is specified as expenditure in excess of £5000 giving benefit for more than one year.

Within the private sector, fixed assets are normally depreciated, ensuring that the profit and loss account bears a charge for the use of the assets and thereby restricting distributable profit and maintaining the organization's original capital. Within local authorities, currently, fixed assets are recorded, but are not depreciated; the charge to the revenue accounts is a reflection of how the asset has been financed by the local authority: for example, if the asset is financed by loan, the Local Government Act 1972 specifies that the interest and principal repayments are charged to the revenue accounts as the loan is repaid. Other methods of financing are: by a direct charge to revenue; from earmarked provisions such as renewals provisions; by grants; and finally by the application of capital receipts. If an asset is financed by loan, the principal repayment in the service revenue account might be regarded as being equivalent to depreciation as long as the life of the asset equals the life of the loan. However, the question of depreciation is not at all irrelevant as CIPFA and local authority treasurers have agreed to implement depreciation with effect from the end of the 1994/95 financial year. A depreciation charge is currently calculated outside the main accounts for specialist direct service organizations (DSOs) and direct labour organizations (DLOs) and is directly relevant to calculating the rate of return.

Within central government assets are currently not recorded as such in the organization's accounts and there is no charge for depreciation to the revenue accounts of the component departments. Expenditure for capital and revenue purposes is strictly segregated, and serve primarily for the allocation of distinct and separate capital and revenue funding to organizations.

Within the NHS assets are now recorded within the accounts at replacement cost and depreciation is recorded within accounts. The revenue accounts of non-trust health units bear a charge for capital consumption equivalent to depreciation plus 6% interest on fixed assets which are held. The managing health authority has a duty to ensure that such health units break even after covering these capital charges. In the case of Trust hospitals there is a requirement of a 6% return after allowing for depreciation.

8.2   The generation of new projects

In practice, every year new investment projects will be proposed within all of these organizations. Almost inevitably, given the infinite demand for capital schemes, there is an inability to satisfy all demands because capital finance is normally restricted. There is one exception to this which is the situation of capital-led revenue. This occurs when specifically targeted capital funding is more freely available than revenue funding and can occur in organizations such as central government in which capital resources are completely separate from revenue resources. For example, there might be sufficient capital funds to acquire a body scanner, but the organization may be unable to find the annual revenue support costs. Apart from this type of situation, the classic case is one of capital rationing which means that we should only accept capital schemes which have been subject to rational processes of project selection and appraisal. A common problem of all public sector organizations is thus the prioritizing and applying of funds to specific projects. In prioritizing, account will be taken of the benefits flowing from the project, the estimated capital costs associated with the project will need to be calculated, as will the annual recurring revenue costs (or benefits) flowing from the project. Thus, a proposal for a new wing of a hospital will establish the patient-related services to be located therein, along with support services. The capital costs will be estimated from construction costs and equipment costs. Land purchase costs will be relevant if the health authority or trust does not already own the land. Before the wing can be up and running, there will need to be consideration of removal costs, the staffing levels will be carefully established, and staffing costs estimated; similarly the whole range of non-staff costs will have to be estimated. Of course, the expenditure will not take place instantly but be phased over a period of time; any income will also be phased, as may the gradual transfer of patients to the wing.

Competing projects require to be prioritized or ranked in order of importance and in many organizations such ranking takes place as a result of the action of a project appraisal team (PAT). This team is usually composed of officers from various disciplines and it is their task to recommend the schemes which conform with the organization's objectives and should be included in the capital programme. In many organizations the inclusion of a scheme in the capital programme is a two-stage process:

1. An outline appraisal which gives approval in principle for a scheme to be included within a multi-year capital programme; at this stage, the need for the project is established, and an estimate of costs is developed.
2. A more detailed project appraisal of those projects within the capital programme. This will establish more detailed estimates, especially of revenue costs, may attempt to measure benefits from competing projects, and examine in detail the financing of the project.

It is also essential that the PAT keeps under review schemes already in the capital programme. Given the time it takes to determine whether schemes should go ahead and to complete work, it is essential that the original justification of the scheme still exists for otherwise scarce resources will be wasted. Reserve schemes should also be available in case project delay or 'slippage' takes place. If central government operates a control on cash spending, there will be a need to introduce schemes quickly to utilize the funds available otherwise the capital allocation may be lost, especially if all opportunities for virement to revenue have already been used up. Such a reserve list might include vehicles which were part of a planned replacement programme but which it was impossible to replace due to inadequate funds. Clearly vehicles can be replaced and paid for rapidly unless there are any specialist requirements.

The planning of schemes by stressing the revenue consequences also enable service managers to identify when a project is coming on stream. In a 'no growth' revenue budget situation they will be identified sufficiently far in advance so that revenue savings may be found to absorb the operational costs of the capital scheme in order that capital assets do not lie idle. The inclusion of a scheme in the capital programme does not mean that the scheme will automatically go ahead. Before final approval is given, detailed specifications will be drawn up and put out to competitive tender. These tenders should be compared to the original estimates before a final decision on proceeding with the scheme is made.

The objectives of capital budgeting

In summary capital budgets are devised to:

1. Express in financial terms the capital works necessary to meet the objectives expressed or implied by an organization's objectives and policies.
2. To set out agreed priorities for the commencement of capital schemes.
3. To facilitate the coordination of plans and resources by:
   (a) allocating financial resources between departments;
   (b) assisting in implementing the capital scheme;
   (c) providing a basis for forecasting capital cash flows and requirements;
   (d) providing a basis for forecasting revenue effects;
   (e) providing a basis for budgetary control;
   (f) satisfying government capital control requirements.

8.3 The multi-year capital programme

As has been outlined above, the two major concerns in the screening of new projects are likely to be, first, the specification and financing of the capital cost involved and secondly, the revenue consequences of such capital expenditure (RCCE). In practice, a number of projects may be under consideration, or in different stages of completion, and one valuable device of forecasting the financial impact is the medium-term capital programme.

Table 8.1 provides a summary indication of the form of such a programme.

In Table 8.1, it is assumed that the current year is 1994/95. The table shows, for example, that the total estimated capital expenditure in 1995/96 is £88 000, that Project 056 incurred expenditure prior to the current year, that only Project 059 is due to commence in the current year, and that Project 061 will incur capital expenditure in years beyond 1997/98. Projected start and finish date information is provided for each project, as is information about the estimated RCCE; all except Project 059 are expected to incur additional revenue expenditure, but 059 is expected to produce savings of £28 000 per year.

Within the public sector in general, most projects *are* likely to result in additional RCCE. For example, an extension to a hospital is unlikely to reduce costs, although it may well increase the level and quality of service provided to patients. Similarly, a new motorway will generate benefits to users, but will result in additional maintenance costs for the Department of Transport. In the competitive services it will inevitably be a prerequisite that a proposed capital scheme will at the very least be self-financing. If the scheme is not self-financing it should be rejected unless the parent organization, for safety or environmental reasons possibly, is prepared to make a specific subsidy towards the new scheme.

Thus, from Table 8.1 it may be seen that the capital programme acts as a valuable planning document. It identifies the projects that will be coming on stream in the future, and provides a summary estimate of the capital costs of each project, year by year and in total. The total capital expenditure for each year is an important indicator of the amount of capital expenditure which will need to be financed. An organization's ability to finance capital expenditure

Table 8.1 An outline capital programme

Project	Start/ end	Capital expenditure (£000s)					Total	Full year RCCE £000s
		1/4/94	94/95	95/96	96/97	97/98		
056	93/95	58	43	10			111	27
059	94/95		120	78			198	28+
060	96/97				27		27	3
061	96/00				30	35	80	9
		58	163	88	57	35	416	11

will itself be a limiting factor, the bottom line for each year may be used as a ceiling, and any new projects may only be accommodated if the ceiling is not breached. If it is desired to re-phase the totality of capital expenditure, then the capital programme is a useful basis for examining the impact of re-scheduling on the annual total expenditure. The programme tends to be of a 'rolling' nature; each year a new year is added and the previous year disappears. Projects also move into and out of the programme; when they come within the current planning horizon of the programme, in this case 1997/98, they are included and are taken out in the year after completion. Similarly, a project may be withdrawn from the programme, for example, due to changes in needs, priorities, estimated engineering problems, or because sufficient financing is unavailable possibly due to a desire by central government to cut public sector capital expenditure.

The capital programme does have one significant weakness. It is purely input orientated; the only values indicated are those of input values. It says absolutely nothing about the outputs – the service improvements, the benefits to taxpayers, that result from the expenditure.

8.4 The detailed project appraisal

Capital costs and their financing

At this stage detailed estimates of capital costs will be provided, as will information as to financing. This will clearly involve the input of a variety of professional skills; in the NHS engineers, builders and doctors will be able to specify the detailed physical requirements and possibly estimated capital costs. It may be difficult to evaluate such estimates other than by examining the *actual* costs of similar projects carried out elsewhere, suitably uprated for inflation. Experience shows that, from defence contractors to tunnel builders, the capital costs are often grossly underestimated. A comparison of previously planned completion dates with actual results may also prove rewarding. There will also be a need to provide detailed phasings, establishing key dates for the work to be carried out, and this may require the use of critical path analysis. Key dates are also important so that the Chief Financial Officer can organize finance to come on stream when it is needed. This is true of capital finance which may be taken up as necessary, and is especially true of RCCE which will typically build up in stages within and between years.

Within central government, funding will originate from the organization's capital allocation, which is fixed for the year. Within NHS trust hospitals there is no specific capital allocation. Instead, the trust must submit a detailed option appraisal, the amount of detail which has to be included is influenced by the scale of the project. For example, for schemes costing more than £1m but less than £10m the following information must be provided:

1. the objectives of the scheme;
2. description of all the options considered for meeting the objectives;
3. the criteria used to evaluate the options and explanation of why the selected option was chosen;
4. details of the selected option;

5. estimates of demand and of income generated by the scheme. This would include evidence of purchasers' intentions. It would also include an examination of the scheme on depreciation, unit costs, prices, rate of return and external financing limit;
6. the total capital and revenue costs and their timing. This would include details of any asset sales which are expected to take place and also the presentation of a discounted cash flow analysis (see Chapter 9);
7. the benefits to patients resulting from the scheme including quality benefits such as reductions in waiting lists, greater throughput or an improved environment;
8. proposals for the financing of the schemes;
9. assumptions, sensitivity analysis and contingency plans.

If the scheme is accepted by the NHS Management Executive and the Treasury, then the trust's external financing limit (EFL), which give it power to borrow, may be increased. Any shortfall in borrowing will need to be funded from internal sources.

As you will have learned in Chapter 7, in a local authority, the Treasurer will need to establish, first that 'approvals' for the project that are available from the DOE, Welsh Office or Scottish Office. Such 'approvals' carry the right to borrow to finance the project. Without such permission, the project can be financed only from revenue or proceeds from the sale of assets (capital receipts). The use of these capital receipts is severely restricted by central government.

If the Treasurer opts to borrow then the specific interest payable on the loan will be charged to the Consolidated Loans Fund (CLF) of the authority. The actual interest costs of the CLF are aggregated and an average rate of interest is calculated. The departments of the local authority then pay this average rate of interest to the CLF, the total annual charge being based upon the loans which the department has outstanding. However, the CLF rate of interest does not reflect the true incremental cost of the project, as it is an average rate based on past as well as current borrowing. You learnt in Chapter 3 that the relevant costs of any decision are the future differential costs. Therefore, the relevant costs in this case are not the average interest costs but the interest costs specific to the project being financed by the loan. The consolidated loans fund on capital expenditure is financed by borrowing. It is possible that DSOs could be charged the real rate of interest to bring home a more realistic cost of financing. When the CIPFA reforms of capital accounting mentioned earlier are adopted more realistic charges for capital expenditure will inevitably appear in service revenue accounts.

Table 8.2 Project X: Home for the age capital payments

Expenditure item	Financing	1989/90 £000	1990/91 £000	Total £000
Land	Loan	120		120
Construction	Loan	110	60	170
Furnishings	Revenue		30	30
		230	90	320

After considering such issues, it will be possible to derive a payments and financing programme for a specific project. The example here is taken from a local authority. A home for the aged is to be constructed; the phasing of payments and their financing outlined in Table 8.2.

The estimation of RCCE

As with capital costs, the specification of items such as staffing levels, provisions, maintenance costs, heating costs and so on will be provided to the Treasurer by the Social Services Department, the Buildings Maintenance Unit and the Energy Officer. However, the Treasurer has an important role in pulling together these diverse costs and providing the financial input to several key areas. The Treasurer will estimate employee costs (pricing the staffing levels and adding an appropriate percentages for employers' national insurance and superannuation contributions), establishing the annual rates payment, converting the energy input into expenditure equivalents, estimating the annual charge for central and technical services and, of course, calculating the estimated capital financing charge. The estimated running costs provided to the Treasurer can be compared to existing unit costs to see if they are realistic.

An annual RCCE estimate for the Home for the Aged would then be established and this is contained in Table 8.3.

There are some specific observations which need to be made statement contained in Table 8.3. The notes below correspond to those in the table

1. *Central departments, technical and support services.* These, abbreviated in Table 8.3 as CDTSS, represent the overhead of management and admin-

Table 8.3 Example of a statement of annual RCCE: Project X: Home for the aged: Estimate of revenue consequences in first full year: 1991/92

	Note	£	£
Income: Fees and charges			
Accommodation charges			40 000
Expenditure:			
Employees: Wages		80 000	
Employers' NI and super annuation		17 600	
			97 600
Premises–related costs		18 500	
Supplies		43 400	
CDTSS	1	12 600	
Miscellaneous		7 000	81 500
Capital financing charges			
Revenue contribution to furniture		30 000	
Principal repayments of loan	2	7 250	
Interest on loan	3	43 500	80 750
Gross estimated costs			259 850
Net costs			219 850

istration required to provide the service. They include, for example, the costs of paying staff and creditors, appropriate legal services, and a share of the administrative costs of the social services department.

2. *Principal repayments of the loan.* It is assumed that the treasurer decides to borrow the money required over 40 years, and that the money is to be repaid in equal instalments of principal (EIP). Therefore, the charge to the revenue account is £290 000/40 = £7250 per year.

3. *Interest on loan.* It is assumed that the money is borrowed at 15% giving an interest payment in the first year of 15% × 290 000 = £43500. As the years pass, the annual interest payment will fall; in the next year, for example, it will reduce because the loan outstanding has been reduced by the first year repayment of an instalment of principal. In 1992/93 it will be 15% × (£290 000 – £7250) = £42 413.

Another feature of Table 8.3 is that it refers to the *first full year*, that is the first year following construction when the home has been in use for a whole year. The home may well accommodate residents during 1990/91, but for only a part-year. Because of the phasing in of use, normally with a part-year, such revenue estimates are normally prepared up to, and including, the first full year. The first full year is an important base for projecting future years' expenditure; the bottom-line figure of £219 850 is also the amount which needs to be financed from the resources of the local authority. Thus, at this stage, the treasurer needs to be sure that the net revenue expenditure figure can be funded from within the authority's resources. A similar consideration will weigh on central government; within the Ministry of Defence, the cost of a new jet fighter is the capital cost, but this has to be supported by an ongoing infrastructure which consumes revenue resources that have to be budgeted and provided for. Exhibit 8.1 contains a worked example relating to the estimation of capital payments and revenue consequences.

The value of this approach

The approach described above is essentially a financially based project appraisal. As such it does have specific values; it concentrates on the financial fundamentals of cost, phasing and financing; it also emphasizes the RCCE. In fact, it deals with almost everything concerned with providing financial support for a project.

However, its value in appraisal *per se* is rather limited unless we are simply comparing two projects with precisely the same output, for example the relative costs of a bridge or an underpass to provide pedestrians with means of crossing a busy road in safety. Where the benefits from projects are not expressed in cash terms, the methodology has no way of integrating these into the appraisal. To take our road crossing example one stage further, a third option might be a pelican crossing, but this causes delays to motor vehicles, and is also less safe to pedestrians than either a bridge or a subway. Such differences cannot be integrated using this approach. Similarly, difficulties occur when competing projects have different lifespans; differences in years of service provided are not readily incorporated within this framework. The difficulties outlined in the last sentence can, however, be tackled using discounted cash flow, an approach which is explained in Chapter 9.

In addition, the absence of strict output measures may lead to a situation where political muscle is the prime determinant of the projects to be selected.

In this situation the newly competitive units may well experience difficulty in promoting their schemes into the programme due to the powerful vested interests of the older established service departments.

Secondly, the approach is only useful for comparing projects with the same mix of financing. For example, if one project is to be wholly financed from revenue (a one-year charge), then comparison of the net RCCE of each is impossible; only by taking out the actual method of financing, and imputing a notional figure, based probably on the notional debt charges, can the two projects be compared.

Finally, the separation of capital and revenue funds which is found in central government and the NHS is itself likely to produce sub-optimal decisions. This is because additional constraints are formulated, namely capital and revenue funding constraints, and, furthermore, the separation means that there is a danger that if capital funds are free there will be a bias to capital projects, some of which may well have uneconomic revenue consequences. These revenue consequences may force out existing schemes which are performing satisfactorily because the prestige capital project must be seen to be operational and must be funded. Again, we find capital-led revenue, a problem identified when we considered the generation of new projects earlier in this chapter. In other words, it does not arrive at necessarily the 'best' project, but the project which best meets the funding sources which are currently most freely available.

8.5 The administrative ranking of projects

The problem of comparing projects with different patterns of service or outputs has led to an approach termed 'goals achievement matrix' or 'desiderata ranking', and is used primarily by health authorities, and also by local authorities in sifting a variety of options to arrive at an optimal decision. The approach taken is as follows:

1. A small multi-disciplinary team will be established to define the desirable service features that they are looking for from different projects. Such service features are known as desiderata or goals.
2. The team then attaches weights to these desiderata to reflect their relative importance. Normally the weights sum to 100.
3. The team scores the performance of each project against the identified desiderata. Different forms of scoring system may be employed but a common system employed within the NHS is as follows:

    +4 Meets the desiderata excellently.
    +2 Meets the desiderata well.
     0 Meets the desiderata adequately.
    –2 Meets the desiderata inadequately.
    –4 Meets the desiderata not at all.

4. For each project, its specific desiderata score is multiplied by the weighting referred to in 2 above.
5. The individual weighted scores are summed, thereby producing a quantified index of non-financial costs and benefits.
6. Such overall scores for each project are then taken into account jointly with the results of the financial appraisal.

Table 8.4 Desiderata and weightings resulting from team discussions

Desiderata	Weights
D1: Improvements to stock control	30%
D2: Improved managerial and financial information	15%
D3: Adaptability to future changes	15%
D4: Ease of introduction	10%
D5: Ease of operation	15%
D6: Total volume of storage space	10%
D7: Reduction of the annual training requirement	5%
	100%

For example, the methodology was used within a health authority to appraise three different options for the establishment of new central stores. A small multi-disciplinary team was established made up of representatives drawn from finance, stores, transport, and end-users from hospitals and community health. In carrying out the non-financial appraisal, the team's discussions were first concerned with agreeing the desiderata and weights with which they would work. The desiderata and relevant weights are set out in Table 8.4. The team then scored the different options as laid out in Table 8.5.

The desiderata rankings summarized in Table 8.5 were at variance with rankings by cost; after lengthy discussion, option 2 was selected. Although this was not the lowest cost option, it was felt to offer best overall value for money on a pound-for-pound basis ('value' being judged by reference to the desiderata ranking).

Table 8.5 The results of desiderata scoring

Desiderata	Weights	Options 1		Options 2		Options 3	
		Score	Weighted	Score	Weighted	Score	Weighted
D1	30%	−4	−1.2	+2	+0.6	+2	+0.6
D2	15%	−4	−0.6	+2	+0.3	+2	+0.3
D3	15%	+2	+0.3	+4	+0.6	0	0
D4	10%	+4	+0.4	0	0	−1	−0.1
D5	15%	+4	+0.6	+2	+0.3	+1	+0.15
D6	10%	−2	−0.2	+3	+0.3	+1	+0.1
D7	5%	+4	+0.2	+1	+0.5	−2	−0.1
Grand total	100%		−0.5		+2.15		+0.65
Project ranking			3		1		2

The value of this approach

Desiderata ranking does allow for the quantitative evaluation of non-financial aspects of the appraisal and does therefore bring into the appraisal a valuable dimension. It also has the merit that it can be carried out quickly by a small team. This team approach, as it is intrinsically multi-disciplinary, also has the

Key points of chapter

1. Within the public sector, there are different approaches to defining capital expenditure and to depreciation.
2. The capital programme is an important aspect of multi-year project planning.
3. Project generation and selection is a multi-year project planning.
4. Projection of net RCCE to first full year is essential..
5. Much current practice ignores outputs; desiderata ranking represents a subjective way of dealing with this problem.

advantage of creating identity with the scheme across departmental boundaries. The costs of implementation are relatively low, but the speed of appraisal is relatively high; these twin advantages explain its popularity in practice.

However, the technique may be criticized because it takes account only of team members' subjective views, and fails to attempt to measure the final outputs from a project. Moreover, the numbers which appear in Table 8.4 and Table 8.5 conceal the inherent subjectivity and falsely suggest objectivity. It may also be more difficult to apply where the schemes being compared are fundamentally different and consensus harder to achieve on the relative weights. As will be seen in the next chapter, there are powerful ways of measuring non-market outputs which are very relevant to the public sector.

8.6 Summary

This chapter first considered the different methods of defining capital expenditure in the public sector and the general absence of a depreciation provision. However, in both local authorities and the National Health Service, policies are changing.

This chapter has examined an essentially finance-based approach to project appraisal. It has stressed that the capital investment decision should be made in a framework of specific objectives and long-term strategy. A capital programme is the major form of expression of an overall plan for the development of a public sector organization's activities and services. The chapter has stressed that the capital programme and the associated revenue effects form an essential part of the planning process of the organization.

The process takes place in stages and is also affected by the time horizon of government funding and grants and the public sector planning process which can be subject to significant changes. Political expediency and the imbalance of capital and revenue funds can also play a major part in the public sector. These factors do not negate the value of planning but they make it more difficult and, in a sense, more essential in that the organization must know what it is attempting to achieve in order to measure how significantly it has failed to achieve its stated objectives.

The chapter has also indicated how a capital programme may be prepared, and how the details of the revenue consequences are obtained. Finally, it has examined an approach by which non-financial factors can also be brought into the analysis.

Exhibit 8.1

This Exhibit contains a brief case study which illustrates the estimation of capital payments and net revenue effects as discussed above.

A public sector organization requires to expand, and, possibly, centralize its office accommodation. It is considering three proposals: either to extend existing offices, to erect a purpose-built office in a run-down part of the city or to rent space in a commercial development in the city centre. Each of the latter options would permit the centralization of office accommodation and management.

The current offices are spread on four sites, three of which are owned by the organization with one being rented. The owned premises are debt free and currently stand in the balance sheet at their cost prices of £80 000, £70 000 and £30 000, while the annual rent of the existing office is £12 500 on a five-year lease, payable annually in advance and subject to review at the beginning of year three when it is expected to double. Average yearly running costs of current premises amount to £185 000 but there are additional costs of £87 500 per year resulting from travelling expenses, postages, etc., consequent upon the split site operation. Unless new accommodation is obtained an extension will be constructed in year four at an estimated cost of £200 000; this will add a further £20 000 to running costs (excluding debt charges) in a full year; it will be occupied at the start of the fourth quarter of the year four with the bulk of the capital expenditure taking place during the first half of year four.

A purpose-built office is estimated to cost £8m; it will take three years to build with capital payments phased as follows:

Year 1: 40%;　　Year 2: 40%;　　Year 3: 20%

Work will commence in June of year one and it is expected to be completed by October of year three.

One-off relocation costs will amount to £150 000 in year three. Running costs for the new offices will amount to £50 000 per annum from the start of January of year three when the premises will be fully occupied.

The three existing offices will be sold immediately staff move to the new offices; sale proceeds are expected to be 15 times their total book value. The proceeds are to be used in redemption of long-term outstanding debt in October of year four.

Rental of centralized office space would amount to £0.65m per year subject to annual rent review, expected to result in rent increases of 15% per annum. One-off relocation costs are expected to amount to £200 000. Running costs will amount to £71 000 per year from the date of occupation, which is identical to the purpose-built option. The sale of the existing buildings is assumed to proceed as with the purpose-built option.

In the event of the existing rented accommodation being vacated before the end of the five-year period, a penalty of three months' rent is payable in addition to the rental for the year in which the accommodation is vacated.

Information on current borrowing rates is as follows:

Temporary　9.75%
Long-term　11.25%

The organization uses the equal instalment of principal method of repayment and has approval to fund all the necessary capital expenditure by borrowing over 40 years. Principal repayments are made half-way through each year, and commence in the year following that in which the borrowing takes place.

The building of new offices has gained initial outline approval and stands in the capital programme of the organization. However, the harsher financial climate has led to a request for a detailed project appraisal of all three options. For this the organization requires the preparation of capital and revenue estimates for each of the three options over a period of five years.

Solution

| | Year | | | | | |
	1 £000	2 £000	3 £000	4 £000	5 £000	Total £000
Capital costs:						
Extension				200		200
Construction	3200	3200	1600			8000

	Year					
	1 £000	2 £000	3 £000	4 £000	5 £000	Total £000
Revenue costs:						
Extension						
Running costs:						
Existing	272.5	272.5	272.5	272.5	272.5	
New				5	20	
Rent	12.5	12.5	25	25	25	
Financing costs:						
Principal					5	
Interest				16.875	22.5	
Totals	285	285	297.5	319.375	345	
Construction of new offices:						
Running costs						
Existing	272.5	272.5	204.375			
New			12.5	50	50	
Rent	12.5	12.5	25			
Penalty			6.25			
Relocation			150			
Financing costs:						
Principal		80	160	200	200	
Interest	150	535.5	837	861.75	839.25	
Totals	435	900.5	1395.125	1111.75	1089.25	
Less: Income:						
Interest				151.875	303.75	
Totals	0	0	0151.875	303.75		
Net revenue effect	435	900.5	1395.125	959.875	785.5	
Rent of new offices:						
Running costs:						
Existing	272.5	272.5	204.375			
New			17.75	71	71	
Rent – old	12.5	12.5	25			
Penalty			6.25			
Rent – new			162.5	674.375	775.531	
Relocation			200			
Totals		285	285	615.875	745.375	846.531
Less Income:						
Interest				151.875	303.75	
Totals	0	0	0	151.875	303.75	
Net revenue effect	285	285	615.875	593.5	542.781	

Notes:

1. *Running costs:*

   Extension: Year 4 One quarter's occupation of the extension giving 25% of £20 000, the full year cost.

   Construction: Year 4 Existing offices are occupied for nine months giving 75% of £272 500, the full year cost. New offices are occupied for three months giving 25% of £50 000, the full year cost.

   Rent: Year 4 Existing offices are occupied for nine months giving 75% of £272 500, the full year cost. New offices are occupied for three months giving 25% of £71 000, the full year cost.

2. *Financing charge calculations:*

   Extensions:

   Year 4: £200 000 advanced in the first half of year 4, on average, the money was outstanding for 9 months. Thus, interest charged is £200 000 $\times$ 0.75 $\times$ 11.25% = £16 875.

   Year 5: £200 000 $\times$ 11.25%.

   Construction of new offices:

   | | Year | | | | |
   | | 1 | 2 | 3 | 4 | 5 |
	£000	£000	£000	£000	£000
Principal b/fwd	0	3200	6320	7760	7560
Borrowed in year	3200	3200	1600		
Repaid in year		−80	−160	−200	−200
Principal c/fwd	3200	6320	7760	7560	7360

   Interest:

   Year 1: £3200K $\times$ 5/12 $\times$ 11.25% = £150 000.

   £3200K was advanced over the ten month period from June to March, so the average time that advances were outstanding was 5 months.

   Year 2: (£3200K + £3200K $\times$ $^1/_2$) − ($^1/_2 \times$ £80K) $\times$ 11.25% = £535 500.

   The year 1 advance of £3200K outstanding for the whole of the year.

   The year 2 advance of £3200K is made evenly over the year, so the average time for which the advance is outstanding is six months.

   The year 2 repayment of £80 000 (1/40 of £3200K) is made mid-way through the year and so represents a reduction in interest for just six months.

   Year 3: (£6320K + (£1600K $\times$ $^3/_4$)) − ($^1/_2 \times$ £160K) $\times$ 11.25% = £837 000.

   The balance b/fwd of £6320 is outstanding for the whole of the year.

   The year 3 advance of £1600K is made in the first half of year 3, so the average time for which the advance is outstanding is 9 months.

   The year 3 repayment of £160 000 (1/40 of £6400K) is made mid-way through the year and so represents a reduction in interest for just 6 months.

   Year 4: (£7760K − ($^1/_2 \times$ 200K) $\times$ 11.25% = £861.750.

   The repayment of principal is 1/40 of £8 millions borrowed.

   Year 5: (£7560K − ($^1/_2 \times$ £200K)) $\times$ 11.25% = £839.250.

3. *Investment of capital receipts:*

   Year 4: Proceeds £180 000 $\times$ 15 = £2 700 000

   Interest savings:

   Year 4: £2 700 000 $\times$ (6 months) $\times$ 11.25% = £151 875

   Year 5: £2 700 000 $\times$ 11.25% = £303 750

8.1 List the benefits of capital programmes.

8.2 Explain one way of taking account of the non-financial aspects of capital schemes.

8.3 A local authority is carrying out an appraisal of a new leisure centre. The following information is available:

Estimated annual costs:	£
Premises costs	14 000
Employees – Manager	16 500
– Centre assistants	32 000
CDTSS	5 500
Supplies and services	11 800
Estimated annual revenue	
Sports hall	19 800
Squash courts	17 700
Equipment hire	3 500
Hire of hall (for functions)	2 500
Estimated capital costs	
Land and construction	545 000

All capital costs are being financed by a loan at 10%. The loan is repayable over 20 years in equal instalments of principal.

Required

Set out the estimated revenue consequences of the scheme in the first full year of operation.

8.4 A county council has 400 places in homes for the elderly. Demand for places exceeded supply in 19X0/X1 by 200 places. This shortfall in places is expected to increase by 50% by the end of the next five years.
In addition one 156-bed home built in 1930 is scheduled to be closed in 19X2/X3. The home has an annual net revenue cost of £320 000 and a disposal value of £600 000.

The council has established a policy to eliminate the shortfall in places by 19X5.

Average income per resident place is £1700 per annum.

It has been decided that only two types of new home will be provided as a matter of policy. These are 40-bed homes and 75-bed homes.

Cost information on the two types of home is as follows:

	40-bed home £	75-bed home £
Capital costs	900 000	1 460 000
Gross revenue costs (including financing costs)	300 000	500 000

The social services committee has been allocated £9 million capital and £1 950 000 additional revenue resources for the provision of new homes in the period 19X1/19X5.

Required

Detail the main conclusions from the above information for inclusion in a financial report on the provision of homes for the elderly.

8.5 In the current period of economic restraint your organization has decided that only of three proposed projects can be started.
You are required to:
(a) Prepare a statement of the annual costs of each project from the information given below.
(b) Discuss the limitations of this method of project appraisal.

		£
Project A	Construction	200 000
	Equipment	60 000
	Furniture	45 000
	Premises	15 000
	Other running expenses	5 000
	Employees	25 000
Project B	Construction	300 000
	Furniture	5 000
	Equipment	25 000
	Employees	30 000
	Premises	10 000
	Other running expenses	14 000
Project C	Employees	60 000
	Other running expenses	30 000
	Premises	5 000

Notes:
(i) Construction costs and professional fees are amortized over 40 years, equipment over 10 years, and furniture over 5 years.
(ii) Annuity factors are: 0.1129 on 40 years
0.1706 on 10 years
0.2714 on 5 years.

(iii) Professional fees are to be charged at 10% of construction costs.
(iv) £5000 of furniture and £10 000 of equipment included in the above figures for project A refers to annual replacements.
(v) A charge is to be made for administration at 5% of annual expenditure exclusive of amortization.

8.6 The following schemes are included in the draft 19X8/X9 capital programme of a service of a local authority.

| Scheme | Total £000 | Programme of capital expenditure | | | | Scheme opens |
		19X7/X8 Revised £000	19X8/X9 £000	19X9/X0 £000	19X0/X1 £000	
Teign Phase 1	150	28	–	–	–	Sept–8
Clyst Vale	230	80	–	–	–	Jan–9
Collompton	160	120	10	–	–	May–9
Ashburton	300	180	100	20	–	Sept–9
Teign Phase 2	400	20	300	80	–	Oct–9
Great Torrington	50	–	20	30	–	June–9
Teignmouth	100	–	75	25	–	June–9
Dawlish	200	–	25	100	75	Sept–0
Holsworthy	40	–	–	40	–	May–0
Tiverton	500	–	–		300	Sept–1

Other information available to you:

1. *Financing*
As much of the capital programme as possible is to be financed from internal sources. It is expected that £50 000 will be set aside annually for revenue contributions to capital outlay. Capital receipts of £160 000 are expected for 19X7/X8 and £200 000 in 19X8/X9.

If it is necessary to borrow to finance the schemes they will all be financed over 60 years with the exception of

Great Torrington	all expenditure	20 years
Teign Phase 2	£200 000 in 19X8/X9	5 years
Holsworthy	all expenditure	5 years

Interest charges are 12.5% and advances are made once a year, at the end of the year. Interest is payable as soon as the money is advanced, principal repayments start at the end of the first year.

2. *Revenue costs other than financing costs*

Running costs in a full year (in addition to financing charges):

Scheme:	£000
Teign Phase 1	60
Clyst Vale	65
Collompton	80
Ashburton	65
Teign Phase 2	50
Great Torrington	–

Teignmouth	100
Dawlish	55
Holsworthy	—
Tiverton	120

3. *Capital expenditure allocations*

The capital expenditure allocation for 19X7/X8 is £380 000. The authority is allowed to supplement this with 30% of capital receipts. The authority may also carry forward the previous year's allocation or anticipate the next year's allocation subject to the total of these being not more than 10% of the enhanced capital expenditure allocation. Capital spending in 19X6/X7 anticipated the 19X7/X8 allocation by £20 000. The capital expenditure allocation for 19X8/X9 has been announced as £360 000. It seems reasonable to assume that the capital expenditure allocation for future years will be even lower. The authority intends to conform to the capital spending regulations.

4. *Priority for schemes*

Council policy dictates that first priority should be given to continuing schemes. This means that the scheme will be allowed to go ahead but not necessarily with the original phasing of expenditure. New schemes are prioritized with a ranking of 1 to 3. Priority 1 is given to schemes that must start in the year. Priorities 2 and 3 are for schemes that may be put back into the next year with Priority 2 being preferred to start over Priority 3.

The priority of the schemes that start after 19X7/X8 are as follows:

Great Torrington	2
Teignmouth	1
Dawlish	2
Holsworthy	3
Tiverton	1

Required

(a) Prepare a revised capital programme for the service for the year 19X8/X9 to include detailed financing for each scheme in the programme and a full year revenue cost for the scheme when completed. Changes made to the draft capital programme must conform to the policies stated in the question.

(8 marks)

(b) Show the impact of the changes made in the capital programme for 19X8/X9 on the capital budgets for future years.

(2 marks)

(c) As the accountant appointed to produce the accounts of the service write a memorandum to the Borough Treasurer to accompany the revised capital programme for 19X8/X9. This should explain the reasons for changes made and justify each change made to the draft budget.

(10 marks)
(Total 20 marks)

8.7 A large comprehensive school has a local sports centre on the same site; both are financed by the same metropolitan authority. Currently, all the heating for the sports centre is supplied from the main boiler house based in the school. This arrangement has been criticized by the authority's Energy Efficiency Officer because the school boiler and heating system has to be activated at weekends and during school holidays. It has also been suggested that, during summer when hot water only is required, there is excessive heat loss in the transmission of hot water between the buildings.

The energy Efficiency Office has proposed two alternative schemes:

(a) The first scheme involves the installation of electric water heaters in the sports centre at a capital cost of £5000. These would require virtually no maintenance but should be replaced every five years. Likely consumption is 5500 therms annually, estimated on the basis of current hot water consumption. Heating would continue to be generated by the school.

(b) The second scheme involves the installation of a gas boiler to satisfy both hot water requirements and to provide space heating when the school system is not in use. The gas boiler would be plumbed directly into the existing system and would incur capital expenditure of £20 000. The estimated consumption would be 12 000 therms annually. Annual maintenance charges under a contract with expected to last for seven years.

Other relevant information is as follows:

(i) Current and estimated thermal demands on the comprehensive school system by the sports centre is as follows:

		Thermal consumption (per annum)
	Current system	28 000
Option (a)	Electric heaters	16 900
Option (b)	Gas boiler	7 600

(ii) The school caretaker is currently paid an allowance of £1000 per annum for boiler lighting during the vacation. This service would not be required if option (b) was adopted.

(iii) The school heating system is oil-fired, and the boiler is expected to last for at least another seven years.

(iv) Contract prices negotiated for each of the four fuels used in the authority are as follows:

	Per therm (pence)
Coal	41.0
Electricity	52.1
Gas	42.6
Oil	44.1

Estimated increases in contract prices for the foreseeable future are 5% per annum for all fuels. However, it is considered that both gas and oil are more vulnerable to fluctuations in prices than the other two fuels.

(v) Both schemes can be accommodated within the capital programme for 19X8/X9.

(vi) It is proposed that in each case financing will be effected by an advance from the authority's Loans Fund, repayable by equal instalments of principal over five years. The current loans fund rate is 9%.

(vii) The authority's policy on Loans Fund advances is to charge a half-year's interest in the year of advance. Principal repayments are made at the end of each financial year, commencing in the year in which the advance is made.

(viii) Current market rates of interest are as follows:

Period of loan	Rate of interest
1 years	9%
5 years	10%
10 years	11%

(ix) The sports centre has displayed a consistent growth in use over recent years.

(x) The Energy Efficiency Working Party has asked the Treasurer to present a report on the financial implications of each option.

Required

Draft a report on behalf of the Treasurer to the Energy Efficiency Working Party recommending the action that should be undertaken.

(24 marks)

9 ▷ Project appraisal

Key learning objectives

After reading this chapter you should be able to:

1. Understand the concept of the time value of money and why future benefits should be discounted to the present time for assessment.
2. Be able to deal with inflation in the capital investment decision-making process.
3. Discuss the applicability of cost-benefit analysis to the public sector.

The previous chapter pointed out that the distinction between capital and revenue expenditure is essentially one that can be based on time. Revenue expenditure is that expenditure on current goods and services the benefits of which are consumed within the present time period, that is the conventional time period of the annual revenue statement. Capital expenditure normally results in expenditure in the framework of the annual time period of the revenue statement but in exchange for the receipt of benefits in future time periods and their annual revenue statements. The essence of this chapter is to use the concept of time and its impact on monetary flows as a basis for the development of a sound framework of investment appraisal in the public sector. The chapter will also consider the technique of cost-benefit analysis which has been developed in the public sector in an attempt to facilitate the finding of better solutions to the problem of resource allocation in the absence of the market mechanism. In order to develop student understanding a number of detailed exhibits are contained within the chapter. These exhibits gradually grow in complexity to ensure student understanding and detailed coverage of this complex topic.

9.1 Discounted cash flow

The objectives of the discounted cash flow model of investment appraisal are to evaluate the net financial benefit of individual projects and to enable an informed financial comparison to be performed between projects. These projects may have different lives and consequently different returns, or the same life but differing returns. The model recognizes that the use of funds has an opportunity cost by the application of a rate of interest to discount future cash flows. If, for example, an individual were offered £100 now or £100 in a year's time the rational individual would accept the £100 today as he could invest it and receive more than a £100 in one year's time as a result of the action of the rate of interest. If, however, the after-tax rate of interest was 10% and the sum offered in one year's time was £110 then the individual would be indifferent between two sums. Finally, if the after-tax rate of interest was 8% but the offer of £110 in the year's time still stood then the rational investor would wait one year as £110 receivable in a year's time is worth £101.86 today, as this is the sum that will amount to £110 one year hence when invested at 8%. Effectively it can be seen that, by discounting the future sum by the rate of interest, it is possible to compare the two cash flows and make a rational investment decision. This essentially very simple, but powerful, technique forms the conceptual basis for a wide range of investment decisions and will be applied in this chapter. It should be pointed out that the technique is concerned with the action of the rate of interest and not the effect of inflation on the value of the sums involved. The effect of inflation in the investment decision is dealt with later in the chapter.

The interest rate used in the discounting process is known as the 'hurdle' or 'cut-off' rate, in that, for a project to be successful, the future benefits when discounted by the cost of capital must exceed the discounted cost associated with the project. The discount rate is thus the required minimum rate of return for a project.

The timing and nature of cash flows

It is a convention for simplicity to assume that cash flows occur only at the beginning or end of a year. Clearly this is unrealistic given the nature of projects and, while it is possible to overcome this objection by more complex analysis, which may be appropriate in certain circumstances, in the majority of cases the results obtained from year-end calculations are adequate.

It is also essential to appreciate that the emphasis in discounted cash flow calculations is on cash flow. There is no place in the technique for the use of accounting concepts such as depreciation. This is because depreciation is an accounting method used to apportion costs to a relevant accounting period over the life of an asset and as such is a bookkeeping entry with no associated cash flow. The cash flows used should also be the incremental cash flows, that is the cash flows which occur as a direct result of undertaking the proposal. It follows from this that any costs already invested in the project at the time that a new investment decision is needed should be treated as sunk costs and similarly ignored except for any salvage or other escape values. Any operating costs estimated to be saved, for example, through installation of a new machine, should be treated as the equivalent of a cash receipt in the analysis. The use of the technique is demonstrated in Exhibit 9.1.

Exhibit 9.1

A public sector organization operates a joinery workshop and is considering buying a new forming machine at a cost of £4000. The machine is estimated to last five years with zero scrap value. It is estimated that the new machine will achieve savings of £1200 in the first three years of operation and £800 in the last two years as maintenance cost increase. The organization has stated the required rate of return is 10%. Should the organization undertake the investment in the new machinery?

Timing of cash flow	Cash flow	10% discount factor	Discounted cash flow
	£		£
Year 1	1200	0.909	1091
Year 2	1200	0.826	991
Year 3	1200	0.751	901
Year 4	800	0.683	546
Year 5	800	0.621	497
			4026
Year 0 (i.e. today)	4000	1	(4000)
Net present value (NPV)			26

The proposal has been appraised using the discounted cash flow method. The discount rate is 10% and factors were obtained from the table in appendix at the end of this book. The discount factor for any sums spent today (i.e. year 0) is £1; quite simply, £1 spent now is worth exactly £1. The incremental savings in operating costs have been treated as the cash flows of the project.

The project has a positive NPV: the discounted savings exceed the discounted costs at 10% and, as such, would prove acceptable to the organization, unless, of course, any competing projects give a higher NPV. It could now go forward for consideration for inclusion in the capital programme.

Exhibit 9.1 illustrates the decision rules for the organization. The project had a positive NPV and thus the organization could consider the proposal for inclusion in the capital programme. If the calculation had revealed that the project had a negative NPV then the proposal would be rejected on financial grounds.

Internal rate of return

An alternative discounting technique to NPV is termed the internal rate of return (IRR). The technique involves an iterative search for the rate of interest which equates the discounted value of cash inflows and cash outflows; calculation is not a problem, not least because most spread-sheet packages incorporate a function to calculate a project's IRR. The resulting IRR is then compared with the appropriate interest rate facing the organization; an IRR in excess of the rate of interest must indicate that the project has a positive NPV at that rate of interest, and vice versa. Surveys have indicated that it is very popular with businessmen within the private sector, and, in most cases, it leads to the same conclusions as NPV. However, the IRR does have certain drawbacks, and, in certain cases, gives an incorrect decision; such drawbacks are well documented and the reader is referred to, for example, Drury (1989).

The decision rules under IRR are:

1. IRR greater than cost or capital – consider the project for inclusion in the capital programme.
2. IRR less than cost of capital – reject the project.

9.2 Ranking projects

The previous chapter indicated how projects might be ranked using a desiderata table to consider non-financial aspects. We now examine the problem of ranking projects, in financial terms only, when investment funds are constrained.

It was stated above that if a project has a positive NPV then it can be considered for inclusion in the capital programme. Almost inevitably, however, the investment requirement of acceptable projects is likely to exceed the funds which are available for investment. Almost certainly, the capital programme for an individual service will be restricted and available funds will need to be rationed. Consequently it is necessary to rank schemes to identify priorities. This is done by the calculation of a 'profitability index' and is simply computed by dividing the present value of the surplus cash inflows by the initial investment. This procedure will only apply to those projects which have a positive cash flow. The greater the value of the index the higher the priority that should be given to the scheme. However, it is insufficient to look at each scheme in isolation; careful analysis should be made of the sum available and possible combinations of projects should be studied to obtain the best NPV for the organization as a whole in order to use the limited resources to the maximum effect.

9.3 Risk and uncertainty

As the process of project appraisal necessarily involves dealing with the future there will be a degree of risk attached to many projections. Therefore, it is essential that consideration be given to these risks; this will be of particular importance to the competitive public sector as in a competitive situation a poor investment decision could have a serious impact. However, it should be remembered that if all possible states of nature were considered, the decision-maker would be overwhelmed with information.

A number of options are available in dealing with risk and these are discussed below:

1. *Standard deviation and probability distribution*. Calculate the standard deviation and probability distribution of the cash flows associated with the project to obtain a measure of the likely risk associated with the possible outcomes.
2. *Simulation techniques*. Undertake simulation using a technique such as Monte Carlo analysis where each factor affecting the investment decision is examined and random numbers used to generate an estimated NPV, probability distribution and standard deviation for the project.
3. *Sensitivity analysis*. Carry out sensitivity analysis by a systematic analysis of the effects of varying the values assumed for certain variables on the

overall result of the proposal. Clearly, by this process it would be possible to identify those factors to which the project is most at risk. If the project does, subsequently, go ahead these factors would be the key statistics to monitor.

4. *Risk premium.* Incorporate a risk premium into the discount rate; this involves increasing the discount rate by a specific percentage so as to reflect risk. The higher the discount rate the lower will be the expected NPV and thus a measure can be achieved of the project's sensitivity to risk with the more marginal projects being rejected. The choice of the risk premium would clearly be crucial to this process. Unfortunately the choice of premium is largely arbitrary, but it has been used within the NHS to appraise 'risky' projects which have been subject to a discount rate 2% higher than for low risk projects.

5. *Limited time horizons.* Limit the time horizon of the appraisal; this is likely to hit benefits more severely than costs as conventional projects are characterized by high cash outflows in the early years in return for future benefits. This procedure is quite arbitrary as would be any decision to inflate costs and/or reduce income.

9.4   The cost of capital

In the simple example given in Exhibit 9.1 earlier, the rate of interest or discount rate was specified as 10%, but considerable debate exists as to the choice of the appropriate discount rate in the public sector. In the private sector the cost of capital of a company can be found using the capital asset pricing model (see, for example, Van Horne, 1988) which uses a basic assumption of profit maximization in its construction. In the public sector no equivalent model is available and a number of possible discount rates are possible. However, there are two main approaches to the solution of this problem:

1. *Social opportunity cost rate.* In so far as funds used for a public sector project come ultimately from the private sector it can be argued that they have displaced either current consumption or investment by private individuals and businesses. To the extent that private sector investment is displaced, the concept of a social opportunity cost rate has been developed. This is defined as the marginal pre-tax rate of return in the private sector, i.e. the rate of return which the funds would have yielded for society, abstracting from externalities, had they not been commandeered by the public sector. One obvious difficulty is defining the private sector return.

2. *Social time preferences rate.* to the extent private consumption is displaced it is argued that the social time preference rate is the relevant concept. This is defined as the after-tax rate of return required by society to induce it to sacrifice present consumption for the promise of future consumption as generated by the investment. The social time preference rate will depend, among others, on factors such as the age structure of the population, which will change over time, expectations about the growth in prosperity and the general level of prosperity, etc. There is an obvious discrepancy between the social time preference rate and the social opportunity cost rate as the latter is before tax and the other is after tax.

The Treasury's approach has been to use the concept of the social opportunity cost rate above, and then exclude inflation from the resulting rate of interest. This rate is known as the test discount rate and is currently 6% for services such as the NHS. As it is a real rate it removes the need to take account of inflation from the discounting process and, as such, removes one complication from an already complicated process. The problem of inflation is a real one, however, and it is discussed more fully later in the next section. The rate of return for nationalized industries was first set at 5% in 1978 but in the light of returns made in the private sector the government announced in April 1989 that it had increased this rate to 8%. This was intended to ensure that the industries made what the government regarded as an appropriate return on the resources invested and that resources were not diverted from areas where they could be used more effectively.

For institutions such as local government, which have day-to-day access to money markets, there is the possibility of using market interest rates as the cost of capital. These market rates include assumptions about future inflation and as such, if they are used, then the cost and income cash flows in the appraisal should include anticipated assumptions about the level of future inflation. Where a combination of sources of finance is used, a local authority would calculate a weighted cost of funds. Local authorities also calculate internal rates on their consolidated loans funds, but these rates are based upon the average historic cost of debt. They also calculate notional interest rates on their capital funds, but these are based purely on internal financing and transfer pricing decisions and may have no relationship with the market rate. There is no justification for using either the consolidated loans fund rate or the capital fund rate in the appraisal exercise as they do not represent the opportunity cost of funds.

9.5 Inflation

If a real discount rate such as the test discount rate is used, then costs and income in future years should be expressed in real terms (i.e. base year prices), and thus exclude the effects of general inflation. If, however, the relative price of different inputs is expected to change, the real price of the inputs will not remain constant. Relative price changes must therefore be considered. Historically, for example, the relative price effect has been particularly important with regard to labour costs given the high percentage of the revenue budget which is consumed by salaries and wages in the public sector. To leave out such a significant factor as pay inflation would weaken the results of the appraisal exercise.

Exhibit 9.2 illustrates three distinct approaches to the problem of inflation.

Exhibit 9.2

A water business has identified that its diversified local stores depots are experiencing difficulty in meeting the demands of its repairs and maintenance division. A study carried out by a firm of consultants has revealed two ways of effecting improvements:

1. *Taking on additional employees at the stores.* This would result in increases in wage costs of £250 000 per annum in the first year (inclusive of employers' National Insurance and Superannuation contributions); such costs are expected to increase by 2% in excess of the rate of general price inflation.

2. *Purchasing stores handling equipment.* This would require an immediate payment of £780 000 and annual maintenance and operating charges of £40 000, increasing in line with general inflation. The equipment is expected to have a five-year life.

General price inflation (measured by the Retail Price Index) is expected to continue at the rate of 5% per annum for the foreseeable future. The company can currently raise finance at 16%. Appraisal is to be carried out over a five-year period.

The calculations illustrate the three alternative methods of accounting for inflation in the capital budgeting process. Method 1 has ignored the specific inflation of 2% above the retail price index and as such is not recommended. Methods 2 and 3 are both acceptable with method 3 being further developed later in this chapter. Technically the Fischer formula should have been applied to arrive at the real rate of interest. This can be calculated by 1.16/1.05 and is 10.5%. The actual effect on the calculations, however, is so small that it can be ignored.

Method 1:

Year	Labour CF	11% factor	PV	Machinery, etc. CF	PV
0				−780	−780
1	− 250			−40	
2	− 250			−40	
3	− 250	3.695	−923.75	−40	−147.8
4	−250			−40	
5	−250			−40	
NPV			−923.75		−927.8

Method 2:

Year	Labour + 7% p.a. CF	16% factor	PV	Machinery, etc. +5% p.a. CF	PV
0		1		−780	−780
1	−250	0.862	−215.5	−40	−34.48
2	−267.5	0.743	−198.753	−42	−31.206
3	−286.225	0.641	−183.470	−44.1	−28.2681
4	−306.261	0.552	−169.056	−46.305	−25.5604
5	−327.699	0.476	−155.985	−48.6203	−23.1432
NPV			− 922.763		− 922.658

Method 3:

Year	Labour + 2% p.a. CF	11% factor	PV	Machinery, etc. CF	PV
0		1		−780	−780
1	−250	0.901	−225.25	−40	−36.04
2	−255	0.812	−207.06	−40	−32.48
3	−260.1	0.731	−190.133	−40	−29.24
4	−265.3	0.658	−174.567	−40	−26.32
5	−270.6	0.594	−160.736	−40	−23.76
NPV			−957.747		−927.84

1. Use a real discount rate, and project cash flows in base year prices, accepting the weakness outlined above.
2. Use a money rate of interest and project cash flows in the money prices estimated for future years.
3. Use a real discount rate and take account of relative inflation.

9.6 Other techniques of investment appraisal

Before turning to a detailed examination of cost-benefit analysis a brief examination will be made of two other techniques used in the private sector. These are:

Payback

This is a simple method of investment appraisal and is frequently used in the private sector. The technique compares the length of time that a project takes to recover its original investment from its net cash flow and then compares this with a laid-down decision rule. If the project fails to pay for itself within, say, a decision rule of two years the project would be rejected. The method can be adjusted to take account of the time value of money but is deficient in its narrow concentration on the payback period. Its only possible use suggested in the public sector is for those competition services which are experiencing cash flow problems as this type of organization would face increased interest charges.

Accounting rate of return

The technique uses the average accounting profit made by an investment divided by the average investment cost, which will depend on the depreciation method used. The method makes no use of the time value of money, considers financial accounting flows rather than cash, and has little to commend it, even in the private sector.

9.7 Cost-benefit analysis

Cost-benefit analysis (CBA) is concerned with economic choice and has as its objective the provision of assistance to decision-makers in their choice concerning the use of scarce resources. It has been defined as follows:

> A practical way of assessing the desirability of projects where it is important to take a long view (in the sense of looking at repercussions in the future, as well as nearer future) and a wide view (in the sense of allowing for side effects of many kinds on many persons, industries, regions, etc.), i.e. it implies the enumeration and evaluation of all the relevant costs and benefits. (Prest and Turvey, 1965, pp. 685–705.)

In the private sector, operating within the market mechanism, the goal of the organization is seen as profit maximization and is thus purely a financial objective. The firm would only consider private costs and benefits in its investment decisions, selecting only those schemes which are within its ability to fund ranked by their contribution to its welfare (i.e. profit). The problem for the public sector is that the market mechanism does not operate for many of its goods and services yet society is faced with major questions when it is considering its use of resources: Is the scheme worthwhile? Are the relative merits of scheme A greater than scheme B? When should a programme be implemented to achieve optimal timing? What scale of operation should be adopted? CBA has been developed to help with these types of decisions.

Intangible items and valuation

CBA attempts to place a value on not only the direct costs of particular programme (e.g. the construction costs of a new road) but also the more intangible benefits that may occur as a result of completing the project (e.g. time savings) or intangible costs (e.g. noise). It is clearly with these more intangible benefits and costs that difficulties of valuation occur although, as will be seen, the direct costs also have their own particular difficulties in this area as well. It should also be remembered that definitive answers will not always be provided by CBA but, to the extent that additional information is provided to decision-makers, it will aid choice concerning complex decisions on resource allocation in the public sector.

In the public sector we are dealing with a wide range of decisions on the potential use of resources. At the heart of government policy will be decisions on the allocation of resources to defence, health, education, etc. Clearly these allocation decisions will be based on political expediency and the political objectives and priorities of the party in power. At the other end of the scale will be day-to-day decisions on, for example, financing, including decisions such as whether or not to lease or borrow money in order to acquire new plant and machinery. This type of resource utilization decision would be one performed using a comparison of cash flows and an appropriate discount rate as discussed earlier. In between these two extremes, we have a large range of decisions for which the technique of CBA has the potential to make a major contribution and it is with these areas that subsequent sections are concerned.

The problem of valuation in CBA

There is a need to examine each item and identify its economic cost to the community. In an attempt to ascribe value to costs and benefits the economist will first resort to market prices, but in some cases market prices may fail to reflect true values due to the presence of market distortions, while in others a relevant market may just not exist, as in the case of environmental factors. In a situation of market imperfections the economist will resort to shadow prices which are simply the values more appropriate for the purpose of economic calculations than the existing price. Certain gains or losses to the project can be valued at zero since, for the economy as a whole, they represent transfer payments, while costs for, say, labour, for example, which would otherwise remain unemployed would be valued at opportunity cost and not at wages actually paid. Two difficulties will, however, be referred to:

1. The shadow price of a particular input, due to interrelationships between commodities, may well require the shadow price of other inputs to be amended but the difficulty is that data on the complex dependency may not exist.
2. The task of measurement may be so difficult as to make the data so unreliable that the base for the exercise becomes questionable.

In practice, therefore, given that the information requirements are such that the fullest information is difficult to achieve, market prices are typically used. It has been pointed out, however, by some economists that observed market prices may be as reliable a measure of economic value as the efforts to derive shadow prices.

As has just been demonstrated, problems exist in the valuation of costs and benefits even where market prices exist. In CBA, however, there is also a need to value those items for which no market exists. Examples include savings in travel time if a new transport system were to be developed, plus the possible reductions in deaths and injuries giving benefits to the economy and the potential loss or gain to the environment if the scheme goes ahead. One approach has been to develop surrogate prices where an attempt is made to derive a cost that consumers would be prepared to pay – to save travelling time, for example. Improvements in transport systems are normally expected to reduce the severity and frequency of accidents. A number of measures have been developed to measure the costs of avoided deaths and injuries. These include a measure of avoided costs, where a measure is made of the income and output not foregone as a result of the system improvement; an examination of defensive expenditure, where a study is made of the past expenditure by society on road safety or the amounts individuals were prepared to pay in terms of insurance cover; or finally by reference to the amount that would be paid for a reduction in the probability of death or injury by reference to indifference curves for a population of individuals. Finally, of considerable concern given today's 'green movement' is the effect of any proposal on the environment.

Clearly this is a difficult area but contingency valuation may have a role to play. Basically, under this proposal, the population is asked directly how much it is prepared to pay for the environment and how much compensation they would require for the loss of the amenity if they were denied. One of the difficulties with this approach is that consumers are being made to measure something which is not as yet within their experience, as they are effectively considering their future reaction to possible extra noise and pollution.

The application of cost-benefit analysis to a road transport scheme

In examining the possibility of building a new road scheme it is necessary to identify the costs and benefits associated with the scheme and these are set out below:

Costs	Benefits
1. Opportunity cost of physical resources	1. Savings in travel time
	2. Reductions in vehicle operating costs
2. Construction costs	3. Reduction in accident costs
3. Maintenance	4. Other benefits – reduced
4. Environmental costs	stress and discomfort

The relative importance of each item will obviously vary between schemes. In terms of valuation, items 1–4 on the cost side of the equation are reasonably easy to value, subject to the discussion on shadow prices earlier. The environmental effect is more difficult but could be considered in terms of the possible effect on crop yields by the examination of historic data, and attempts could also be made to estimate health damage as a result of consulting medical opinion. The Roskill Inquiry into the third London airport made an attempt to value the social cost of the loss of historic churches by reference to their fire insurance value. This process was held up to ridicule and probably detracted from the Committee's work in measuring the physical distributional effect of noise on the area if the airport were to be built.

In an examination of the benefits associated with a road or any public transport scheme the major objective of the scheme is probably time saving. Indeed in such schemes as the construction of the M1 motorway and the Victoria Line it was the time saving which was the major benefit of the proposals. Two categories of time can be identified. These are work and leisure time and therefore the question has to be addressed as to what value should be given to these savings. The conventional approach is to measure the value of work time in terms of the average gross salary for the type of work time saved plus an additional sum for extra costs associated with the costs of employing labour (e.g. National Insurance and pension costs). This of course assumes that the time saved can be converted directly into additional output. The problems of valuing non-work time (commuting and leisure) are, however, more difficult as no equivalent market price in terms of direct wage rates exist. For the value of non-work time it is necessary to impute values from choices which people make regarding the use of time (the behaviour observation method) or to use a questionnaire or other experiments to derive a value (the contingent valuation method). The Ministry of Transport has suggested a standard figure of 25% of the national average gross hourly rate as a measure of commuting time but there are obvious difficulties in the application of one figure in a range of differing situations. The Department's figures is also restricted to commuting time and does not cover leisure travel.

With a new road it would be hoped that savings could be generated by the reduction in vehicle operating costs as wear and tear on vehicle is reduced. However, it is necessary to consider the distinction between generated and non-generated traffic. While data is available in respect of vehicle operating costs it is the level of traffic that it is difficult to estimate. Generally, the larger the generated or extra traffic, the greater will be the effect on the original estimated time savings of the scheme. The M25 indicates that generated traffic will have a major impact on the success or failure of a scheme; in this particular case, additional generated traffic may actually reduce (or even eliminate) total time savings!

The question of accident costs has already been touched upon above. The physical costs of treatment, for example, will be available from health authorities and in the M1 study costs were input for accident savings in terms of loss of output, medical expenses, property damage and administration costs. However, the authors of the study admitted the difficulties of placing a monetary value on death itself and personal distress. Some writers have suggested the use of court awards but inevitably there will always be disagreement on the value of this element of the cost-benefit equation. Finally there is a need to consider the value of such benefits as reduced stress and strain on drivers and passengers if congestion can be reduced. If can be argued, however, that such factors are related to time in that time pressures cause stress and discomfort. This factor might therefore be included in the general framework of time valuation.

Summary of cost-benefit analysis

It can be seen from the previous statements that there are considerable difficulties in the application of cost-benefit analysis. The method does, however, require a systematic analysis of a problem and its potential solutions. It focuses on the important issue in any project appraisal and is based on focuses on techniques consistent with economic principles including the discounting of future monetary flows. Decision-makers are being called on to exercise judgement with imperfect knowledge but partial or approximate information is better than no information at all. In each step assumptions have been made but, given the earlier discussion on probability, all investment decisions inevitably entail risk and the public sector cannot be protected from a fact of life.

9.8   Cost-effectiveness analysis

This technique has been developed in an attempt to overcome the difficulties of gathering and valuing information in a complete CBA exercise. Cost-effectiveness analysis identifies all costs and benefits but concentrates on measuring the measurable and provides a description of the non-quantifiable factors only. The technique, therefore, does not provide an absolute measure of the value of the project. In the field of housing and inner-city renewal the provision of a given standard of accommodation at minimal cost could be the subject of a cost-effectiveness exercise. The exercise may thus be considered to be more realistic than a full cost-benefit exercise as no attempt has been made to measure the unmeasurable.

A form of cost-effectiveness analysis is the technique of option appraisal as developed in the health service, although it has the potential for application in the public sector in general. Option appraisal can be defined as a method of project appraisal which systematically informs the decision maker of all the advantages and disadvantages of the practical alternatives for achieving an objective by providing all relevant information. It is a process of informing rather than actually determining the decision. On some occasions option appraisal will change the decision makers mind about the best way of deploying resources while on others it will merely confirm that solutions arrived at intuitively are correct. It is a team approach in that it is multi-disciplinary and inevitably involves value judgements.

The steps in optional appraisal are:

1. *Identify the strategic planning context* as this will put any proposals for change in the context of the overall organization's goals and objectives.
2. *Set the objectives, constraints and performance criteria* for the proposed changes.
3. *Formulate options*, this should include doing nothing as this will provide a reference point to assess how successfully the options considered meet the current service problems.
4. *Evaluate options*, this involves a preliminary sift to eliminate options which are not practical in that they fail to satisfy step (2). For remaining options:
    (a)   prepare a detailed description of each option giving full background;
    (b)   assess benefits describing the quantifying where possible the effectiveness of each option in satisfying the objectives of the scheme;
    (c)   assess revenue and capital costs;

(d) discount to take account of the timing of cost flows.
(e) assess any significant costs and benefits in the wider non-organizational context.
(f) carry out sensitivity analysis to assess the relative importance of particular assumptions to the options under consideration.

5. *Select the preferred option.*
6. *Monitor results.*

The organizational environment in which appraisal takes place is clearly important and this point lends support to the accusation that appraisals can be used for political purposes to advance a case or protect an organization from outside interference rather than for purely evaluation reasons (McAlister, 1990, p. 49). Clearly, in a political environment the political consequences of any decision cannot be ignored but the technique of option appraisal has the potential to bring all relevant factors to the attention of the decision maker and thus inform him/her of the full consequences of any decision.

In summary option appraisal has the potential to provide:

1. a disciplined approach to ensure that all relevant factors are considered in a multi-disciplinary framework before a decision is reached;
2. a mechanism to ensure that all feasible alternative methods of meeting an objective are considered;
3. a framework to marshall the arguments for and against potential solutions;
4. the opportunity to take account of risk and uncertainty in the decision-making process;
5. full information to decision makers on the consequences of the choice of a particular option.
6. after the decision has been taken a basis to monitor progress in achieving the original objective(s) set.

The application of the technique is now demonstrated in Exhibit 9.3 in relation to a proposed capital project by a central government department, and also draws on the 'desiderata' principles demonstrated in Chapter 8 on capital budgeting.

Exhibit 9.3

A government department is considering developing new office accommodation and has assembled an appropriate team to examine in full the alternatives available to it (the options). The department currently operates on a split site in two office buildings in the heart of a town centre in the south-east of England. Only one of these sites has adequate land to build additional offices although the remaining site could be redeveloped by internal modernization of the current office layout and the addition of an extra floor on top of the present structure. The only other alternative is the purchase of land and the building of new office accommodation on the outskirts of the town. Relocation to other parts of the United Kingdom is not possible due to the work of the department. It is also not possible to do nothing as the work of the department is suffering from the split site and the public is seriously dissatisfied with the service resulting in political pressure to act.

In summary the options are thus:

1. develop existing site by the utilization of surplus land for new offices; (site A).
2. modernize present offices and add new floor to existing structure; (site B).
3. purchase new site and use sale proceeds of selling sites A and B to reduce capital costs;
4. relocate – impractical;
5. do nothing – operationally and politically unacceptable.

It is first necessary to cost the feasible alternatives:

	Land £000	Building costs £000	Annual revenue cost £000	NPV
Option 1		2300	750	13 321
Option 2		2000	680	11 998
Option 3	300	2200	670	12 038

Notes:

1. The discount rate is 6% with the life of the buildings estimated at 50 years (i.e. cumulative discount factor year 51 at 6% is 15.813).
2. Building costs are spread over one year with payment assumed at the end of year one (i.e. discount factor 0.943).
3. The annual revenue costs of the buildings once complete (i.e. cumulative discount factor 15.813 − 0.943) = 14.87.
4. Capital cost after income from sale of other sites. It is assumed that the sites are sold for £530 000 in one year's time. The total capital cost of the land is estimated at £800 000 payable upfront. (Total capital cost = £800 000 × 1 − (£530 000 × 0.943) = £300 210.)

On the basis of the above financial appraisal option 2 is the cheapest and would appear to be the one that should be adopted. There is a need, however, to consider the other benefits that would occur. At this stage the team might draw up the desiderata matrix shown in Table 9.1. (It will be noted that this desiderata exercise is presented differently to that in Chapter 8. This is to indicate that alternative formats are available.)

Clearly in this exhibit the weights given to each of the criteria plus the criteria themselves will be those identified by the team. It can be seen that while option 2 is the cheapest it scores badly on the non-financial appraisal. Option 1 is the most expensive but scores well on the non-financial appraisal. Option 3 costs marginally more than 2 but is significantly better in terms of its effectiveness. On the basis of this appraisal option 3 should be choosen subject to detailed tenders to ensure the original cost estimates were realistic.

All options can be subjected to sensitivity analysis to test the strength of the assumptions on which they are based and to recognize the uncertainty of capital investment.

Table 9.1 Desiderate table for option appraisal exercise

Criteria	Weights	Option 1	Option 2	Option 3
Lack of disruption to existing workload	10	7	3	9
Car parking	5	3	2	5
Access to public transport	5	4	4	3
Suitability for future expansion	10	7	1	8
Staff perceptions	5	3	2	3
Total benefits		190	80	225

Key points of chapter

1. The importance of considering the time value of money in the capital investment decision has been stressed.
2. The problem of inflation was discussed and illustrated.
3. The potential for cost-benefit analysis was explored.
4. The value of option appraisal in the public sector was explored.

9.9   Summary

This chapter has examined techniques which take account of the time value of money in project appraisal. It also developed economic concepts of investment appraisal in the calculation of the cost of capital and the development of cost-benefit analysis. The difficulties of the cost-benefit approach were discussed but the conclusion reached was that the technique is of considerable value in public sector investment appraisal. Cost-effectiveness analysis was also examined but it was pointed out that this technique is less ambitious than CBA but can make a valuable contribution to the capital investment decision-making process.

Exhibit 9.4

Chilly County Council is considering installing a new central heating system in one of its older offices. As part of its long-term plan this office will be sold in three years' time on 31/12/X3. The authority believes that installing the central heating system will make the building easier to sell and add £100 000 to the final selling price. Three systems are regarded as feasible and the estimated capital costs of each are set out below:

	£
Gas	170 000
oil	150 000
Solid fuel	140 000

Annual fuel costs are dependent on the severity of the winter each year and the rate of increase in fuel price. At the prices expected to be in force during 19X1 the annual fuel costs are estimated at:

	Severe winter £	Mild winter £
Gas	40 000	24 000
Oil	53 000	37 000
Solid fuel	45 000	36 000

The authority estimates that in each year there is a 70% chance of a severe winter and a 30% chance of a mild winter. The chance of a mild or severe winter in any year is considered to be independent of the chance of a mild or severe winter in the previous year.

Fuel prices are expected during 19X2 and 19X3 to increase by either 8% (probability equal to 0.4) or 10% (probability equal to 0.6%). Whichever rate of increase applies in 19X2 will be repeated the following year. Maintenance costs (payable at the end of year) are expected to be:

	£
Gas	2 500
Oil	2 000
Solid fuel	10 000 (in 19X2)

Maintenance costs are fixed.

There is no difference in performance between the systems.

The authority uses the monetary cost of capital as its hurdle rate. This rate is currently 12%.

Which system should be purchased by the authority?

The following solution uses expected value to calculate risk, and expresses project costs in monetary terms, permitting discounting using the monetary cost of capital.

Gas heating

Expected value of fuel costs, based upon the probabilities of a mild (0.3) or severe (0.7) winter:

$$= (0.7 \times £40\,000) + (0.3 \times £24\,000)$$
$$= £35\,200$$

Annual fuel costs:

Year	12% discount factor	8% inflation		10% inflation	
		Cash flow	PV	Cash flow	PV
		£	£	£	£
1	0.893	35 200	31 433	35 200	31 433
2	0.797	38 016	30 298	38 720	30 860
3	0.712	41 057	29 234	42 592	30 326
			£90 965		£92 619

Expected value of discounted fuel costs, allowing for probabilities of 8% inflation (0.4) and 10% inflation (0.6):

$(0.4 \times £124\,561) + (0.6 \times £126\,825)$

	£
	91 960
Capital costs	170 000
Maintenance (£2000 per annum for 3 years)	6 005
= £2000 × 2.402	
NPV of gas option	£−267 965

Oil heating

Expected value of fuel costs, based upon the probabilities of a mild (0.3) or severe (0.7) winter:

$$= (0.7 \times £53\,000) + (0.3 \times £37\,000)$$
$$= 48\,200$$

Annual fuel costs:

Year	12% discount factor	8% inflation		10% inflation	
		Cash flow	PV	Cash flow	PV
		£	£	£	£
1	0.893	48 200	43 043	48 200	43 043
2	0.797	52 056	41 489	53 020	42 257
3	0.712	56 220	40 029	58 322	42 257
			£124 561		£126 825

Expected value of discounted fuel costs, allowing for probabilities of 8% inflation (0.4) and 10% inflation (0.6):
(0.4 × £124 561) + (0.6 × £126 825)

	£
	125 920
Capital costs	150 000
Maintenance (£2 000 per annum for 3 years)	4 804
= £2 000 × 2.402	
NPV of oil option	£280 724

Solid fuel heating

Expected value of fuel costs, based upon the probabilities of a mild (0.3) or severe (0.7) winter:

= (0.7 × £45 000) + (0.3 × £36 000)
= £42 300

Annual fuel costs:

Year	12% discount factor	8% inflation Cash flow £	PV £	10% inflation Cash flow £	PV £
1	0.893	42 300	37 774	42 300	37 774
2	0.797	45 684	36 410	46 530	37 084
3	0.712	49 339	35 129	51 183	36 442
			£109 313		£111 300

Expected value of discounted fuel costs, allowing for probabilities of 8% inflation (0.4) and 10% inflation (0.6):
(0.4 × £109 313) + (0.6 × £111 300)

	£
	110 505
Capital costs	140 000
Maintenance (£10 000 in 2 years time)	7 970
£10 000 × 0.797	
NPV of solid fuel option	£258 475

Based on the above calculations, the solid fuel option has the lowest NPV of costs, and on financial grounds would appear to be the favoured option. It also requires less capital investment than the other two options, which may be important if there are severe constraints on capital expenditure.

The main limitations on this type of analysis are that the expected value will never occur and we are ignoring the decision-maker's attitude to risk. A possible alternative would be to attempt to redefine the problem in terms of utility but clearly this is difficult ground to read. A decision must be made and therefore we have to take into account uncertainty whatever decision-making technique is used, and there is inevitable compromise. The comparison between the three systems must also taken into account both financial and so-called non-financial factors. A selection of these are set out below:

1. How reliable are the estimates of cost, the probabilities of fuel price inflation and the chances of a mild or severe winter?
2. Is there a legal obligation to instal a new system?
3. While the increase in the selling price has been ignored since it is common to all three systems the question must arise as to the validity of this assumption due to the possible views of potential buyers.
4. There is no mention of storage problems or extra employees to check deliveries of the appropriate systems.
5. Gas may be an environmentally cleaner fuel.

Exhibit 9.5

A town centre is heavily congested with road traffic. It has been suggested that a bypass be constructed to relieve the congestion.

The projected road will be 2.5 miles long and will require a capital cost of £0.3 million per mile and annual maintenance costs of £12 000 per mile. The projected route is via rich agricultural land which was acquired by the Department of Transport in anticipation of the road scheme being built for £0.5m some five years ago. In its present use it yields crops worth £60 000 per year. The new road will result in higher noise levels and houses will require to be soundproofed at a cost ranging between £2500 and £3500 each. One hundred houses are affected.

It is predicted that there is a:

0.2 probability of 1.5 million journeys per year
0.5 probability of 2.0 million journeys per year or
0.3 probability of 3.0 million journeys per year

along the new road.

In each case approximately 40% of the journeys will compromise generated traffic and 50% of the journeys will be for leisure purposes. The average mileage saved per journey will be 1.2 miles and the average time saved will be 12 minutes per journey.

It is expected that there will be a reduction in accidents from 30 per year to 14 year:

		Fatal	Serious	Minor
Town	centre	2	6	22
route		2	8	4
Bypass				

During construction of the bypass there will be considerable delays to users of the existing route.

Notes:

1. Generated traffic is weighted 0.5 of existing traffic. This is to reflect the impact that generated vehicles currently using other routes will have on traffic flow. The case of the M25 might suggest that generated traffic be treated as a cost due to its potential to remove the benefits of time savings and increase operating costs.

2. Time savings are to be valued as follows:

   Work time   £2.25 per hour
   Leisure time   £1.00

3. Recent court awards for loss of life range from £50 000 to £250 000, and for serious accidents from £5000 to £85 000.

4. Hospital statistics reveal that the cost per case is £1500 for serious accidents and £80 for minor accidents.

5. The project is to be appraised using the test discount rate of 6%.

6. The project is to be evaluated over a 30-year time horizon.

7. Vehicle operating costs amount to £0.10 per mile.

   Should the bypass be built?

The problem examines the role that CBA can play in a decision-making situation. The calculation below illustrates how the costs and benefits of the scheme can be calculated once the difficult conceptual issues of valuation have been addressed.

Years		Cost £000	Discount factor	NPV £000
Costs:				
0	Construction Costs	750.00	1.00	750.00
1–30	Maintenance	30.00	13.76	412.80
1–30	Land–opportunity Cost	60.00	13.76	825.60
0	Soundproofing	300.00	1.00	300.00
1–30	Serious injuries	90.00	13.76	123.84
1–30	Additional hospital costs	3.00	13.76	41.28
	Total costs			2453.52

Benefits:				
1–30	Time saved	577.50	13.76	7870.72
1–30	Vehicle operating costs	198.00	13.76	2906.11
1–30	Minor accidents	1.44	13.76	19.81
Total benefits				10 796.94
Net benefits				8343.12

The discount factor of 13.76 was taken from annuity tables for 6%. The incremental changes resulting from building the road were used as appropriate. Where a range of values was given, as for soundproofing, the average value was calculated. The number of journeys undertaken is based on the expected value calculated by multiplying the probability factor by the expected number of journeys associated with that factor and taking the sum of the three resultant figures (i.e. 2.2 million). This was then multiplied by the anticipated number of generated journeys (0.4). The balance of 60% is the number of non-generated journeys. This results in generated journeys of 880 000 and non-generated journeys of 1 320 000; 50% of each of these journeys are for work and 50% are for leisure. It is now possible to calculate the time factor saving (12/60) at the appropriate rate for work (£2.25) and leisure (£1.00) and to take account of note 1 on the weighting of generated journeys. A similar calculation was then undertaken for operating cost savings using the appropriate distance saved and note 7.

Questions

9.1 (a) Indicate briefly why discounted cash flow techniques are used in the public sector.

(b) Following a review by the Fire Prevention Officer the Chief Building Works Manager has recently presented an adverse report on an operational building in your public sector organization. To bring the existing building up to standard would cost capital expenditure of £90 000 next year, and extra maintenance expenditure of £15 000 in each of the next three years, commencing next year. Alternatively if the building were replaced after those three years there would be no need for capital expenditure, and additional maintenance expenditure of only £4000 in each of those three years would be required.

The Management Board suggests that it would be more economic to replace the building as, because of the nature of the building, staffing and running costs are also high.

The figures are as follows:

Annual cost	Existing building £000s	Replacement building £000s
Staffing	130	96
Running costs	42	26
	172	122
Income	51	51
	121	71

The cost of building and furnishing a new building on an adjacent site owned by the organization would be £630 000, spread evenly over the next three years. The present building could be sold for £40 000.

The Chief Accountant asks you to:

(i) Assess whether it would be economic over a 20-year period to replace the building on the basis of the above costs (assuming a discount rate of 6% in real terms).

(ii) Indicate the other factors to be taken into account by the organization in considering whether to go ahead with the proposal.

9.2 (a) Discuss the view that payback is a more appropriate investment appraisal technique than net present value for public sector organizations, since liquidity is of critical importance.

(b) Metroland County Ambulance Service is considering changing from petrol to liquified petroleum gas (LPG) as the primary fuel for its ambulance fleet of 208 vehicles. Some of the costs and benefits involved with the change have been identified, allowing a preliminary evaluation of the financial viability of the proposal to be made. All costs and benefits are at November 1987 prices, and a 5% discount rate is normally used in appraisals.

Capital costs so far established can be categorized as vehicle conversion costs, bulk installation costs and training costs.

Vehicle conversion costs have been calculated as averaging £540 per vehicle. It is assumed that 40 vehicles will be converted now, payment being made immediately, then 100 vehicles during the first year, payment to be made at the end of the year, and the remaining vehicles during the second year, with payment at the end of the year. From then on there will be no need for conversion, and no additional costs, as replacement ambulances will be fitted to run on LPG.

Bulk installation costs arise form the need for bulk storage tanks to contain LPG. It will be necessary to purchase 21 tanks, all of which are initially presumed to be of a two-tonne size. The cost of each tank and its installation is estimated at £7650. Purchase will be phased at seven year with payment assumed to be made at the beginning of each year.

Training costs arise from the need to retrain maintenance staff and operational staff who number 520. For maintenance staff it is assumed that the retraining programme will cost £2200, payable immediately. It is estimated that on average £10 will be incurred on training for each member of the operational staff, with the training programme taking two years. Assume that the payment is made in two halves, at the end of the first and second years.

Revenue costs involve maintenance and insurance costs per year for the tanks of £25 per tank, and additional maintenance for each vehicle of £12 per year, both payable at the end of the year.

The financial benefit of LPG is its price advantage over petrol. Given the size of deliveries and quantities likely to be required for the fleet, it is estimated that LPG would produce a saving of 4p per litre, for a range of consumption between 1.15 million and 1.35 million litres per annum when all the vehicles have been covered. It has been decided to assess the change to LPG over a ten-year period.

9.3 Midlands Airport Authority is considering the construction of a new airport terminal building to handle international passenger traffic.

The following estimates of the most likely increase in passenger movements and cost data have been derived from the preliminary feasibility study, just completed by consultants at a cost of £100 000:

(i) The increase in international passenger movements is anticipated to be 3m per annum.

(ii) It would be necessary to spend £2m immediately on infrastructure before construction of the terminal could commence.

(iii) The estimated capital development cost of the terminal building is £52m. The construction period is anticipated to be 2 years. Payments would be phased and £26m would be paid at the end of the 2 years.

(iv) Expected annual running costs are:

Fixed costs	£4 million
Variable costs	£10 per passenger movement

(v) Competitive considerations suggest that landing fees should be fixed at £12 per passenger movement. In addition, each passenger will generate £2 average net income from duty-free sales.

(vi) Advances in air travel technology indicate that the useful life of the terminal building could be as short as 18 years.

(vii) Capital can be readily obtained at a cost of 10% per annum.

Required

(a) You are required to prepare a report to the Board of the Authority indicating whether the construction of the new terminal building is likely to be worthwhile. Your report should include an assessment of the sensitivity of the proposals to the annual level of passenger movements.

(15 marks)

(b) What are the limitations of using the above information for assessing the desirability of the airport extension from the viewpoint of society as a whole. What other factors should be taken into consideration and to what extent can they be quantified in financial terms? (5 marks)

(Total 20 marks)

9.4 Your council is concerned at the substantial amounts paid in car allowances for the reimbursement of officers who use their own vehicles for the provision of services and wishes to investigate alternative methods of provision. The objective of this exercise is to provide a comprehensive report on the most cost-effective alternative method(s) for the provision of car transport for its employees with high car mileage.

Option 1 considers contract leasing for the hire of 37 vehicles at a rental of £120 per month whatever the mileage. Maintenance costs are included in the agreement.

Option 2 considers operating a vehicle fleet financed from the Renewal and Repairs Fund. Ford Escorts and Flestas are selected and the average cost per vehicle is £4550; initial outlay from the R & R fund will be made this year. Annual repayments of principal are to be made over three years and the cost of internal finance is 12%. Residual value at the end of year 3 is £67 340.

Option 3 is the finance leasing option. A lease for the purchase of 37 vehicles totals £188 520. Annual repayments are made evenly over three years. A commission of 0.5% of capital expenditure is normally charged at the beginning of the agreement. The residual value of the vehicles is £67 340 less 5% paid to the lessor at the end of the third year.

To make a valid comparison maintenance costs must be taken into account. One local garage has expressed an interest in contract maintenance and has quoted £20 per month per vehicle as an indication of their charges. In their quotation they say a 7% inflation factor must be built into the figures and payment made yearly in advance.

(a) Calculate which of the three options is the most cost-effective. It is suggested that a discount factor of 7% should be built into the calculations. Base your calculations on a fleet of 37 vehicles.

(b) Although discounting procedures are a recommended method of investment appraisal many organizations use the simple payback method of evaluation. Why should this be the case and what are the disadvantages of payback.

Note: Year	Discount factor 7%
0	1.0000
1	0.9346
2	0.8734
3	0.8163

9.5 The National Mining Corporation extracts and sells coal using open-cast mining methods. This involves three major operations:

(a) First, the removal and setting aside of the topsoil covering the coal to be excavated.
(b) Secondly, the extraction, preparation and sale of the minerals.
(c) Finally, the restoration of the site by filling in the excavation and replacing the topsoil with general restoration to at least the same condition as before the operation commended.

The corporation owns a site and is faced with two possible alternatives for the use of the site. These are:

1. To sell the site immediately for £350 000.
2. To develop the site for mining purposes.

If alternative 2 is adopted the following data will need to be considered:

Physical data
Volume of topsoil: 2 500 000 cubic metres
Coal in site: 1 500 000 tonnes
Extraction rate: 300 000 tonnes per annum

Cost data
Equipment costs: £800 000 (paid at end of first year)
Topsoil removal by private contractor: £1.30 per cubic metre.
Mining costs: £8.00 per tonne.
Restoration: £1 250 000 (paid at end of seventh year).

Income
Mineral sales: £15.00 per tonne.

Other data
Equipment will be sold at the end of year seven at 10% of the original cost. The value of the restored site at the end of the seventh year is estimated at £450 000.

The corporation uses a 20% discount rate as its cost of capital.

The payments to the private contractor are spread evenly over the first 12 months of the scheme.

Required

Advise the corporation as to which of the two alternatives it should follow in a report to the Management Board, including any non-financial factors they might consider.

Ignore inflation.

Discount factors
Year 1   0.833
Year 2   0.694
Year 3   0.579
Year 4   0.482
Year 5   0.402
Year 6   0.335
Year 7   0.279

9.6   Deptford Health Authority is planning to change its geriatric care service. The proposals of the Geriatric Health Care Planning Committee (composed of medical staff) are set out in the following paper which has been presented directly to the Area Management Team.

Extract from Geriatric Care Paper to Management Team

The Geriatric Health Care Planning Committee has considered the need to improve services to the elderly given the increasing trend towards a more elderly population. It is considered three alternatives exist:

1.   to build a new specialist unit;
2.   to convert part of an existing hospital;
3.   to improve the current units and also to offer wider ranging care in the community to prevent admission to hospital. The Revenue Allocation would be increased each year by £5000 over the current allocation for each of the next ten years.

After due consideration the Committee has decided to recommend the adoption of Scheme (A) as on the basis of the Cost Statement set out as it is the only scheme that will pay for itself in ten years (i.e. the period of the current planning cycle).

Cost Statement

	Schemes		
	(A)	(B)	(c)
	£000	£000	£000
Capital Cost	1050	700	
Additional Revenue Running Cost	—	—	50
	1050	700	50
Income from Sale of Redundant Property	(60)	(40)	—
Net Reduction in Annual Revenue Costs			
£100 000 p.a.	(1000)	—	—
£63 000 p.a.		(630)	—
Total Income/Savings	(1060)	(670)	—
Surplus	10	—	—
Deficit	—	30	50

The Report has only just been sighted by the Area Treasurer who is to attend the Management Team meeting and he has asked you for your comments on the proposals.

The following additional information is available to you.

(i) The life of the buildings are as follows

Scheme (A)   60 years (Annuity factor 0.1201)
Scheme (B)   30 years (Annuity factor 0.1241)

(You should assume that loan repayments are due to begin at the end of the first year on Schemes (A) and (B), the Capital Works taking one year to complete.)

(ii) The reduction in administration costs are achieved in the first year after the completion of the Capital Works, this is the same year as the increased Revenue funding would commence for Scheme (C).

(iii) The income from the sale of property is received in the third year after completion of the Capital Works. The figures have been confirmed by independent valuers.

(iv) Present value tables for £1 receivable at the end of each year at 12% are:

1	0.89	6	0.51
2	0.80	7	0.45
3	0.71	8	0.40
4	0.64	9	0.36
5	0.57	10	0.32

Prepare a Report to your Treasurer commenting on the appraisal performed by the Geriatric Care Committee, identifying which solution in your view should be adopted, and including any other factors which you consider important.

9.7 A town centre is heavily congested with road traffic. It has been suggested that a bypass be constructed to relieve the congestion.

The projected road will be three miles long and will require a capital cost of £0.5 million per mile and annual maintenance costs of £25 000 per mile. The projected route is via rich agricultural land which was acquired by the Department of Transport in anticipation of the road scheme being built for £0.5m some five years ago. In its present use it yields crops worth £160 000 per year. The new road will result in higher noise levels and houses will require to be soundproofed at a cost ranging between £2500 and £3500 each. One hundred houses are affected.

It is predicted that there is a:

0.1 probability of 1.5 million journeys per year
0.5 probability of 2.0 million journeys per year
0.4 probability of 3.0 million journeys per year

along the new road. In each case approximately 30% of the journeys will comprise generated traffic and 40% of the journeys will be for leisure purposes. The average mileage saved per journey will be 2.2 miles and the average time saved will be 20 minutes per journey.

It is expected that there will be a reduction in accidents from 30 per cent to 14 per year:

	Fatal	Serious	Minor
Town centre route	2	6	22
Bypass	2	8	4

During construction of the bypass there will be considerable delays to users of the existing route.

Notes:

1. Generated traffic is weighted 0.2 of existing traffic.
2. Time savings are valued as follows:

   Work time   £2.25 per hour
   Leisure time £1.00

3. Recent court awards for loss of life range from £50 000 to £250 000, and for serious accidents from £5000 to £85 000.
4. Hospital statistics reveal that the cost per case is £1500 for serious accidents and £80 for minor accidents.
5. The project is to be appraised during the test discount rate of 6%. The appropriate factor is 13.76.
6. The project is to be evaluated over a thirty-year time horizon.
7. Vehicle operating costs amount to £0.14 per mile.

Required

Prepare a report for the Ministry of Transport advising whether or not the bypass should be built.

9.8 Aqua Water Authority is to provide a water supply to part of a new town development comprising partially of industrial units and partially of domestic dwellings. The following information is available to you:

1. Land acquisition costs amount to £145 000 and will be incurred at the commencement of the project.
2. Construction costs of laying the supply are £110 000 and will be incurred 50% at the commencement of the scheme and the balance one year later.
3. A pumping station will operate from the beginning of year two. Annual costs of maintenance are estimated at £33 000 per annum and will increase by 10% from the beginning of year three and the beginning of each year thereafter.
4. When developed the area will comprise:
   (a) 3000 dwellings of which 1000 will be completed by the start of year two and the remaining 2000 by the start of year three. Each property will yield an income of £25 per annum increasing by 10% per annum from the start of year four and from the beginning of each year thereafter (assume all properties occupied on completion).
   (b) The industrial estate will consume water at the rate of 2.5 million gallons from the commencement of year three, 4 million gallons from the commencement of year four and 10 million gallons per annum thereafter. This will be charged for at the rate of 0.3p per gallon for the whole period under review.

Required

(i) The Water Authority uses a 7-year time cycle in calculating the returns on capital projects. You are required to calculate the net present value of the project using discount rates of 10% and 20%. Indicate the approximate internal rate of return.

(ii) What other factors should be considered by the Authority? Present the results in report form to the Management Board of the Authority.

10 The audit of public organizations

Key learning objectives

After reading this chapter you should be able to:

1. Understand the development of auditing in the public sector.
2. Contrast the increased importance of value-for-money auditing today with the decline of emphasis on stewardship auditing in the public sector.
3. Explain what is meant by the term value for money and discuss the difficulties of achieving value for money in the public sector.
4. List the audit processes necessary to achieving value for money.

Highly important to accountability in the public sector is the function exercised by the external audit of public sector organizations and today's increased demand for value-for-money appraisal placed upon it. This chapter examines the development of audit in the public sector and its changing role over time. It then turns to examine the role that value-for-money audit exercises contribute in the current role played by the auditor. External audit in the public sector is performed by the National Audit Office for government departments and other *ad hoc* bodies such as the Arts Council which are financed by central government, and by the Audit Commission for local government and the National Health Service, the Commission having taken over this duty from the Department of Health. The private sector audits on the 'true and fair view' basis those nationalized industries that remain in the public sector under the original Acts which established them. It should, however, not be forgotten that as important as the role of the external auditor is, a vital role is also played by internal audit. Increasingly the internal audit section is being required to undertake value-for-money assignments and it can be seen that pressures on the external auditor are reflected in the demands placed on internal audit staff. The opportunity has also been taken in this chapter to develop a number of exhibits which apply what might seem to be theoretical issues in a practical context. This effectively concludes what has been a theme of the book — the development of student understanding of complex financial management issues in the challenging environment of the public sector.

10.1 The audit of central government

The National Audit Office was established by the National Audit Act 1983 which represented the first major amendment to the role of the central government auditor since the statutory changes of 1921. The 1921 Act had itself only modified the original Exchequer and Audit Department Act of 1866. The Act of 1866 provided for the appointment of the Comptroller and Auditor General (C and AG) and the appointment of staff to carry out the statutory duties of the examination, certification and reporting on government department accounts. Under the 1866 Act the audit was to be a 100% check of the transactions of government departments but this was amended in 1921 to allow test checking. The 1921 Act also provided for the preparation and audit of trading accounts and the extension of powers to examine the revenue accounts of government. The C and AG's full title is the 'Comptroller General of the Receipt and Issue of Her Majesty's Exchequer and Auditor General of Public Accounts'. This rather long title covers, however, two main functions:

1. As Comptroller General he is responsible for the issue of public funds to appropriate bodies.
2. As Auditor General he is required to certify the accounts, carry out value-for-money studies and report on these matters to Parliament.

In practice these matters are referred to the Public Accounts Committee which was established in 1861 and by tradition is chaired by a leading member of the Opposition. The Committee has a maximum of 15 members but, again by tradition, does not question the policy of the government and tends not therefore to divide on party lines. An example of the work of the Public Accounts Committee can be found in its report on the recent developments on community care. It expressed doubts about the level of financial controls exercised over joint financing schemes by the Department of Health and was also critical of the differences in planning timescales between health authorities and local authorities. It is interesting to note that this was the Committee's second report into this area only to discover similar problems.

By the early 1980s pressure had built up such that a review of the functions of the C and AG was called for. Underlying this pressure were greater demands for accountability, not in the traditional narrow stewardship sense for the proper use of resources, but rather for a wider interpretation of stewardship to include economy, efficiency and effectiveness in the use of resources provided. The result of this pressure was the passing of the 1983 National Audit Act which established a National Audit Office and a Public Accounts Commission to strengthen independence. Prior to this the Treasury had significant influence over the C and AG in that it could direct the area and nature of his work. Traditionally the Treasury had supplied from its ranks the C and AG, it audited the accounts of the Exchequer and Audit Department and it exerted influence over the level of remuneration and conditions of service of staff. The Act also provided for a discretionary power to undertake examinations of the economy, efficiency and effectiveness with which departments used resources.

The C and AG is independent of the Executive as is shown by the following:

1. The appointment is made by the Queen and he can only be dismissed by a vote of both Houses of Parliament. Advice for the appointment is given by the Prime Minister after discussion with the Chairman of the Public Accounts Committee.
2. The salary for the post is paid from the Consolidated Fund.
3. The C and AG decides his own objectives within the statutory framework and the extent to which those objectives will be carried out.
4. The C and AG sets and appoints the number and conditions of service of his staff.

The powers of the C and AG are not, however, all-embracing in that there is no power to disallow expenditure and give legal rulings; there is no right of access to the accounts of public corporations or local authorities; he cannot 'follow public money wherever it goes' as there is no right of access to any other than government accounts; he cannot question policy; and finally maladministration affecting individual members of the public is a matter for the Ombudsman.

In central government there are numerous internal audit sections which have been given a stimulus by such events as the development of the Financial Management Initiative and the publication of *Improving Management in Government: The Next Steps*. During this period internal audit has moved from a regularity function to being integrated within the drive to promote economy, efficiency and effectiveness. The stronger are these internal audit sectors the more reliance that the C and AG will be able to place on their work.

The importance of value-for-money audit undertaken by the C and AG is illustrated in his report on the *Property Services Agency and Department of Energy, New Headquarters Building for the Department, 1990*, where it was identified that £2.8m was paid for eight months rent on an empty building and £3.6m in penalties was incurred due to poor planning by the Property Services Agency. The National Audit Office has also completed an investigation into civil service training (*Training of Non-Industrial Civil Servants; Report by the Comptroller and Auditor General*). It found that non-industrial civil servants were trained in 1988–89 at a cost of approximately £350m but found that there was little evidence of strategic planning to support training policies (see Table 10.1 which gives the unit costs of training calculated by department). The basic conclusion was that training was 'erratic' and that until attitudes to training matched policy statements training was not likely to achieve its full potential.

Table 10.1   Civil service training 1989

	Average	MAFF	LR	ODA	DHSS
Trainee days per tutor	412	1273	403	279	140
Costs per trainee day (£)	174	201	145	283	224
Costs per head of staff (£)	712	606	828	782	437

Source: National Audit Office.

10.2   The health service

The Health Service was audited by auditors appointed by the Secretary of State for Health but under new legislation this work has been taken over by the Audit Commission (from 1.10.90 under Statutory Instrument 1990/1329). The powers of the external auditors are now contained in three Acts of Parliament; The National Health Service Act 1977, The Local Government Finance Act 1982, and The National Health Service and Community Care Act 1990. The National Health Service and Community Care Act 1990 made provision for the following changes to the Local Government Finance Act 1982:

1. The name of the Commission was changed to the Audit Commission for Local Authorities and the National Health Service in England and Wales. Membership of the Commission increased from 15 to 20 members (s. 11).
2. The Commission is responsible for the appointment of auditors of the Health service but need not by law consult with the component bodies of the Health Service (s. 13).
3. The Commission is to prepare a Code of Audit Practice for the Health Service (s. 14).
4. The Auditors must satisfy themselves that the accounts comply with directions issued under the NHS Act and that value for money is achieved (s. 15).
5. Gives auditors the right of access to documents held by GP fundholders (s. 16).
6. There is no right of question of the auditor or inspection and objection to the accounts. Powers of illegally, prohibition orders and surcharge do not apply (Ss. 17, 19, 20 and 24). Under S. 20 (3) the auditor must report immediately to the Secretary of State where unlawful expenditure may occur.

Under the former system the audit system was an in-house service which reported directly to the Minister of Health. Essentially this procedure could be summarized as an examination of the systems of accounting and control and an assessment of their effectiveness, the undertaking of studies on the economy, efficiency and effectiveness of procedures and the verification of assets and liabilities. There was a close relationship between the centre (i.e. the Department of Health) and the individual health authorities and the concept of independence could be questioned. Also, as the audit was not conducted by the Comptroller and Auditor General, there was no direct accountability to Parliament.

In 1987 it was announced that in addition to the Audit Directorate use would be made of the private sector to carry out the statutory audit. The National Audit Office is responsible for examining and certifying the summarized accounts of the health authorities but they relied on the role of the Directorate in performing this task. The National Audit Office does, however, attempt to monitor the quality of the audit undertaken and has access if necessary to the books and records of all health authorities, the Department of Health and the Welsh and Scottish Offices. Internal audit in the NHS has been criticized and has been given low priority in the past. Some health authorities have privatized their internal audit services. Recent examples of value-for-money work undertaken by the Department of Health's auditors include enquiries into central sterile supplies departments and energy use. The National Audit Office has also undertaken value-for-money studies on a rolling programme using a sampling approach to select authorities, and, for example, in its report Management of the Family Practitioner Service found a wide variation in the quality of information available to the service.

10.3 Local government

Local government has a long tradition of audit. The earliest known reference is dated 1430 when an audit was conducted into the application of monies to build a town wall. Modern audit in the form of the district audit was established by the Poor Law Amendment Act 1844, but the system, as the Act implies, only related to the Poor Law. The history of local government audit is one, however, in which the district auditor gradually gained more influence over the accounts of local government until the abolition of the service and the establishment of the Audit Commission in 1982. In its earliest days the district audit was primarily a stewardship audit but this did not prevent value-for-money questions from raising their head. The case of Roberts v. Hopwood (1925) AC 578 is a case in point. (For a fuller discussion on the development of the district audit see Coombs and Edwards, 1990.)

By 1979 the government was becoming increasingly concerned about the effectiveness of the audit of local government, in particular the lack of detailed economy, efficiency and effectiveness studies. Indeed this concern was not only confined to the government as, in 1976, the Layfield Commission had recommended the appointment of an independent auditor with the same status as the C and AG. The result of this concern was that in 1982 the Local Government Finance Act established the Audit Commission. The role of the Commission from 1 April 1983 included the duties of:

1. appointing auditors to local authorities either from their own staff or the professional firms;
2. fixing the level of fees for audits;
3. preparing and maintaining an audit code of practice;
4. retaining the previous duties of auditors with regard to financial and regularity audit with specific reference to illegality and wilful misconduct. With the passing of the Local Government Act 1988 auditors gained new powers to apply for the judical review of possible unlawful actions by authorities or to issue a prohibition order;
5. ensuring auditors satisfy themselves that adequate arrangements are made for 'securing economy, efficiency and effectiveness' in the discharge of functions by authorities.

In addition the auditor has a duty to consider whether in the public interest he should make a report on any matter coming to his attention.

The main section of the 1982 Act is section 15 and paragraph 1 is reproduced below. This requires that:

(1) An auditor shall by examination of the accounts and otherwise satisfy himself:
   (a) That the accounts are prepared in accordance with regulations ... and all other statutory provisions applicable to the accounts.

(b) That proper practices have been observed in the compilation of the accounts.

(c) That the body whose accounts are being audited has made proper arrangements for securing economy, efficiency and effectiveness in its use of resources.

The local government elector has a right of inspection of the accounts including a right to make copies of most information. The Freedom of Information Act 1985 also aids the local elector by greater publicity of material. The local government elector also has the right of objection to the accounts and may appeal to the auditor if any matter is considered to be illegal. On application to the courts by the auditor the sum may be declared illegal and the sum recovered from the individual.

The chief financial officer (the responsible officer) of a local authority has a statutory obligation to make proper arrangements for the conduct of a local authority's financial activities (Local Government Act 1972, SS. 151). This has normally meant that an in-house internal audit section has been established as the accounts and audit regulations stipulate the need for the responsible officer to provide an adequate internal audit (the Audit Commission verify that this duty has been properly discharged). It should be pointed out, however, that this function does not have to be provided internally only that the function must be adequate. It is often stated that the internal audit section is the 'eyes and ears' of the chief financial officer although clearly there is the potential for conflict with service officers and the function is not independent of his own department. The main advantage to the external auditor is that a strong active internal audit section will reduce workload. This should help keep the external audit fees lower than they might otherwise have been as relevant information is exchanged sufficient to maximize audit performance.

A number of public sector organizations, including local government, have market tested the provision of services such as internal audit in advance of compulsory competitive tendering. Others have established service level agreements between internal audit sections and client departments. Both these steps represent a major challenge to internal audit as, under the first, there is the potential for the loss of the in-house function and, under the second, the need to perform to agreed standards as set out in the internal contract. In addition, a further threat to the future of the internal audit department/section is the reduction in audit activity as services leave the control of the organization. In local government, for example, the loss of colleges of higher education in local government, resulted in lower income and a consequent inability of the section, unless replacement work was generated, to support existing staff numbers. Internal audit therefore faces numerous challenges while, service managers, will need increasingly to appreciate the role that internal audit performs in order to achieve high standards in terms of the service they need and demand.

The major steps that internal audit must take to prepare for competitive tendering or to prepare a realistic service level agreement are:

1. establish the level of work necessary to achieve the basic statutory obligations of the director of finance and agree the level of service required by the organization in terms of those areas regarded as non-mandatory;

2. build up a long-term plan for the future of internal audit based on a risk index. A rolling plan for a three-year period is probably the minimum necessary;

3. establish quality standards with clients to ensure that the client is fully conversant with the role and function of internal audit;
4. cost all activities such as accommodation and computer services and in any tender situation ensure that all non-audit costs are excluded and that there are no costs attributable to the client function;
5. prepare a business plan which, during the process of preparation, fully identifies the strengths, opportunities, threats and weaknesses of the section. Appropriate action should be taken to build on the strengths, exploit the opportunities and overcome the threats and weaknesses identified;
6. establish systems to advise the client on the costs of audit work to date, feedback systems to ensure audit reports are followed up and quality is maintained and to monitor progress against the business plan.

Internal auditors may find that marketing is part of the departmental/sectional strategy as new opportunities are identified in the business planning process. Clients can then be targeted as they may not be fully aware of what the service has to offer (Jones, p. 15, 1993).

Service managers need to be aware of the range of audit activity. While financial probity is a major function, the internal audit 'toolkit' includes systems development work, value for money activities, performance review, consultancy and possibly training. In deciding which services to accept service managers should be fully aware of the costs of these services and the quality required. In negotiating a service level agreement for internal audit services the service manager could consider, for example, the inclusion of the following:

1. extent of agreed duties;
2. the hourly rate to be charged for a particular service and the agreed maximum number of hours;
3. the level and basis of charges for additional work and the authorization procedure necessary for that work to be carried out;
4. the quality standard to be achieved;
5. response times;
6. redress procedures for work which is below standard and possible access to audit staff timesheets;
7. reporting practices;
8. timing of invoices and payment procedures.

A number of internal audit sections have adopted quality British Standard BS5750 (Connor, pp. 10–12, 1993) as a means of ensuring customer satisfaction and competitive edge. BS5750 provides a quality assurance system possibly as part of a total quality management system. The basic objective of operating such a system is to develop a clear understanding of the necessity to provide clients with a high quality service, increase customer satisfaction, have greater control over operating costs due to the constant drive to improve quality and uniformity of working practice.

10.4 The public corporations

The nationalized industries are audited by the private sector under the provision of the original nationalization Acts and as such are subject to the 'true and fair' view concept. The accounts of these industries therefore are prepared on the lines of best commercial practice as set out in the Companies Act 1989, the relevant Statements of Standard Accounting Practice and any advisory pronouncements of the professional accounting bodies.

10.5 Value-for-money auditing

The earlier sections of this chapter have shown the increasing importance of value-for-money auditing in the public sector for the role of the external auditor. This role is not only confined to the external auditor, however, as in its Statements on Internal Audit Practice in the Public Sector CIPFA identifies the following responsibilities of reviewing, appraising and reporting for internal audit:

(1) the soundness, adequacy and application of internal controls;
(2) the extent to which the organization's assets and interests are accounted for and safeguarded from losses of all kinds arising from:
    (a) fraud and other offences;
    (b) waste, extravagance and inefficient administration, poor value for money or other cause;
(3) the suitability and reliability of financial and other management data developed within the organization.

(*Source*: CIPFA Statements on Internal Audit, 1979)

It can be seen that item (2) (b) specifically refers to value for money, but sound systems of internal control also imply that adequate steps be taken within the organization to achieve it.

As outlined in chapter one the achievement of value for money is no longer seen as a virtue but a necessity for public sector managers. It must be pointed out, therefore, that the search for value for money is not confined to either internal or external auditors but should permeate through the organization. This section of the text should thus be seen in this wider context and consequently develops general concepts which can be applied by both auditors and managers in their attempts to achieve the better use of limited resources. As previously explained value for money has come to be associated with the three Es' – economy, efficiency, and effectiveness.

It must be emphasized that no value-for-money exercise can be considered to be complete unless it has considered all three elements. The main problem is obviously with effectiveness due to the great difficulty in expressing and quantifying the often multiple goals and objectives of many public sector organizations and activities. It must also be pointed out that it is not the duty of the auditor to question policy. It is his duty to consider the effects of policy and to examine arrangements by which policy decisions are reached. The government has recently announced that in any future examination of the Health Service the Audit Commission will examine the effect of ministerial policy decisions on value for money. To this end the auditor will need to consider whether:

1. objective have been set for the policy to achieve;
2. all relevant data was considered in arriving at the decision, including the examination of any feasible alternatives;
3. there is any conflict between policy objectives;
4. there is a monitoring and review procedure.

10.6   Sources of value-for-money studies

Policy areas for review are identified in a number of ways. These include:

1. *Comparative statistics.* The Audit Commission has identified similar authorities by devising expenditure profiles and using multiple regression techniques. CIPFA also publishes comparative statistics for various services and these may provide a guide to over-spending. These statistics are only indicators and need to be treated with caution. In the case of the CIPFA statistics differences in accounting treatment may explain even significant variations.
2. *General audit activities.* In carrying out normal audit activities the auditors may identify waste and extravagance. This may then be invest- igated as resources permit.
3. *Special studies.* Each year specific target areas may be identified for study as is the case with the Audit Commission. Past studies include rent arrears, central purchasing and vehicle maintenance. If this policy is adopted then the appropriate man-days must be set aside in the audit plan.
4. *Miscellaneous.* Includes specific requests from departments, direction by elected members and information from professional journals, e.g. the results of investigations in similar public sector bodies.

Clearly there is a need to build these factors into the audit strategic plan, whether for the internal or external auditor. Figure 10.1 sets out a possible procedure for this.

As each year proceeds the auditor will be able to examine the action taken on any previous recommendations and build any appropriate action into his ongoing plan. In devising and amending the plan on value-for-money work the audit should take into account the activity of complementary parties to avoid duplication of effort (for example, the work of an organization and methods unit).

In carrying these out studies, however, hindsight should not be seen as a virtue. Decisions should be judged on the information available at the time the decision was made. The actual studies can be broken down into two categories. Single-loop learning studies where the goal of the policy is not questioned but

Figure 10.1   *Incorporating VFM studies in the overall audit plan.*

the method of achieving the goal is examined, and double-loop learning exercises where the policy goal itself is questioned and if necessary changes as a result of the outcome of the exercise.

10.7   Undertaking a value-for-money study

In carrying out a successful value-for-money assignment it is essential, as with all audit activity, that sound planning takes place. Detailed planning begins with a thorough examination of the area to be examined. This would include the need to:

1. obtain past audit reports on the area to be examined;
2. check policy decisions to identify if policy objectives have been set and how their effectiveness is to be measured;
3. examine the efficiency yardsticks for appropriateness;
4. review the allocation of overheads to the activity under scrutiny;
5. establish the level of delegation to managers and their relationship to the existing department structure;
6. establish the current level of activity;
7. review the budget and budget control procedures within the activity.

Clearly the above is background work and the list is by no means exhaustive. Having established the necessary information the next step is then to set the audit objectives and to identify the appropriate level of staff and the man-days to be committed to the study. It almost goes without saying that there will be a need to monitor progress to prevent drift.

The next stage is the conduct of the exercise. It must be remembered that the auditor is dealing with people who traditionally have associated audit as a checking function and may have difficulty adjusting to the new demands placed on them by audit staff. One way of overcoming resistance may be to make all concerned fully aware of the benefits of the exercise – communication can break down barriers. Where there is a need for the agreement of the client department in undertaking the exercise the appointment of a coordinating officer may help alleviate problems quickly. Where a sensitive issue is being examined the choice of staff in the planning stage may be crucial to success. Clearly these staff must be properly briefed and must fully understand the nature of the task in hand and their part in it. The importance of good working papers cannot be overemphasized as is the cross-checking of material facts, as any factual errors in reports will distract from a generally sound exercise, especially in a politically sensitive area.

In carrying out the study various investigatory techniques will be used. These include:

1. Input-based reviews where the resources devoted to a particular activity are expressed in terms of the output of that activity (for example, the cost per mile of street cleaned). There is a danger here, however, that least cost is seen as giving value for money when all we have is an expenditure measure which says nothing about quality of service.
2. System-based reviews where the concentration is on the systems and procedures of the organization. This might include how marketing strategies for leisure centres are developed and reviewed with specific reference to pricing policy.

Table 10.2 Guide to carrying out a value-for-money exercise

1. Begin by properly planning the exercise. Identify specific goals and objectives avoiding any inbuilt bias that the area covered by the investigation fails to provide value-for-money.
2. Establish proper systems to record the facts. In order to form a reasoned judgement these will provide a basis for any conclusions and recommendations.
3. Ensure that a structured approach is adopted to the collection of facts in order that all relevent information is gathered and that there is a detailed understanding of the reasons for the current system. Any pilot study should be consulted to verify that the results are consistent or otherwise.
4. In obtaining information use all the skills available to the auditor. These should include the use of ICQs, interviews, analysis of the underlying accounting and non-financial records, and observations of procedures.
5. Flowchart systems if information is not available, and identify weaknesses.
6. At interviews make interviewee aware, as far is reasonable, of the nature of the exercise and try to establish enthusiasm for the task in hand. Attempt to attend interview with list of points and ensure that all are covered.
7. Review results of interviews and data collection to identify any missing factors. Consider the implications for the study of statements which may have been made but which 'were off the record'.
8. Divide conclusions into factual matters and those resting on opinion. Ensure that there is no error of fact as the higher the strategic value of the report the greater is the probability that political capital will be made to embarass the auditor.
9. Base recommendations on content of the report. Ensure that any recommendations represents a practical solution to the problem in hand.

---

3. Comparison with the private sector where data is available.
4. Internal comparison as with those organizations having various divisions set up on a regional basis. It will be possible to compare between regions and adjust for price and cost differentials.
5. Output measurement by the use of trained specialists as with incentive bonus schemes and the use of work study techniques.

Table 10.2 provides a guide to fact finding, recording and interpreting information gained in carrying out the above exercises.

10.8 Effectiveness auditing

It has already been pointed out that the great difficulty for the auditor in carrying out value-for-money studies lies in the area of effectiveness. The problem for the auditor, however, is that Parliament and public sector organizations expect that this criteria will be measured. It is also probably true to state that surveys on vehicle maintenance and the collection of rent arrears are bound up more with economy and efficiency than the major question of the effectiveness or a policy, say, on homelessness. Clearly, the major reviews that can be undertaken are fraught with political difficulty and definition problems with regard to objectives. There is also the problem of the difficulty of measuring inputs. For example, direct inputs such as money can be measured for the education service but quasi inputs such as parental support also play a part.

There is also the question as to whether or not the output of the education system rests solely, for example, with examination results, or does it include wider objectives, and if so, what are they and how do you measure them? In this type of situation it will be necessary for some form of consensus to be reached with management and policy-makers if the auditor is to attempt to measure value for money. Clearly, in any policy decision the decision-makers must have had an objective in mind. It is defining this objective which is the challenge to the auditor and subsequently relating the output of the decision to it. On the positive aspect of effectiveness auditing there are many value-for-money studies which can be carried out without major debate. Examples would include refuse disposal and the effectiveness of an incentive bonus scheme. The problem for the auditor is that these are not necessarily at the strategic level of policy-making and as such as auditor is not providing a positive contribution at the highest level.

Key points of chapter

1. There is an increased emphasis on economy, efficiency and effectiveness in all areas of auditing in the public sector.
2. The role that both internal and external auditors have to play in seeking economy, efficiency and effectiveness was explored.
3. The challenging nature of this work was examined with specific reference to the measurement of effectiveness.

10.9   Summary

This chapter has examined the evolution of the external audit in the public sector and pointed out the increasing importance of the search for economy, efficiency and effectiveness in its role. It has also stressed that internal audit has a vital role to play in this process and suggested that this role may expand as 'agencies', for example, develop in the provision of central government functions. The section on value for money indicates that the difficult area for the auditor in terms of value-for-money auditing lies in evaluating effectiveness but that this problem must be solved if a contribution is to be made at the strategic policy level. The exhibits attempts to illustrate the challenge that faces the auditor in carrying out an actual assignment and draw together concepts from earlier chapters of the text.

Exhibit 10.1

Tayside University is investigating its refectory services and has requested a value-for-money audit be undertaken of the service to students. The refectory is of the self-service type offering a choice of several meals at various counters. There is a separate buffet bar in the refectory with its own till. Customers collect their meals at the service counters and pay at centralized tills prior to the consumption of meals. There is limited competition to the University's service in the area.

Identify the major items that would be considered in undertaking a VFM study of the refectory.

The first step would be to identify the objective of providing the service as clearly any set profit margin will have implications throughout the exercise. There is of course the option of closing the refectory and this may be a possibility if alternative facilities were available to staff and students. It might then be considered desirable solely to operate a small cafeteria system to meet residual demand. If this were a school meals exercise there would be a need to consider statutory implications such as a possible duty to provide free meals. All feasible options would need to be costed and this provides a link with much of the previous text.

It is possible in the University refectory exercise to identify five key areas for detailed examination. These are:

1. provisions
2. staff costs
3. overheads and administration
4. revenue generation
5. management

Each of these areas is examined in turn below to indicate the type of factors that would be considered.

Provisions

Clearly there will be a need to examine the manner in which items are purchased, stored and issued. Competitive tendering should be under taken on all major purchases with appropriate contracts negotiated. Storage areas should be adequate to cope with quantities consumed and to provide conditions conductive to storing the commodities involved. Security should be adequate for the risks involved. Menu and portion controls should be in operation and comparative unit cost exercises should be undertaken. Quality of meals should be investigated as this will have an impact on consumption of meals. The level of waste should be monitored and the possibility of sale for agricultural use considered.

Staff

Staff are normally the major cost in any public sector operation and as such the area needs detailed examination. Clearly appropriate rates of pay should be paid which may be laid down in national agreements, but consideration can be given to flexible local arrangements subject to union negotiation. Working arrangements should be flexible, possibly to include a core staff available at peak demand periods with casuals employed as appropriate. Investigate labour-savings devices such as the purchase of ready-prepared vegetables, cook-chill meals (though this may need a significant capital investment unless shared facilities are used with another organization) and the use of microwaves. Investigate workload, for example number of meals prepared per cook. Investigate till operation procedures to ensure sufficient staff are on duty to avoid creating a queue and deterring return custom. Investigate the number of supervisors in relation to direct employees and compare with available standard data and trends over time. Examine cleaning staff to consider competitive tendering. Examine method of cleaning as 'flow' cleaning is more efficient than floor-space allocation. (In the public sector it is a common practice to allocate cleaners a floor to clean on which they undertake all cleaning duties. In the private sector the alternative is for one cleaner to start with, say, emptying bins and for another cleaner to follow behind undertaking another cleaning task. The flow of work is thus not interrupted.) It might be possible for this service to be put out to competitive tender, in which case it is essential to put it in sound economic shape if it is considered desirable that an in-house bid be successful.

Overheads and administration

Some overheads may be allocated to the refectory on an arbitrary basis and as such will need examination. This review would include factors such as whether or not such services are necessary. This would include the need to consider the contribution that administrative staff make to the service and whether such services can be provided in an alternative manner.

Income generation

It is obvious that pricing and marketing strategies must be examined and it is here that the objectives set for the refectory will play a major role. Careful consideration has to be given to the choice on offer. Do the several counters, for example, include a vegetarian dish? Check prices of the competition, and if different meals are on offer which could be produced by the refectory investigate the feasibility of production. Increased take-up means increased contribution. Students should be aware of what is on offer so undertake a client survey to obtain their views on improvements. Consider a 'no smoking' policy and its implications for patronage.

Management

There is a need to strengthen commercial management which implies delegating responsibility to ensure greater accountability. This may also imply additional rewards being paid for enterprise. If this policy is adopted the financial information system must be geared to meet the needs of managers with appropriate time periods for production and level of aggregation. Margins on meals would need to be identified and monitored.

Exhibit 10.2

One of the major considerations in any stores exercise is whether or not the store/s is/are really needed for the smooth and efficient running of the organization. The existence of local suppliers willing to deliver on call could reduce or eliminate the need to hold items in stock as a store results in capital being tied up in goods rather than being available for investment. The exercise should therefore have the mutually exclusive options of stores or no stores in mind in considering the alternatives. There is also an intermediate stage where only emergency items are held.

The main items to be examined in considering the stores managed by the organization will be the systems and procedures operated by the stores and their physical properties. The following sections identify a selection of relevant questions to which answers will need to be sought.

Systems and procedures

1. Are maximum and minimum stock levels clearly identified for each item and reviewed at appropriate periods?
2. Are economic order quantities identified and reviewed at appropriate periods?
3. Is there an adequate system for emergency orders and are goods ordered and received by different persons?
4. Is there a proper procedure for the issue of goods on authorized requisitions?
5. Are inventory procedures adequate?
6. Does the coding system provide adequate information?
7. Are computer stores-records received promptly in the store and do they identify slow-moving stock?
8. Are operational and financial procedures defined in writing and stores managers and other appropriate staff aware of their responsibilities? Does senior management take an active interest in the stores at least to the minimum extent of requiring an annual summary of performance to be prepared and acted upon?
9. Do procedures exist to monitor major changes in operational needs such that the stores are able to respond quickly?

Physical properties

1. Is security adequate for the value of items retained at the stores?
2. Is the location appropriate to the demands placed on the stores and for deliveries?
3. Is the stores layout appropriate for the materials stored there? Does it facilitate stock-checking?
4. Is stock deterioration prevented?
5. Is there adequate storage of scrap materials returned from jobs appropriate to the value of that material?

Finally the auditor will be keen to examine all available statistics, including stock turnover ratios, number of requisitions handled per storeman, number of times stock-outs have occurred and slow-moving stock to see if a smaller store could be used if these items were removed. It will also be necessary to examine stores overhead costs to judge their reasonableness.

Exhibit 10.3

As marketing and proper pricing policies are becoming increasingly important to the public sector this final exhibit examines the major areas in this field with which a value-for-money study would be concerned. Typical areas to be examined might be:

1. the extent to which pricing policy is constrained by government. An income register should be kept which details at a minimum all charges, the extent of statutory control and the date of last review;
2. whether all charges reflect the organization's policies and are set on the fullest information of costs;
3. that an analysis is carried out of the effect of different pricing policies with reference to demand changes;
4. whether pricing policies reflect seasonal variations, peak demand periods, etc;
5. if no charges are set for services, that this policy is regularly reviewed and decision-makers were fully aware of the implications of this policy when making the decision to provide the free service.

10.1 The Director of Social Services of a large county council is a socially deprived area is concerned to achieve value for money in the provision of the home-help service to the elderly. He has directed you to examine the service with this objective in mind. Prepare a report for the Director of Social Services explaining what you understand by the term value for money and the main areas you would examine.

10.2 You are employed as team leader of the management audit team for the Clueless Health Authority. The following information gives a summary of the costs of providing the hospital meals service together with comparative costs for a similar authority. A member of the authority has gained access to the figures and requested that a VFM study be undertaken. Suggest explanations for the differences and suggest ways of improving the VFM of your hospitals meals service by analysis of the major variables.

| | Clueless HA | | 'X' HA | |
| | Total cost | Unit cost | Total cost | Unit cost |
	£m	p	£m	p
Provisions	2.0	23	1.89	21
Kitchen staff	3.4	38	3.06	34
Supervision	0.7	8	0.81	9
Administrative staff	0.4	5	0.54	6
Overheads	1.3	14	0.9	10
Gross expenditure	7.8	88	7.2	80
Income from meals	2.8	32	3.6	40
Notional income duty meals*	1.7	19	1.26	14
Net cost of service	3.3	37	2.34	26

* Notional income duty meals is the value of free meals issued to staff while on duty shifts.

10.3 Compare and contrast the roles that the internal and external auditor play in achieving economy, efficiency and effectiveness in the provision of a public sector organization's services.

10.4 What do you understand by the terms economy, efficiency and effectiveness? Outline the difficulties experienced by the value-for-money auditor in measuring these three elements. Illustrate your answer with practical examples.

10.5 How are auditors able to assist management in attaining value for money in meeting the growing need to allocate scarce resources among the many demands placed on public sector organizations?

10.6 Under the 1936 Public Health Act amended by the Control of Pollution Act 1974, it is the statutory duty of Mid-Norton Borough Council to collect refuse from domestic and commercial premises and transport it to the Eastham County Council landfill waste disposal site.

Mid-Norton's gross expenditure on refuse collection during 19–4/–5 was £860 000 (see table below) and 28 800 tonnes of refuse was collected. The Borough Council are empowered to charge for trade refuse and it has been the Council's policy to levy a flat-rate charge of £3 for commercial premises for the last three years: this yielded income of £21 000 in 19–4/–5.

Mid-Norton BC: Waste collection service expenditure actuals
19–0/–1–19–4/–5

	19–0/–1 £000s	19–1/–2 £000s	19–2/–3 £000s	19–3/–4 £000s	19–4/–5 £000s
Employees	292	401	472	574	628
Running expenses	81	91	109	114	117
Debt charges	17	18	49	92	115
Gross expenditure	390	510	630	780	860
Income	15	17	19	20	21
Net expenditure	375	493	611	760	839
Tonnes (000s)	27	27.6	28.1	28.6	28.8

The method of operation is the collection of bins by the 'task and finish' system: as soon as the task of work is complete the employees are free to leave. With the expansion of the UK motorway programme, Mid-Norton is becoming a growth area. Over the past five years there has been a steady increase in the population, coupled with a rapid development of light commercial industries and an expanding shopping centre.

Between 19–0 and 19–4 this has resulted in refuse tonnage increasing from 27 000 to 28 800 tonnes. In addition, there has been a change in the composition of refuse with decreasing quantities of heavy solid fuel waste and increasing quantities of more bulky plastic and paper packaging material. The trend over the last four years has been to increase both the weight and volume of waste, leading to increasing use by householders of larger 3.25 cu. ft. bins replacing the old 2.5 cu. ft. bins, and by a significant number of households now having two bins.

Faced with this increasing pressure on the waste disposal service at a time when the Authority was also under pressure to restrict spending, the Council decided in 19–1 to introduce an incentive bonus scheme in order to increase the productivity of the waste disposal service.

A firm of management consultants were brought in to review operations and measure the workload. Their conclusions (see the following appendix) indicated that a bonus scheme was viable after an initial two-year lead-in period. (NB: The Authority has a long-term 'no redundancy' arrangement with the trade union.) A measured day-work (stint) bonus scheme was implemented on 1 April 19–1, on completion of a 'stink' or 'task' of work resulting in a flat rate of 25% bonus on basic wages.

Recent developments

The changing density of refuse, together with advances in technology, has had an effect on the design of refuse collection vehicles and over the three years

19–1 to 19–4 Mid-Norton have replaced their fleet of 18 vehicles with 15 larger vehicles. These have filling and compacting mechanisms which operate with automatically closing hoppers and are capable of high ratios of refuse compaction.

The external auditors submitted a report to the Council in 19–4/–5 about the adverse trend in Mid-Norton's expenditure in comparison with authorities in the same family group and national statistics (see table below).

National statistics – waste collection service

	19–0/–1	19–1/–2	19–2/–3	19–3/–4
Gross expenditure per tonne	15.5	18.0	21.7	24.0
Net expenditure per tonne	14.8	16.7	20.0	22.0

Required

As the Management Auditor of Mid-Norton Borough Council, prepare a formal report for the Authority, analyzing the performance of the Council's refuse collection service, explaining possible reasons for this performance, and making practical recommendations on how the efficiency on the service may be improved. (40 marks)

Appendix

Reference period data for proposed productivity scheme in the Mid-Norton refuse collection service

Prepared by: Anon & Partners, Consultants
Date: 31 December 19–0

	Actual		Expected Estimated				
	19–8/9	–9/–0	–0/–1	–1/–2	–2/–3	–3/–4	–4/–5
Annual tonnage (000s)	23	25	27	29	30	32	34
Density (cu. yds per tonne)	7.7	7.8	7.9	8.1	8.2	8.3	8.3
Bulk (000s cu. yds)	177	195	213	235	246	266	282
Index of bulk	83	92	100	110	116	125	132
No. of operatives	65	70	75	75	75	75	75
No. of vehicles	16	17	18	18	18	18	1

A flat-rate bonus of 25% to all operatives from 19–1/–2 would result in a net loss for the Authority during the first two-year lead-in period. However, in 19–3/–4 the Authority would break even and from 19–4/–5 onwards the quantity/bulk of refuse collected will increase by more than the 25% bonus payment and the Authority will gain by not recruiting any more additional operatives.

10.7   Compact City Health Authority serves a population of 400 000 and operates an in-house building and maintenance service to its 19 hospital locations.

Builders and engineers in the authority are based at 10 of the 19 hospitals and from their bases they also carry out maintenance work in the remaining nine hospitals, community health centres, clinics and ambulance stations.

There are currently separate stores for building and engineering supplies at each of the 10 hospital bases which are controlled by 10 storekeepers at a total staff cost of £62 000 p.a. The value of issues of building and engineering materials is £950 000 p.a. As each store only employs one storekeeper the building foreman and engineers have tended to be involved in the day-to-day operation of the stores.

The last audit of these stores was undertaken two years ago, but recent preliminary audit investigations have revealed the following:

1. past two year's year-end stock levels were £450 000 and £550 000;
2. stores reordering is based on visual inspection of bins or racks;
3. order quantities are based on estimates of future usage by the builder or engineer concerned;
4. the accounting system is based on the 'end-user' charges whereby materials are charged directly to the ultimate end-user and held in stock until they request it;
5. monthly management information is provided only on total stock balances and total expenditure for each of the 10 stores.

You are a principal internal auditor in Compact and you have been requested by your Chief Internal Auditor to the following task:

Prepare a draft report for the general management team of Compact proposing a value-for-money investigation into the building and engineering stores.

Your proposal should include:

(i)   The objective of the investigation.
(ii)   An outline of the process which you intend to follow to achieve this objective.
(iii)   An initial analysis of the weak areas of the present stores system which your future investigation will be focused on.

Appendix: Present value of 1

					Rate of interest %					
	1	2	3	4	5	6	7	8	9	10
Year										
0	1.0000	1.0000	1.0000	1.0000	1.0000	1.0000	1.0000	1.0000	1.0000	1.0000
1	0.9901	0.9804	0.9709	0.9615	0.9524	0.9434	0.9346	0.9259	0.9174	0.9091
2	0.9803	0.9612	0.9426	0.9246	0.9070	0.8900	0.8734	0.8573	0.8417	0.8264
3	0.9706	0.9423	0.9151	0.8890	0.8638	0.8396	0.8163	0.7938	0.7722	0.7513
4	0.9601	0.9238	0.8885	0.8548	0.8227	0.7921	0.7629	0.7350	0.7084	0.6830
5	0.9515	0.9057	0.8626	0.8219	0.7835	0.7473	0.7130	0.6806	0.6499	0.6209
6	0.9420	0.8880	0.8375	0.7903	0.7462	0.7050	0.6663	0.6302	0.5963	0.5645
7	0.9327	0.8706	0.8131	0.7599	0.7107	0.6651	0.6227	0.5835	0.5470	0.5132
8	0.9235	0.8535	0.7894	0.7307	0.6768	0.6274	0.5820	0.5403	0.5019	0.4665
9	0.9143	0.8368	0.7664	0.7026	0.6446	0.5919	0.5439	0.5002	0.4604	0.4241
10	0.9053	0.8203	0.7441	0.6756	0.6139	0.5584	0.5083	0.4632	0.4224	0.3855
11	0.8963	0.8043	0.7224	0.6496	0.5847	0.5268	0.4751	0.4289	0.3875	0.3505
12	0.8874	0.7885	0.7014	0.6246	0.5568	0.4970	0.4440	0.3971	0.3555	0.3186
13	0.8787	0.7730	0.6810	0.6006	0.5303	0.4688	0.4150	0.3677	0.3262	0.2897
14	0.8700	0.7579	0.6611	0.5775	0.5051	0.4423	0.3878	0.3405	0.2992	0.2633
15	0.8613	0.7430	0.6419	0.5553	0.4810	0.4173	0.3624	0.3152	0.2745	0.2394
16	0.8528	0.7284	0.6232	0.5339	0.4581	0.3936	0.3387	0.2919	0.2519	0.2176
17	0.8444	0.7142	0.6050	0.5134	0.4363	0.3714	0.3166	0.2703	0.2311	0.1978
18	0.8360	0.7002	0.5874	0.4936	0.4155	0.3503	0.2959	0.2502	0.2120	0.1799
19	0.8277	0.6864	0.5703	0.4746	0.3957	0.3305	0.2765	0.2317	0.1945	0.1635
20	0.8195	0.6730	0.5537	0.4564	0.3769	0.3118	0.2584	0.2145	0.1784	0.1486
21	0.8114	0.6598	0.5375	0.4388	0.3589	0.2942	0.2415	0.1987	0.1637	0.1351
22	0.8034	0.6468	0.5219	0.4220	0.3418	0.2775	0.2257	0.1839	0.1502	0.1228
23	0.7954	0.6342	0.5067	0.4057	0.3256	0.2618	0.2109	0.1703	0.1378	0.1117
24	0.7876	0.6217	0.4919	0.3901	0.3101	0.2470	0.1971	0.1577	0.1264	0.1015
25	0.7798	0.6095	0.4776	0.3751	0.2953	0.2330	0.1842	0.1460	0.1160	0.0923
26	0.7720	0.5976	0.4637	0.3607	0.2812	0.2198	0.1722	0.1352	0.1064	0.0839
27	0.7644	0.5859	0.4502	0.3468	0.2678	0.2074	0.1609	0.1252	0.0976	0.0763
28	0.7568	0.5744	0.4371	0.3335	0.2551	0.1956	0.1504	0.1159	0.0895	0.0693
29	0.7493	0.5631	0.4243	0.3207	0.2429	0.1846	0.1406	0.1073	0.0822	0.0630
30	0.7419	0.5521	0.4120	0.3083	0.2314	0.1741	0.1314	0.0994	0.0754	0.0573
31	0.7346	0.5412	0.4000	0.2965	0.2204	0.1643	0.1228	0.0920	0.0691	0.0521
32	0.7273	0.5306	0.3883	0.2851	0.2099	0.1550	0.1147	0.0852	0.0634	0.0474
33	0.7201	0.5202	0.3770	0.2741	0.1999	0.1462	0.1072	0.0789	0.0582	0.0431
34	0.7130	0.5100	0.3660	0.2636	0.1904	0.1379	0.1002	0.0730	0.0534	0.0391
35	0.7059	0.5000	0.3554	0.2534	0.1813	0.1301	0.0937	0.0676	0.0490	0.0356
36	0.6989	0.4902	0.3450	0.2437	0.1727	0.1227	0.0875	0.0626	0.0449	0.0323
37	0.6920	0.4806	0.3350	0.2343	0.1644	0.1158	0.0818	0.0580	0.0412	0.0294
38	0.6852	0.4712	0.3252	0.2253	0.1566	0.1092	0.0765	0.0537	0.0378	0.0267
39	0.6784	0.4619	0.3158	0.2166	0.1491	0.1031	0.0715	0.0497	0.0347	0.0243
40	0.6717	0.4529	0.3066	0.2083	0.1420	0.0972	0.0668	0.0460	0.0318	0.0221
41	0.6650	0.4440	0.2976	0.2003	0.1353	0.0917	0.0624	0.0426	0.0292	0.0201
42	0.6854	0.4353	0.2890	0.1926	0.1288	0.0865	0.0583	0.0395	0.0268	0.0183
43	0.6519	0.4268	0.2805	0.1852	0.1227	0.0816	0.0545	0.0365	0.0246	0.0166
44	0.6454	0.4184	0.2724	0.1780	0.1169	0.0770	0.0509	0.0338	0.0226	0.0151
45	0.6391	0.4102	0.2644	0.1712	0.1113	0.0727	0.0476	0.0313	0.0207	0.0137
46	0.6327	0.4022	0.2567	0.1646	0.1060	0.0685	0.0445	0.0290	0.0190	0.0125
47	0.6265	0.3943	0.2493	0.1583	0.1009	0.0647	0.0416	0.0269	0.0174	0.0113
48	0.6203	0.3865	0.2420	0.1522	0.0961	0.0610	0.0389	0.0249	0.0160	0.0103
49	0.6141	0.3790	0.2350	0.1463	0.0916	0.0575	0.0363	0.0230	0.0147	0.0094
50	0.6080	0.3715	0.2281	0.1407	0.0872	0.0543	0.0339	0.0213	0.0134	0.0085

Year	11	12	13	14	15	16	17	18	19	20
0	1.0000	1.0000	1.0000	1.0000	1.0000	1.0000	1.0000	1.0000	1.0000	1.0000
1	0.9009	0.8929	0.8850	0.8772	0.8696	0.8621	0.8547	0.8475	0.8403	0.8333
2	0.8116	0.7972	0.7831	0.7695	0.7561	0.7432	0.7305	0.7182	0.7062	0.6944
3	0.7312	0.7118	0.6931	0.6750	0.6575	0.6407	0.6244	0.6086	0.5934	0.5787
4	0.6587	0.6355	0.6133	0.5921	0.5718	0.5523	0.5337	0.5158	0.4987	0.4823
5	0.5935	0.5674	0.5428	0.5194	0.4972	0.4761	0.4561	0.4371	0.4190	0.4019
6	0.5346	0.5066	0.4803	0.4556	0.4323	0.4104	0.3898	0.3704	0.3521	0.3349
7	0.4817	0.4523	0.4251	0.3996	0.3759	0.3538	0.3332	0.3139	0.2959	0.2791
8	0.4339	0.4039	0.3762	0.3506	0.3269	0.3050	0.2848	0.2660	0.2487	0.2326
9	0.3909	0.3606	0.3329	0.3075	0.2843	0.2630	0.2434	0.2255	0.2090	0.1938
10	0.3522	0.3220	0.2946	0.2697	0.2472	0.2267	0.2080	0.1911	0.1756	0.1615
11	0.3173	0.2875	0.2607	0.2366	0.2149	0.1954	0.1778	0.1619	0.1476	0.1346
12	0.2858	0.2567	0.2307	0.2076	0.1869	0.1685	0.1520	0.1372	0.1240	0.1122
13	0.2575	0.2292	0.2042	0.1821	0.1625	0.1452	0.1299	0.1163	0.1042	0.0935
14	0.2320	0.2046	0.1807	0.1597	0.1413	0.1252	0.1110	0.0985	0.0876	0.0779
15	0.2090	0.1827	0.1599	0.1401	0.1229	0.1079	0.0949	0.0835	0.0736	0.0649
16	0.1883	0.1631	0.1415	0.1229	0.1069	0.0930	0.0811	0.0708	0.0618	0.0541
17	0.1696	0.1456	0.1252	0.1078	0.0929	0.0802	0.0693	0.0600	0.0520	0.0451
18	0.1528	0.1300	0.1108	0.0946	0.0808	0.0691	0.0592	0.0508	0.0437	0.0376
19	0.1377	0.1161	0.0981	0.0829	0.0703	0.0596	0.0506	0.0431	0.0367	0.0313
20	0.1240	0.1037	0.0868	0.0728	0.0611	0.0514	0.0433	0.0365	0.0308	0.0261
21	0.1117	0.0926	0.0768	0.0638	0.0531	0.0443	0.0370	0.0309	0.0259	0.0217
22	0.1007	0.0826	0.0680	0.0560	0.0462	0.0382	0.0316	0.0262	0.0218	0.0181
23	0.0907	0.0738	0.0601	0.0491	0.0402	0.0329	0.0270	0.0222	0.0183	0.0151
24	0.0817	0.0659	0.0532	0.0431	0.0349	0.0284	0.0231	0.0188	0.0154	0.0126
25	0.0736	0.0588	0.0471	0.0378	0.0304	0.0245	0.0197	0.0160	0.0129	0.0105
26	0.0663	0.0525	0.0417	0.0331	0.0264	0.0211	0.0169	0.0135	0.0109	0.0087
27	0.0597	0.0469	0.0369	0.0291	0.0230	0.0182	0.0144	0.0115	0.0091	0.0073
28	0.0538	0.0419	0.0326	0.0255	0.0200	0.0157	0.0123	0.0097	0.0077	0.0061
29	0.0485	0.0374	0.0289	0.0224	0.0174	0.0135	0.0105	0.0082	0.0064	0.0051
30	0.0437	0.0334	0.0256	0.0196	0.0151	0.0116	0.0090	0.0070	0.0054	0.0042
31	0.0394	0.0298	0.0226	0.0172	0.0131	0.0100	0.0077	0.0059	0.0046	0.0035
32	0.0355	0.0266	0.0200	0.0151	0.0114	0.0087	0.0066	0.0050	0.0038	0.0029
33	0.0319	0.0238	0.0177	0.0132	0.0099	0.0075	0.0056	0.0042	0.0032	0.0024
34	0.0288	0.0212	0.0157	0.0116	0.0086	0.0064	0.0048	0.0036	0.0027	0.0020
35	0.0259	0.0189	0.0139	0.0102	0.0075	0.0055	0.0041	0.0030	0.0023	0.0017
36	0.0234	0.0169	0.0123	0.0089	0.0065	0.0048	0.0035	0.0026	0.0019	0.0014
37	0.0210	0.0151	0.0109	0.0078	0.0057	0.0041	0.0030	0.0022	0.0016	0.0012
38	0.0190	0.0135	0.0096	0.0069	0.0049	0.0036	0.0026	0.0019	0.0013	0.0010
39	0.0171	0.0120	0.0085	0.0060	0.0043	0.0031	0.0022	0.0016	0.0011	0.0008
40	0.0154	0.0107	0.0075	0.0053	0.0037	0.0026	0.0019	0.0013	0.0010	0.0007
41	0.0139	0.0096	0.0067	0.0046	0.0032	0.0023	0.0016	0.0011	0.0008	0.0006
42	0.0125	0.0086	0.0059	0.0041	0.0028	0.0020	0.0014	0.0010	0.0007	0.0005
43	0.0112	0.0076	0.0052	0.0036	0.0025	0.0017	0.0012	0.0008	0.0006	0.0004
44	0.0101	0.0068	0.0046	0.0031	0.0021	0.0015	0.0010	0.0007	0.0005	0.0003
45	0.0091	0.0061	0.0041	0.0027	0.0019	0.0013	0.0009	0.0006	0.0004	0.0003
46	0.0082	0.0054	0.0036	0.0024	0.0016	0.0011	0.0007	0.0005	0.0003	0.0002
47	0.0074	0.0049	0.0032	0.0021	0.0014	0.0009	0.0006	0.0004	0.0003	0.0002
48	0.0067	0.0043	0.0028	0.0019	0.0012	0.0008	0.0005	0.0004	0.0002	0.0002
49	0.0060	0.0039	0.0025	0.0016	0.0011	0.0007	0.0005	0.0003	0.0002	0.0001
50	0.0054	0.0035	0.0022	0.0014	0.0009	0.0006	0.0004	0.0003	0.0002	0.0001

11 ▷ **Case studies**

11.1   Service level agreement – ambulance service

The Darwen Ambulance Service serves a population of approximately 300 000 in a semi-rural district of the United Kingdom covering an area of 1800 square miles. The ambulance service is, at present, a directly managed service under the control of the district health authority, employs 130 staff, has 50 ambulances and 12 ambulance stations. The service delivers both an emergency and a non-emergency transport services to patients. The total expenditure of the service for the last financial year was £8m. Following the enactment of the NHS and Community Care Act 1990 the ambulance service operates on a purchaser and provider split. The ambulance service acts as the provider of services and bills its expenditure on the provision of the service directly to the district health authority.

An emergency service is delivered by a block contract with the district health authority and is recovered on a full cost basis. In the last financial year the emergency service achieved its financial target of break even. At the end of the last financial year, however, the non-emergency service was under recovered on its block contract against the original budget by £95 000. This service must be provided on the basis of clinical need under statutory obligations. The service is demand led and at present is provided on request to hospitals, doctors, and so on. The costs of the non-emergency transport operation were intended to be recovered under the block contract based on a flat rate call-out fee to each user. This fee covered call-outs over the whole of the service's geographical area but inadequate information on cost and estimated demand caused the under recovery mentioned above.

GPs and directly managed units are unconcerned regarding the over-spend. The financial target of the ambulance service for the non-emergency transport service is break-even point. The NHS trust hospitals in the district have negotiated contracts with private ambulance services for non-emergency transport for the next three years despite a bid by Darwen Ambulance Services. While the service, clearly, knows who its clients are there is also little or no monitoring of the quality of service, both users of that service and the ambulance service itself. A number of patients have, however, complained about late arrival of ambulances, cancellation (often at very short notice) of the service and a poor standard of cleanliness in some of the older vehicles in the fleet.

The ambulance service is considering setting itself up with trust status but, as a first step, wishes to establish a service level agreement with each of its non-emergency clients. The financial objective of this process is that all costs will be recovered from clients on an equitable basis.

Tasks

Outline how you would undertake the exercise of establishing a service level agreement with clients concentrating on the manner in which you would identify the full cost of the non-emergency ambulance service and what costs you should include.

1. What problems do you think you might encounter?
2. Discuss the alternative ways in which you might charge users for the service.
3. What advantages and disadvantages do you see in introducing a system of service level agreements.
4. Outline the main features you would expect to see in any service level agreement for the ambulance service.

11.2   Staff travel costs

A local authority reimburses staff mileage costs incurred when acting on official business according to national agreed rates. These rates are divided between essential users, who get a lump-sum payment and a rate per mile, and casual users who get a higher rate per mile travelled. The rates paid are based on the engine capacity of the car used. The actual expenditure incurred by the authority over the past three years compared with the original estimate is set out below.

Department	19x1/x2	19x2/x3	19x3/x4
	£	£	£
Chief Executive	10 250	12 000	13 500
Finance	30 500	32 500	40 000
Environmental health	60 250	75 000	72 250
Leisure services	18 250	18 500	19 500
DSO	25 000	25 250	25 350
Total	144 250	163 250	170 600
Original estimate	£135 000	£150 000	£155 000

At present there are 110 posts which are designated as essential users and approximately 65 casual users. In addition there are 10 chief officers who receive enhance lump-sum allowances. All essential and casual users are entitles to reduced rate finance to purchase new vehicles from the authority. The latest mileage rates paid are as follows:

Casual user		Engine capacity		
Miles per annum	<999cc	1000–1200 cc	1201–1450 cc	>1450
0 – 1 500	44.0p	52.5p	60.0p	70p
1501 – 5 500	30.5p	35.5p	41.0p	50p
5501 – 11 000	25.0p	27.0p	31.0p	35p
After 11 000	10.5p	10.9p	12.0p	13p
Essential User	<999cc	1000–1200cc	1201–1450cc	>1450
Lump sum	£600	£750	£885	£1009
Per mile <11 000	24.0p	26.9p	31.8p	33.5p
Per mile >11 000	10.5p	10.9p	12.0p	13p

*Chief Officers receive an additional 5%.

The costs of car mileages are not allocated to departments in the first instance but charged to central administration and only recharged to departments at the end of the financial year. These recharges are based on the percentage that the salary costs paid by service departments represent as a percentage of total service department salary expenditure and not car allowances actually paid by departments. The only monitoring information available on mileage allowances for departments is a six-monthly estimate of costs incurred to date for central administration coupled with an estimate out-turn for the year provided by the Finance Department. Within the information provided it is difficult for departmental staff to separate which part of the central administration charge actually relates to mileage expenses.

Employees fill in claim forms monthly and these are certified by their immediate supervisors. They are then forwarded to the central service departmental offices for further certification and recording of mileage claimed. This recording of mileages provides departments with their main control information. The claim form is then sent to the Finance department where payment is made by cheque to the employee on average two months after the claim for payment was first submitted.

Council policy on the designation of employees for the two categories of car user allowances was established 12 years ago. These designations are:

Casual users are those individuals for whom it is desirable that a car should be available when required.

Essential users are those employees whose duties are regarded as being of such a nature that it is vital that they have a car available whenever required.

Members and Chief Officers are becoming increasingly concerned about the cost of the mileage allowance scheme and have requested that it be examined with a view to achieving greater value for money. They have requested that an investigation be undertaken into all aspects of the scheme including its possible replacement by a car leasing scheme which they are aware other public sector bodies operate.

Tasks

1. Identify what you believe is wrong with the present scheme on the basis of the information given above.
2. Outline how you might go about improving the scheme as presently operated by the authority.

3. Consider how you would approach setting up a replacement to the current scheme and the type of information that you would need. Discuss the non-financial aspects of any proposals you might have.

11.3 Central administration charges finance section

Hopeless District Council treasurer's department recharges for services it provides on the basis of a central holding account. All costs of the treasurer's department are charged to this account. These costs include all salaries and salary related overheads, travelling and subsistance allowances and office accommodation expenses. At the end of the financial year all the costs held on the treasurer's department's central administration holding account are charged to the various service committees of the authority and other holding accounts both capital and revenue.

The functions provided by the department are accountancy, internal audit, council tax and national non-domestic rates (business rates), housing benefits, general revenue collection and corporate management. The cost of the treasurer's department for the last financial year is set out below.

Treasurer's Department Costs 19x3/x4

Category of expense	Original estimate	Revised estimate	Actual	No. of staff
	£	£	£	
Accountancy	420 150	425 000	425 500	25
Audit	295 000	297 000	297 250	16
Council tax/business rate	415 000	415 000	412 000	28
Housing benefits	400 000	405 000	403 000	25
Revenue collection	250 000	255 000	253 250	20
Corporate management	130 000	130 000	130 000	4
	1 910 150	1 927 000	1 921 000	118
Travel allowances	159 000	145 000	140 000	
Accommodation costs	500 000	500 000	525 000	
Total cost	2 569 150	2 572 000	2 586 000	118

Salary costs of the treasurer's department for the previous three years, beginning with the last financial year, were £1 814 000, £1 707 760 and £1 535 180. Employee numbers starting with the previous financial year, were 105, 101 and a 100 respectively.

To establish the costs to be recharged to departments each member of staff completes a timesheet to show the amount of time spent on each activity by service department. These timesheets are completed by activity (e.g. accountancy) as no costs are collected by cost centre (for example, housing accountancy team) as they do not exist. At the end of the financial year these completed timesheets are then used as the basis for the recharge. The budget for recharges is based on last year's timesheet allocation uprated for inflation. Travel expenses and accommodation costs are allocated to service departments on the basis of the percentage of total direct service department salaries that each individual service department represents. These costs are allocated at the end of the financial year with no previous notification to chief officers. They are, however, treated as outside the service manager's control. In addition, as these costs form part of the global recharge of central administration costs, the service manager has no easy way of separating the cost of financial services from other central services for example legal services.

Matters regarding the charging of central finance costs (and in reality other central services) came to a head following the complaints of the direct services manager. She feels that the addition of £90 000 in the previous financial year to her budget to pay for the treasurer's costs was totally unjustifiable. This cost represented an addition of 5% of the original total budget of the DSO and was totally unexpected. She believes this is not justifiable as she has to meet competitive pressures and such figures could make the difference between profit and loss. She feels finance and other central services are 'feather-bedded' being divorced from the real world and could do with a dose of competition. Of particular concern to her is that the current year is expected to be very difficult for the DSO and the budget could not absorb a similar increase. No accurate estimate of the level of charges likely to be imposed is yet available for the current year despite the fact that it is now January.

The recent announcement of the possible extension of competitive tendering to the treasurer's department (granting the DSO manager's wish) has also meant that the current system of recharging appears to be indefensible in the immediate future.

Tasks

1. Identify what you consider to be the advantages and disadvantages of the current system of recharging the treasurer's administration costs.
2. Consider what other system of charging for financial services might be introduced, what information you would require to appraise the alternatives and how you might go about introducing an alternative system.
3. Outline the advantages and disadvantages of any alternatives you consider viable.
4. Consider the non-financial implications of any proposed change.

11.4   Vehicle replacement

The Highways Department of the Covert County Council has spent the sums of money disclosed by the table below in financing its vehicle replacement policy over the last five years.

Comparison of planned expenditure on vehicle replacement with actual expenditure 19x9/0 to 19x3/4.

	19x3/4 £	19x2/3 £	19x1/2 £	19x0/1 £	19x9/0 £
Capital estimate	600 000	500 000	550 000	400 000	350 000
Actual expenditure	580 000	650 000	750 000	200 000	150 000
	(20 000)	50 000	200 000	(200 000)	(200 000)
Cutbacks				200 000	200 000
Capital Virements		40 000	195 000		
Transfers (to) from revenue	(20 000)	10 000	5000		
	(20 000)	50 000	200 000	(200 000)	(200 000)

Due to the anticipated high level of demand for capital finance in 19x4/5 no provision for replacement vehicles has been made in that year. The fleet size is 150 vehicles.

In October prior to the new financial year a capital allocation is normally made to cover the cost of vehicle replacement in the next financial year. It is set on the basis of what can be afforded with no account taken of the actual physical condition of the vehicles. Some vehicles are purchased from revenue. The amount of money available from this source is dependent on the hourly rate charged to jobs to recover vehicle operating costs achieving a surplus. A surplus arises if more hours are worked than estimated or running costs are lower than anticipated. Any deficit on operating cost recovery is carried forward into the next financial year. Vehicle operating hours for this calculation are based on each vehicle being available for 1200 productive hours in any one year. On purchase an estimate is made of the anticipated useful life of the vehicle but no commitment to replace is implied at that time. The fleet is thus larger than is probably required in order to have spare vehicles to cover for the downtime of vehicles under repair.

The total estimated cost of replacing the fleet is over £5m and with the increased pressure on financial resources the authority recognizes that it is increasingly important that capital assets are managed effectively. The fleet is, however, in a generally poor condition with many vehicles requiring major repairs or renewal. It is estimated that a sum pf £450 000 is needed immediately to bring the fleet into an efficient operating condition. The authority recognizes the crisis situation and wishes to consider a number of ways of financing the fleet. The alternatives identified by the management accountant for the authority include establishing a renewals and repairs fund, borrowing, leasing and funding from revenue.

Tasks

1. Identify the type of replacement policy adopted by the authority from the above information.
2. Outline the advantages and disadvantages of such a policy. What alternatives are available?
3. Outline the major features of the alternative methods of financing that the authority has identified.
4. The management accountant has obtained a number of quotations for the alternative methods of funding available. These are

Leasing	Borrowing
Primary period	

3 years £380 per £1000 in advance.	Rate of interest 10%.
4 years £320 per £1000 in advance.	Equal instalment of principal
5 years £280 per £1000 in advance.	Repayable at the end of each
8 years £255 per £1000 in advance.	year.

The breakdown of the capital requirement for new vehicles is:

	£
3-year finance	100 000
4-year finance	50 000
5-year finance	150 000
8-year finance	150 000
Total finance needed	450 000

Calculate the cost of the alternative methods of funding and compare, Which would you advise?

11.5   Computer recharges

The computer section of the Glamwent Health Authority employs twenty full time staff and costs £903 000 a year to operate. At present the costs of running the section are apportioned to user departments on annual basis. There is no interim billing and no analysis of the charge is provided to users. The recharge to users takes place some three months into the next financial year and thus users have difficulty incorporating these charges into their budget plans. Computer charges for the last three years are shown below.

	19x3/4 £	19x2/3 £	19x1/2 £
Finance section	210 000	190 000	195 000
Legal services	90 000	100 100	85 000
Estates	175 000	170 000	160 000
Medical and dental	190 000	195 000	198 000
Nursing	75 000	75 000	75 000
Catering	50 000	55 000	48 000
Pharmacy	15 000	14 000	13 000
Physiotherapy	8 000	7 500	7 000
Other	90 000	81 000	75 000
	903 000	887 600	856 000

Costs are apportioned to departments on the basis of the number of times the department has accessed the central mainframe computer. In addition there is an element of 'manger's discretion' whereby costs are reallocated between users to reduce the cost to certain users.

The computer department is organized into four teams under the computer manager. These teams are development services (five staff), computer operators (six staff), support staff (four staff) and data preparation staff (four staff). Staff do not complete timesheets for any category of work. No external work to the authority is performed by the section although it is felt that there is some spare capacity. The work done by the teams is broadly as follows:

System development is carried out at the request of departments to either improve existing systems or design new systems. Much of this work recently has been designing a new financial information system in conjunction with the Finance department. Computer operators are concerned with the maintenance and operation of the mainframe computer.

Data preparation is the section concerned with inputting the relevant information into the mainframe. There is no distributed data input. Remote terminals are only allowed 'read' only facilities.

Computer support is an advice unit. The increasing use of remote terminals has meant an increase in workload. The section also runs a number of short courses in basic computing. Demand for these courses is rising as more staff seek to become computer literate in, for example, spreadsheet packages.

The costs for the last financial year are broken down into the following categories:

	£
Machines – Maintenance	80 000
– Lease	18 000
Support staff	120 000
Operators	100 000
Support	140 000
Development	95 000
Applications software	68 000
Consumables	40 000
Purchase of PCS and printers	80 000
Total cost	903 000

The authority is concerned about the cost of the computer section and the lack of accountability and is considering the possibility of contracting out the work. It wishes first, however, to put the in-house operation right and is examining four possibilities:

1. retaining the current system of apportionment as it stands;
2. retain the present system of apportionment but improve the basis of apportionment;
3. adopt a non-commercial basis for charging aiming only to breakeven;
4. charge users on a normal commercial basis with a set target for the section to achieve.

Tasks

Identify the advantages and disadvantages of the alternatives open to the health authority.

Consider:

1. how you would improve the system of apportionment;
2. what methods exist for recharging the computer section on commercial lines and how you would carry out this exercise;
3. whether full commercial charging is appropriate for the section;
4. what recommendation you would make.

11.6   Falling school rolls

Clueless County Council is responsible for the management of 40 secondary schools. The total budgeted expenditure of these schools in 19–3/4 is £80m. The county is primarily industrial although this industry is concentrated in the southern part of the county. The northern half of the county is primarily a commuter area but with a high percentage of agricultural land and strong village communities. This part of the county also has a large elderly population. No schools within the county have, to date, opted out of local authority control.

Concern has been expressed both within the authority and externally at the number of surplus places that exist within the county's secondary schools. In 19–3/4 there are an estimates 5000 surplus places with a projected rise to 7500 surplus places over the next four years. The Department of Education is calling for the removal of 70% of these surplus places by the end of the four years. In addition the Audit Commission is known to be concerned at the potential waste of resources.

In their last audit report the Audit Commission identified the cost of surplus places as £0.75m for the financial year 19–2/3. This figure was based on 4500 surplus places and related to premises cost per comprehensive school place. In addition to external pressures the authority has to cope with the problems of formula based funding where school budgets are based primarily on a calculation in which a major component is the number of pupils on roll. As school rolls are projected to fall this will clearly place additional pressure on resources. In addition another component of the authority's formula is floor area of schools. This means that the authority will effectively be funding inefficiency unless it takes action on surplus places.

The education service is arranged on a district basis and the following table shows the cost per district based on premises costs only for 19x3/4:

District cost	District A £	District B £	District C £	District D £
Premises cost	900 000	850 000	825 000	1 025 000
School capacity	5 500	5 750	6 500	7 100
Premises cost per place	163	147	126	144
Surplus places	1 100	1 450	900	1 550
Cost of surplus places	179 300	213 150	113 400	223 200

A number of options have been identified by the authority to deal with the problem. These are:

1. the closure of certain schools with possible amalgamation. Premises could then either be sold or mothballed;
2. closure of one or more schools and the building of new purpose built units;
3. closure and mothballing of a part of a school;
4. removal of temporary mobile classrooms;
5. establishing of six form colleges as all current secondary schools have retained their six form and make the necessary adjustments outlined in points (1) to (4).

Tasks

1. Outline what you consider to be the major financial implications for Clueless in implementing a policy of reducing surplus places under each of the above alternatives.
2. Consider how you might calculate the costs associated with the above alternatives identifying clearly the basis for the calculation of any costs identified.
3. Identify the non-financial implications of the policy of reducing surplus places.
4. How might you take account of these factors in any options you identify as being feasible?

 11.7 Capital financing policy

Drift County Council is considering reviewing its capital financing policy. Capital expenditure amounts to £50m in the current financial year (19x4/x5). Capital expenditure in each of the next three years is planned at £60m, £65m and £70m respectively. Revenue expenditure in the current year is planned at £300m of which capital charges represents £20m. This compares with actual revenue expenditure in the previous financial year of £290m and capital charges of £7.4m. The authority feels politically that expenditure on its capital programme is essential due to the high level of social deprivation within the authority's area. In previous years it also had a history of failing to achieve its planned capital expenditure programme and there now exists political pressure to ensure that this does not happen again. It would also like to finance as large a capital programme as possible as there are many priority schemes which are not included in the capital expenditure plans set out above. The authority would fund these schemes if it has the resources to do so.

Actual capital expenditure over the last five years has been financed as follows:

	Value of Capital exp. £m	Revenue £	Financed by Borrowing £	Leasing £	Grants* £
19–3/–4	45 (48)	9	28	6	2
19–2/–3	50 (55)	12	25	8	5
19–1/–2	42 (41)	13	20	6	3
19–0/–1	40 (46)	12	18	7	3
19–9/–0	35 (38)	10	17	5	3

(Figures in brackets represent the original planned levels of capital expenditure for the years shown.)

*external grants were largely from the European Community's Regional development Fund.

The authorities policy has been to invest capital receipts in the and earn interest on this balance.

External borrowing is limited by the annual credit approvals set by central government. While these are difficult to predict the authority anticipates credit approvals of £35m for 19x4/x5 and £37m, £40m and £38m for each of the next three years. The level of grants for capital expenditure is also seen as falling to £1m per annum for the current year and each of the next three years due to a change in EC rules. The authority in setting its original capital spending plans was hoping to make greater use of external borrowing in order to finance its expenditure plans.

Tasks

1. Discuss the legal constraints under which the above local authority must operate its capital financing policy.
2. From the information given comment on the capital financing policy adopted by the authority to date and the strengths and weaknesses of that policy.
3. What objectives would you set for a capital financing strategy?
4. What advice would you give to the authority in planning how it will finance its proposed capital expenditure programme?

11.8   NHS case costing

Under the NHS and Community Care Act 1990 provider units in the NHS are required to enter into contracts for services with their own health authority, other health authorities and general practitioner fundholders for the provision of health care. Trauma (i.e. injury or wound) and orthopaedic services at the Getwell Hospital (currently a non-trust hospital) are charged out under this system on the basis of the average cost per case. The current cost of these services are £15m per annum. The typical patient can be classified into inpatients (5000 per annum) outpatients (35 000 per annum) and day patients (500 per annum). It is estimated that inpatients cost £9m, outpatients £5m and day patients £1m. Management is particularly concerned with the cost and recovery of inpatient services due to the high level of expenditure and the complexity of the surgery involved.

The trauma and orthopaedic unit has 90 beds and occupies a complete wing of the hospital. Contracts have been entered into with the 'parent' health authority, three other health authorities and two GP fundholders. The following costs have been calculated for inpatient services in the current year:

	£
Direct patient costs	7 250 000
General overheads	1 750 000

Direct patient costs represent the following:

Nursing	–	charged directly to the trauma ward.
Medical staff	–	charged directly to speciality but costs are split over inpatients, outpatients and day cases. This allocation takes place on the basis of doctor workload returns completed at the end of each month. This split is based simply on the number of patients treated in each category.
Dressings	–	charged on the basis of actual use.
Drugs	–	recharged by the hospital pharmacy on an estimate of use by each speciality in the hospital at the end of the financial year.
Other specialities	–	based on the estimated time spent dealing with cases referred by trauma.
Surgical supplies theatre	–	actual cost (e.g. of replacement hip joints). Costs are apportioned on the average amount of theatre time devoted to the speciality.
Pathology/radiology	–	apportioned on the basis of the number of tests carried out for the speciality.

General overheads are apportioned as follows:

Catering	–	apportioned to the speciality on the number of inpatient days.
Laundry/linen	–	as catering.
Building costs	–	repairs, heating, maintenance etc. are allocated on the basis of floor area.
Other costs	–	administration, training, general management, etc. are apportioned on the basis of inpatient days.
Capital charges	–	the capital charges are based on the value of the buildings and equipment. The total capital charges are spread over specialities by the number of inpatient days.
Non-emergency ambulances	–	based on number of patients using the service.

The contract price was then based on the total costs allocated to the speciality for the current calculated by the above methods divided by the anticipated case load. This resulted in a single flat rate charge for all patients regardless of the complexity of any single operation.

Tasks

1. Identify what you believe is wrong (if anything) with the present system of charging for trauma and orthopaedic services.
2. Taking each of the methods of allocating costs set out above comment on the suitability of each method of allocating both direct and indirect costs.
3. What changes would you propose?
4. Consider what alternatives exist for the pricing of trauma services.

11.9 Library service

Sally Evans is the manager in charge of the Library Service of Readhall District Council. She is under considerable pressure in her job to perform to targets and control her expenditure within strict cash limits. The budgeting system is primarily incremental but swinging cuts have been introduced often late in the budget cycle. The Library Service is regarded as a 'Cinderella' service by the authority.

It is the end of the financial year and she has over-spent on a number of budget heads and is coming in for severe criticism for this. At the same time she has under-spend on other heads of expenditure so that on balance she will balance her budget in terms of planned expenditure.

She complains that she is never involved in the budget process. She produces her figures which she never sees again and then they are handed back to her changed out of all recognition in her final budget. Targets are imposed based on these figures which she is expected to achieve. The finance department when reporting back then claim achieving these targets are her responsibility and in any case there are proper channels for questioning targets and budgets with her own management. Sally is unaware of these channels.

At the end of the financial year central charges are added to her budget (legal services, financial services and personnel). Sally feels these charges are excessive particularly, as in her view, she never uses the services to the extent to which she is charged. These charges are also treated as a cost she can control and they are always above target. This year there is a proposal by the finance section to add 5% to her original notified figure. The finance section is seen as budget policemen rather than as financial advisers.

Financial information consists of large computer printouts produced weekly although the form of the information causes consternation among her staff as the information never agrees with staff perceptions of the situation. Sally keeps a little black book covering her expenditure and income. She never looks at the computer printout.

The Library has been starved of capital finance and there is a need for significant capital investment. Loan charges are charged to the budget at the end of the financial year but are considered controllable by Sally. No new capital expenditure is planned for at least three years. The current level of debt charges is very low.

Book expenditure has been low for a number of years. The clientele of the service is generally elderly. Various exhibits have been held in the libraries on local history and have been a success. Some income has been raised from the exhibits and the library service wish to reinvest this income in more exhibits. They been informed that it must be paid into general authority funds.

Tasks

1. Identify the problems facing Sally.
2. Suggest solutions to the problems identified under (1).
3. Fully explore the advantages and disadvantages of each proposed solution.
4. Recommend what you think to be the best course of action.

11.10   An occupational health unit

A Health Authority currently administers an occupational health unit. The unit has a budget of £300 000 and employs the following staff:

1   consultant
1   senior medical officer
4   nursing officers
3   other nursing staff
6   administrative and clerical staff

The unit is based in three locations: a hospital in the south of the area, a hospital in the north of the authority about 25 miles distant, and at a large county council.

The work undertaken falls into three main areas of activity, pre-employment examinations, medical examinations (primarily for long-term sickness assessment and for drivers of public carrying vehicles), and immunization services. In recent years the unit has also reacted to an increasing volume of tests on VDU operatives and work is also increasing due to health and safety at work legislation. The client base includes health authority staff, the county council, two district councils, and various companies.

It is planned that the unit will become a self-financing entity from 1 April, 19–2 and it will need to cover its costs from the income which it is able to generate.

It is June 19–1. The accounts for the unit for the previous financial year have just been made available. They demonstrate that the unit has underspent its staffing and non-staffing budgets by £20 000 largely because a nurse vacancy was left unfilled for nine months.

Investigation reveals that a variety of costs are not currently charged to the unit. These include cost apportionments from the pathology and radiology departments, capital charges, energy costs, postal costs, telecommunication costs and the health authority's charges for financial services. These are estimated to amount to £112 000 in the current financial year. If these costs are charged, the unit spends considerably in excess of budget.

Services are not costed in any systematic way by the authority. Prices for services are set by the consultant occupational health physician. A comparison of the unit's current prices currently charged with the BMA recommended fees for the specific services reveals that prices are between 20–40% below the recommended levels. However, a recent audit exercise has revealed that if all costs were taken into consideration then prices would need to be 20% in excess of the BMA figures. The audit investigation also came up with the following conclusions:

1. Cost of inputs suggest uneconomic practice: salaries are high because of high grade clinical staff.

2. Non-productive time is high; to some extent this is due to the split site operation.
3. There is often a duplication of work and roles, especially in the administration of the unit.
4. Work done for some local authorities in the area, and the fire service is carried out well below current cost.
5. The in-house service to the County Council is the result of an agreement dating back to when the service was in part provided by the local authority sector. The County Council receive 400 free sessions per annum (a session is defined as 3.5 hours of a doctor's time) and pay for any service over and above this level at the prices charged by the authority.

The Unit is preparing a business plan as part of its preparation for the environment within which it will operate from 1 April 19–2. As the first stage in the preparation of the business plan the Unit is identifying its strengths, weaknesses, opportunities and threats (SWOT analysis).

Tasks

Assist in the preparation of the SWOT analysis by the Occupational Health Unit.

11.11   Blood collection service

A regional blood collection service is responsible for collecting, processing and distributing all blood and blood products required by the district health authorities and hospital trusts within the region. Its annual collection cost is about £2.8 millions.

The centre of operations is in the more densely populated south-eastern part of the region. In the area surrounding the centre of operations, blood is collected using daily visits to establishments where blood donation is taking place (generally work places, local halls or by means of the mobile collection service). The blood from outlying areas is collected by 'tours', whereby staff stay away from home in hotel accommodation for several days. All blood is shipped back to the centre for processing on a daily basis. Good road communications are essential and they are generally excellent between the regional centre and the outlying areas.

The regional blood collection service has an agreed collection target annually which is specified in its business plan. In order to achieve this target:

1. There is an annual planning cycle and most blood collection sessions are organized four months in advance. Each visit is preceded by support work which has access to a database holding information for each location, detailing donors, staffing requirement, transport requirement and any overnight accommodation requirement.
2. Total care of the donor has the highest priority during the blood donation process. This is ensured by the training of all staff, whose performance is carefully monitored by nursing staff and by team leaders. (Nursing staff are drawn from local hospitals). Each donor on a local list is requested to contribute about every six months.

The blood collection service is currently faced with a number of challenges:

1. First, it is faced with an annual cost improvement target, and in the current year this amounts to 2.3%.

2. Secondly, its market is becoming increasingly competitive and its customers are becoming increasingly demanding about the prices charged for blood as they themselves come under increasing cost pressure.

3. Thirdly, the demands for blood are increasing but it is having to make increasingly effective use of donors in order to maintain blood supplies at past levels. There are a variety of reasons for this last challenge; generally only 50% of a local donor list turn up to sessions and this has been declining; annually about 10% of donors leave the local lists; and an increasing number of donation attendances provide below normal levels of donation because of weakness resulting from a poor diet.

There are six donor teams in operation with, on average, ten people in each team: a team leader, six donor attendants, a receptionist, medical officer and driver. There is also cover provided for other staff for sickness, emergencies and annual leave. There is always a medical officer present at each session to ensure that there is medical cover in the event of any problems. The teams work four weeks at collection sessions and one week in the regional centre which is used for leave purposes (due to the high number of hours worked whilst on duty) and for training.

Tours themselves tend to be organized on a yearly basis to ensure a fair distribution to each team. There are usually no tours in December or January because of the difficulties of finding hotel accommodation. On average four of the teams are on tour at any one time. Tours are, of course, a far more expensive way of collecting blood than daily visits; the average cost of collection per donation is £17.31 for tours and £11.96 for daily visits.

Managers of the collection service are currently reviewing the cost-effectiveness of the service with particular reference to outlying areas. A small multi-disciplinary group has been formed to address the problem and they have come up with two additional options for the service:

1. The collection in outlying areas could be provided by the establishment of a few locally-based and recruited collection teams. All team members would reside in the area and operate from a local base to provide the blood collection service. Blood would be transported back to the regional centre on a daily basis.

2. The new area teams could come under regional management or they could operate local management, undertaking all planning, recruitment and collection activities.

You are a key member of the multi-disciplinary team.

Tasks

1. List the primary financial costs and savings associated with the options to be examined.
2. Produce a list of non-financial derisderata which can be used in the appraisal. Justify your selection of desiderata.

11.12 The bridge

A County Council is responsible for a toll bridge which crosses an estuary in an outlying but well populated area of the county. The bridge was constructed some ten years ago and its eventual capital cost was well over budget. Since opening it has made a loss; furthermore, it does not cover the annual interest charge on the construction of the bridge so that the initial loan is being increased by the amounts of unpaid interest. The County Council itself is not in a position to subsidize the bridge and the accumulated revenue deficit is projected to increase by £100 000 per annum to £1.2M within ten years.

Approximately 40% of the costs are staffing and 60% are capital related. In five years time there will be a bridge-strengthening programme which will cost £750 000. It is planned to fund this expenditure by borrowing.

The Council has increased tolls above the rate of inflation in recent years, and there has been some downturn in traffic as compared with ten years ago but this may reflect the relative economic decline of the country rather than the impact of the price increases. No attempt has been made to measure price sensitivity. The bridge saves a ten-mile round trip and it currently charges £2 to cars for each single journey. This toll was increased by 40 pence six months ago. There are other tolls for motorcycles, lorries and coaches. The Council gives a discount for pre-payment and a booklet of ten tickets may be purchased for £18.

There are some internal control problems as well. The bridge is a four-lane construction and there are two ticket collectors at each end of the bridge, one for each lane, and each pair is supervised by an inspector. There are three shifts per day. There is also a bridge manager. The supervision by inspectors is occasioned by the collection system. Different classes of users pay different rates, as indicated above, and different coloured tickets are available for this purpose. There is an under-road counter but this is incapable of discriminating between classes of vehicles. There is no way of ensuring that each user pays, or pays the correct amount or receives the correct coloured ticket. Hence the inspectors are required.

Finally there is strong political pressure from the area in which the bridge is located and this pressure is directed against the increase of toll prices.

Tasks

Examine how the Council may resolve the problem of the bridge deficit.

References

Argyris, C. (1953) 'Human Problems with Budgets', *Harvard Business Review*, **31**, 1, pp. 97–110.

Armstrong, C, (1992) 'Base Budgeting: a Modified Approach', *Public Finance and Accountancy*, 10 July, pp. 13–15.

Budgetary Reform (1992) Cmnd 1867. London: HMSO.

CIPFA (Chartered Institute of Public Finance and Accountancy) (1971) *Programme Budgeting – the Approach*. London: CIPFA.

CIPFA (Chartered Institute of Public Finance and Accountancy) (1979) *Statements on Internal Audit*. London: CIPFA.

CIPFA (Chartered Institute of Public Finance and Accountancy) (1991a) *The Management of Overheads in Local Authorities*. London: CIPFA.

Citizen's Charter (1992) First Report, Cmnd 2101. London: HMSO.

Connor, S. (1993) 'Accounting for Quality in Audit', *Public Finance and Accountancy*, 23 July, pp. 10–12.

Coombs, H. M. and Edwards, J. R. 1990, The Evolution of the District Audit, Financial Accountability and Management, 6 (3).

Department of Health (1989) '*Working for Patients*'. London: HMSO.

Dopson, S. (1993) 'Are Agencies an Act of Faith? The Experience of HMSO', *Public Money and Management*, 13, 2, pp. 17–24.

Drury, C. (1989) *Management and Cost Accounting*, 2nd edn. London: Van Nostrand Reinhold.

Efficiency Unit (1988) Improving Management in Government: The Next Steps. London: HMSO.

Efficiency Unit (1991) Making the Most of Next Steps, Report to the Prime Minister. London: HMSO.

Giddings, P. (1991) 'Cash Management: Joining Forces with the Specialists', *Public Finance and Accountancy*, 25 October, pp. 14–15.

Hardcastle, A. (1990) 'Financial Accountability and Reporting in Central Government', *Public Money and Management*, 10, 1, pp. 23–8.

Henley, D., Likierman, A., Perrin, J., Evans, M., Lapsley, I. and Whiteoak, J. (1992) *Public Sector Financial Accounting and Control*, 4th edn. London: Chapman and Hall.

HM Treasury (1976) Cash Limits on Public Expenditures, Cmnd 6440. London: HMSO.

HM Treasury (1978) The Nationalised Industries, Cmnd 7131. London: HMSO.

HM Treasury (1988) A New Public Expenditure Planning Total, Cmnd 441. London: HMSO.

HM Treasury, 1989, Public Expenditure Management. London: HMSO.

HM Treasury (1990) The Government's Expenditure Plans, Cmd 1021. London: HMSO.

HM Treasury (1993) Public Expenditure Analyses to 1995–96, Statistical Supplement to the Autumn Statement, 1993. Cmnd 2219, London: HMSO.

Horngren, C. T. (1987) *Cost Accounting a Managerial Approach*, 6th edn. Englewood Cliffs, NJ: Prentice-Hall.

Jones, R. (1993) 'Customers, Financial Services and the Competitive Edge', *Public Finance and Accountancy*, 4 June, pp. 14–15.

Jones, T. and Prowle, M. (1988) *Health Service Finance: an Introduction*, 2nd edn. London: Certified Accountant Educational Trust.

Kemp, P. (1990) 'Can the Civil Service Adapt to Managing by Contract', *Public Money and Management*, 10, 3, pp. 25–32.

Knights, A. (1991) 'Investing Within a Framework', *Public Finance and Accountancy*, 13 December, pp. 12–14.

Likierman, A. (1988) *Public Expenditure: Who Really Controls It and How*. London: Penguin.

Masters, S. (1993) 'Financial Management in the NHS', *Public Money and Management*, 13, 1, p. 4.

McAlister, D. (1990) 'Option Appraisal: Turning an Art Into a Science', *Public Money and Management*, 10, 4, pp. 27–34.

Morgan, T. and M. Weaver, 'Budget making – Is There a Better Way', *Public Finance and Accountancy*, 11 June 1993, pp. 51–6.

National Audit Office (1986b) The Rayner Scrutiny Programmes, 1979–1983, HCC 322. London: HMSO.

National Audit Office (1986a) The Financial Management Initiative. London: HMSO.

Pendlebury, M. W. (1985) Management Accounting in Local Government: A Research Study. London: The Institute of Cost and Management Accountants.

Plowden Report (1961) The Control of Public Expenditure, Cmnd 1432. London: HMSO.

Prest, A. R. and Turvey, R. (1965) 'Cost Benefit Analysis: a Survey', *Economic Journal*, LXXXV, 300, pp. 685–705.

Simon, H. A. (1953) *Administrative Behaviour*. London: Macmillan.

Simon, H. A. (1959) 'Theories and Decision Making in Economics and Behavioural Science', *American Economic Review*, XLIX, June, pp. 253–83.

Thain, C. and Wright, M. (1990) 'Haggling in Mr Clarke's Turkish Bazaar', *Public Money and Management*, 4, pp. 51–6.

Treasury and Civil Service Committee (1982) Efficiency and Effectiveness in the Civil Service: Cmnd 8616. London: HMSO.

Treasury and Civil Service Committee (1991) The Next Steps Initiative, 7th Report, session 1990–91, HC 496. London: HMSO.

Treasury and Civil Service Committee (1992) Banking Supervision and BCCI: The Role of Local Authorities and Money Brokers. London: HMSO.

Van Horne, J. C. (1986) *Financial Management and Policy*, 6th edn., Englewood Cliffs, NJ. Prentice-Hall.

Wildavsky, A. (1974) *The Politics of the Budgetary Process*, 2nd edn, Boston: Little Brown.

Further reading

Anthony, P. (1993) 'Healthcare Resource Groups in the NHS: a measure of success', *Public Finance and Accountancy*, 23 April, pp. 8–10.

Armstrong, W. (1980) *Budgetary Reform in the United Kingdom*, Oxford: Oxford University Press.

Barnett, J. (1982) *Inside the Treasury*, London: Andre Deutsch.

Boyfield, K. (1992) 'Private Sector Funding of Public Sector Infrastructure', *Public Money and Management*, 12, 2, pp. 41–6.

Buttery, R. and Simpson, R. (1989) *Audit in the Public Sector*, 2nd edn. London: Woodhead Faulker.

Capon, B. (1992) 'The Inevitability of the Internal Trading Market', *Public Finance and Accountancy*, 8 May, pp. 16–18.

Cargill, R. (1991) 'Investing surplus funds', *Public Finance and Accountancy*, 13 December, pp. 10–12.

Caulfield, I. and Schultz, J. (1989) *Planning for Change: Strategic Planning in Local Government*. London: Longman.

Chartered Institute of Management Accountancy (1987) *Management Accounting – Official Terminology of the CIMA*, London: CIMA.

CIPFA (Chartered Institute of Public Finance and Accountancy) *Financial Information Service*, various volumes. Regularly updated manual.

CIPFA (Chartered Institute of Public Finance and Accountancy) (1990) *Financial Information System: Vol. 4, Budgetary Processes*: London: CIPFA.

CIPFA (Chartered Institute of Public Finance and Accountancy) (1991b) *Service Level Agreements: A Compendium*. London: CIPFA.

Citizen's Charter (1991) *Raising the Standard*, Cmnd 1599. London: HMSO.

Cowan, N., 1993, 'Marketing for Survival', *Public Finance and Accountancy*, 28 May, pp. 8–9.

DHSS (1982) Investment Appraisal in the Public Sector, NH(82)34, London: DHSS.

Dixon, R. (1991) 'Local Management of Schools', *Public Money and Management and Management*, 11, 3, pp. 47–52.

Edwards, P. (1992) 'Formula Funding: Three Years On', *Public Finance and Accountancy*, 6 March, pp. 27–8.

Gray, M. (1992) 'Business Planning', *Public Finance and Accountancy*, 10 April, pp. 12–14.

Haring, P. (1993) 'Restructuring Debt', *Public Finance and Accountancy*, 22 January, pp. 14–15.

Henderson, J. (1984) *Appraising Options*. Health Economics Research Unit, Aberdeen University.

Hennessy, P. (1989) *Whitehall*. London: Secker and Warburg.

Jones, R. and Pendlebury, M. (1989) *Public Sector Accounting*, 2nd edn. London: Pitman.

Korner, E. (1984) Report of the Steering Group on Health Service Information. London: HMSO.

Lapsley, I. and Llewellyn, S. (1993) 'Costing Care Packages: Dilemmas and Difficulties', *Public Money and Management*, 13, 3, July, pp. 15–17.

Lapsley, I. (1986) 'Investment Appraisal in UK Non-trading Organisations', *Financial Accountability and Management*, 2, 2, pp. 135–51.

Lapsley, I. (1986) 'Investment Appraisal in Public Sector Organisations', *Management Accounting*, June 1986, pp. 28–31.

Morley, D. (1992) 'The Citizen's Charter and a 21st-century Vision', *Public Money and Management*, 12, 1, p. 6.

Public Accounts Committee (1976–77) Cash Limits, 3rd Report, HC 274. London: HMSO.

Public Accounts Committee (1986–87) Financial Reporting to Parliament, 8th Report, HC 383. London: HMSO.

Pendlebury, M. (ed.) (1989) *Management Accounting in the Public Sector*. London: Heinemann.

Perrin, J. (1988) *Resource Management in the NHS*. London: Chapman Hall.

Phyrr, P. (1970) 'Zero Based Budgeting', *Harvard Business Review*, 43, 12, pp. 111–21.

Preddy, B. (1993) 'Performance Targets for Managing Cash', *Public Finance and Accountancy*, 9 April, pp. 13–14.

Puxty, A. G. and Dodds, J. C. (1988) *Financial Management Method and Meaning*. London: Chapman and Hall.

Rutherford, B. A. (1983) *Financial Reporting in the Public Sector*. London: Butterworth.

Robinson, R., (1991) 'Health Expenditure: Recent Trends and Prospects for the 1990s', *Public Money and Management*, 11, 4, pp. 19–24.

Sugden, R. and Williams, A. (1978) *The Principles of Practical Cost Benefit Analysis*. Oxford: Oxford University Press.

Walker, D. (1993) 'A Private Style at the Heart of Whitehall'.

While, R. (1993) 'How to live with SSAs', *Public Finance and Accountancy*, 25 June, pp. 20–2.

Index